W9-AUJ-944

BUDDHISM

Its Essence and Development

Other books by Edward Conze include

Buddhism: A Short History
Buddhist Meditation
Buddhist Thought in India
Further Buddhist Studies
Memoirs of a Modern Gnostic
Selected Sayings from the Perfection of Wisdom
Thirty Years of Buddhist Studies
The Way of Wisdom

Translations:

Buddhist Wisdom Books: The Diamond and the Heart Sūtra
The Buddha's Law Among the Birds
The Perfection of Wisdom in a few words
The Perfection of Wisdom in 700 words
The Perfection of Wisdom in 8,000 Lines and Its Verse Summary
The Larger Sūtra on Perfect Wisdom
Vajracchedikā Prajñāpāramitā
Aṣṭasāhasrikā Prajñāpāramitā

EDWARD CONZE

BUDDHISM

Its Essence and Development

WINDHORSE PUBLICATIONS

Published by Windhorse Publications
11 Park Road
Birmingham
B13 8AB

© The estate of Edward Conze 1951
First published by Bruno Cassirer, Oxford, 1951
First Windhorse edition 2001

Printed by Interprint, Marsa, Malta
Cover images © Getty Images
Cover design Vincent Stokes

The publishers wish to acknowledge with gratitude permission from the Sri
Aurobindo Ashram Trust to quote from Sri Aurobindo, *Bases of Yoga.*

British Library Cataloguing in Publication Data
A catalogue record for this book is available from the British Library

ISBN 1 899579 40 0

CONTENTS

About the Author

Eberhart Julius Dietrich Conze was born in London in 1904 of mixed German, French, and Dutch ancestry. His father belonged to the German landed aristocracy, and his mother to what he himself would have called the 'plutocracy'. His background was Protestant, though his mother became a Roman Catholic in later life.

He was educated at various German universities and developed a command of fourteen languages, including Sanskrit, by the age of 24. He came into contact with Theosophy, but he also took up astrology, and remained a keen astrologer all his life.

During the rise to power of Hitler, Conze found himself so strongly opposed to the Nazi ideology that he joined the Communist Party and made a serious study of Marxist thought. For a while, he was the leader of the communist movement in Bonn, and his life was consequently in some danger.

In 1933 he returned to England, having earlier taken the precaution of renewing his British nationality, and arrived at the age of 29, virtually without money or possessions. In London he married a German Jew, Dorothea Finklestein, partly in order to save her from the Nazis. He supported himself by teaching German and became very active in the British socialist movement, lecturing and writing books and pamphlets, until he eventually became disillusioned with politics. At the age of 35 he found himself in a state of intellectual turmoil and collapse. At this point he discovered – or rather re-discovered – Buddhism. At the age of 13 he had read *Gleanings in Buddha Fields* by Lafcadio Hearn. However, Conze's first significant contact with Buddhism came at the beginning of the Second World War, through the writings of D.T. Suzuki. They were literally his salvation, and after this there was no turning back. Conze devoted the rest of his life to Buddhism. He wasn't just a scholar in the academic sense; during the war he lived on his own in a caravan in the New Forest and practised meditation, following the instructions given in the *Visuddhimagga*, and achieving some degree of success.

After the war he moved to Oxford and remarried, this time to Muriel Green, and in 1951 *Buddhism: Its Essence and Development* was first published. However, his major achievement over the following twenty years was to translate more than thirty texts comprising the *Prajñāpāramitā* sūtras, the fundamental scriptures of the Mahāyāna, including two of the most well-known of all Buddhist texts, the *Diamond Sūtra* and the *Heart Sūtra*.

In the sixties and seventies he lectured at several universities in the United States, and went down well with the students, but he was very outspoken, and gained the disapproval of the university authorities and some of his colleagues. With the combination of his communist past and his candid criticism of the American involvement in Vietnam, he was eventually obliged to take his talents elsewhere. He died at his home in Sherbourne in 1979.

He is representative of a whole pre-war generation in the West which became disillusioned with Marxism, especially in its Soviet form. Where he differed from others was in the fact that he did not really lose his sense of faith. He did not simply become disillusioned while carrying on within the milieu with which he was familiar. He transferred his uncompromising idealism from politics to Buddhism.

Dr Conze was one of the great Buddhist translators, comparable with the indefatigable Chinese translators Kumārajīva and Hsüan-tsang. It is especially significant that as a scholar of Buddhism he also tried to practise it, especially meditation. This was very unusual at the time he started his work, and he was regarded then – in the forties and fifties – as something of an eccentric. Rather than have any personal involvement in their subject, scholars were supposed to be 'objective', so he was a forerunner of a whole new breed of Western scholars in Buddhism who are actually practising Buddhists.

Adapted from Sangharakshita, *Great Buddhists of the Twentieth Century*, Windhorse, Birmingham 1996

PUBLISHER'S NOTE

In the fifty years since this book was first published, Buddhism has firmly established itself in many parts of the Western world. As the Buddha's teaching has begun to take root in the soil of modern culture, its truths have been increasingly interpreted in ways that are relevant to people from a wider range of lifestyles and backgrounds than were current in the Buddha's own lifetime. Life as a homeless wanderer, for example, is not a practical alternative for most Westerners, and Dr Conze's assertion that 'monks are the ... only Buddhists in the proper sense of the word' (p.38) would today be disputed by dedicated Buddhists choosing, none the less, to follow the lifestyle they find most appropriate.

It is clear that Conze was addressing himself to a readership that would have been at least nominally Christian, and his translation of some Buddhist concepts into Christian terms, while not unreasonable in those days, looks rather odd fifty years later. But the Dharma, whether taken as a description of the human condition or the ultimate truth, is not a religion as the word is generally understood, and any parallels with Christianity are intended to be illustrative rather than taken literally. For this new edition, a few endnotes have been added to clarify Conze's occasionally idiosyncratic or outdated choice of word.

Conze's original references for most of the quotations are given as footnotes. Unless indicated otherwise, translations from Sanskrit and Pali works are assumed to be Conze's own. Most of the other quotations have been checked and the references updated where necessary, but it was not always possible for us to trace and compare source material. We have also taken the opportunity to make the charts and diagrams clearer, and compile a more comprehensive index. The inconsistent transliteration and use of diacritics in the original, and the spellings of proper names, have been regularized in line with modern usage. Apart from a few minor corrections no other changes to the text have been made.

Shantavira
Windhorse Publications
November 2001

AUTHOR'S NOTE

The idea of this book originated with friends of mine in 1941, when I lived in Godshill in Hampshire and attempted to find out how much of Buddhist meditation could actually be practised in this present age. The first chapters represent lectures that I gave some years ago in Oxford at St Peter's Hall, and some traces of the spoken word still cling to them. In 1948 Dr William Cohn, of Oxford, suggested to me that a work covering the whole range of Buddhist thought would be much appreciated, and encouraged me to complete the book. Dr Cohn and, at a later stage, Mr Arthur Waley and Mr Christmas Humphreys, have eliminated many errors. Mr Claud Sutton and Mr Arthur Southgate have watched over the English style. Discussions with various scholars have, I hope, put me right on a number of difficult and controversial points. In this connection, I must mention, with gratitude, Prof. F.W. Thomas, Dr E.J. Thomas, Prof. Murti of Colombo, Prof. Lamotte of Louvain, Prof. Demieville of Paris, Prof. Tucci of Rome, and Dr Pott of Leyden. Many of the texts on which my account is based have never been translated into English. It may one day be possible to offer the reader a selection from the main documents of Buddhist thinking which would substantiate much that is merely stated here.

Edward Conze
Ewelme
January 1951

INTRODUCTION

BUDDHISM AS A RELIGION

Buddhism is an Eastern form of spirituality. Its doctrine, in its basic assumptions, is identical with many other teachings all over the world, teachings which may be called 'mystical'. The essence of this philosophy of life has been explained with great force and clarity by Thomas á Kempis in his *Imitation of Christ*. What is known as 'Buddhism' is a part of the common human heritage of wisdom, by which men have succeeded in overcoming this world, and in gaining immortality, or a deathless life.

During the last two centuries, spiritual interests have in Europe been relegated into the background by preoccupations with economic and social problems. The word 'spiritual' seems vague nowadays. It is, indeed, not easy to define. It is easier to state by what means one gets to the spiritual realm than to say what it is in itself. Three avenues of approach to the spiritual are, I think, handed down by the almost universal tradition of the sages: to regard sensory experience as relatively unimportant; to try to renounce what one is attached to; to try to treat all people alike – whatever their looks, intelligence, colour, smell, education, etc. The collective effort of the European races during the last centuries has gone into channels which by this definition are not 'spiritual'.

It is often assumed that there is some fundamental and essential difference between East and West, between Europe and Asia, in their attitude to life, in their sense of values, and in the functioning of their souls. Christians who regard Buddhism as unsuitable for European conditions forget the Asiatic origin of their own religion, and of all religions for that matter. A religion is an organization of spiritual aspirations, which reject the sensory world and negate the impulses which bind us to it. For 3,000 years Asia alone has been creative of spiritual ideas and methods. The Europeans have in these matters borrowed from Asia, have adapted Asiatic ideas, and, often, coarsened them. One could not, I think, point to any *spiritual* creation in Europe which is not secondary, which does not have its ultimate impulse in the East. European thought has excelled in the elaboration of *social* law and organization, especially in Rome and England, and in the *scientific* understanding and control of sensory phenomena. The indigenous tradition of Europe is inclined to affirm the will to live, and to turn actively towards the world of the senses. The spiritual tradition of mankind is based on the negation of the will to live, and is turned away from the world of the senses. All European spirituality has had to be periodically renewed by an influx from the East, from the time of Pythagoras and Parmenides onwards. Take away the Oriental elements in Greek philosophy, take away Jesus Christ, Saint Paul, Dionysius Areopagita, and Arabic thought – and European spiritual thinking during the last 2,000 years becomes unthinkable. About a century ago the thought of India began to exert its influence on Europe, and it will help to revivify the languishing remnants of European spirituality.

Some features distinguish Buddhism from other forms of wisdom. They are of two kinds: (1) Much of what has been handed down as 'Buddhism' is due not to the exercise of wisdom, but to the social conditions in which the Buddhist community existed, to the language employed, and to the science and mythology in vogue among the people who adopted it. One must throughout distinguish the exotic curiosities from the essentials of a holy life. (2) There are a number of methods for winning salvation by meditation, of which Buddhist tradition gives a clearer and fuller account than I have found elsewhere. This is, however, largely a matter of temperament. Properly studied, the literature of the Jains, of the Sufis, of the Christian monks of the Egyptian desert, and of what the Catholic Church calls 'ascetical' or 'mystical' theology, yields much of the same kind.

To a person who is thoroughly disillusioned with the contemporary world, and with himself, Buddhism may offer many points of attraction – in the transcending sublimity of the fairy land of its subtle thoughts, in the splendour of its works of art, in the magnificence of its hold over vast populations, and in the determined heroism and quiet refinement of those who are steeped into it. Although one may originally be attracted by its remoteness, one can appreciate the real value of Buddhism only when one judges it by the results it produces in one's own life from day to day.

The rules of wholesome conduct recommended in the Buddhist scriptures are grouped under three headings: *Morality, Contemplation*, and *Wisdom*. Much of what is included under *Morality* and *Contemplation* is the common property of all those Indian religious movements which sought salvation in a life apart from ordinary everyday society. There we have, in addition to rules of conduct for the laity, regulations for the life of the homeless brotherhood of monks; many yoga practices – rhythmical and mindful breathing, the restraint of the senses, methods for inducing trance[1] by staring at coloured circles, stages of ecstasis, the cultivation of unlimited friendliness, compassion, sympathetic joy, and even-mindedness. Further, meditations of a generally edifying character, which could be found in any mystical religion, such as meditation on death, on the repulsiveness of the functions of this material body, on the Trinity of the Buddha, the Dharma (Truth), and the Sangha (Brotherhood). Few could be expected to practise all those methods in one lifetime. There are many roads to emancipation. What is common to all of them is that they aim at the belief in individuality.

When taken in its present-day vagueness, the word 'individuality' does, however, fail to convey the Buddha's meaning. According to Buddhist teaching, as we shall see in more detail later on, man, with all his possible belongings, consists of five 'heaps', technically known as *skandhas*. They are: the body, feelings, perceptions, impulses and emotions, acts of consciousness.

Anything a person may grasp at, or lean on, or appropriate, must fall within one of those five groups, which make up the *stuff* of 'individuality'. The *belief* in individuality is said to arise from the invention of a 'self' over and above those five heaps. The belief expresses itself in the assumption that any of this is 'mine', or that 'I am' any of this, or that any of this is 'myself'. Or, in other words, in the belief that 'I am this,' or that 'I have this,' or that 'this is in me,' or that 'I am in this.' The fact of individuality disappears with the belief in it, since it is no more than a gratuitous imagination. When the individual, as constituted by an arbitrary lump taken from those five heaps, ceases to exist, the result is Nirvāṇa, the goal of Buddhism. If one wishes to express this by saying that one has found one's 'true individuality', the word 'individuality', as understood at present, is elastic and vague enough to permit this. The Buddhist scriptures do, however, distinctly avoid this or any equivalent expression.

The various schools of Buddhism spring, as I will try to show, from differences in the approach to the Buddhist goal. Already in the early Order, men of different temperament and endowment are reported to have reached the goal by different roads. Śāriputra was renowned for his wisdom, Ānanda for his faith and devotion, Maudgalyāyana for his magical potency. In later times, different-minded people formed different schools, and, in addition, the spread of the doctrine led to geographical separation and to separate organizations. Some of the methods for achieving de-individualization, which we shall discuss in the later chapters of this book, are not mentioned at all in the oldest strata of the tradition as it has come down to us, or are no more than dimly foreshadowed, but, as many of the later Buddhists would have argued, in his love for beings the Buddha would have excluded nothing that could help anyone who wanted the right thing. A great deal of this book will be devoted to explaining what each of the chief schools stood for, what method it chose as its own particular way, how it can be thought to lead to the same goal as the others, and how it fared in the world of history.

BUDDHISM AS A PHILOSOPHY

Philosophy, as we understand it in Europe, is a creation of the Greeks. It is unknown to Buddhist tradition, which would regard the enquiry into reality, for the mere purpose of knowing more about it, as a waste of valuable time. The Buddha's teaching is exclusively concerned with showing the way to salvation. Any 'philosophy' there may be in the works of Buddhist authors is quite incidental. In the ample vocabulary of Buddhism we find no word to correspond to our term 'philosophy'. An analogy may clarify the position. The Chinese language, as the Chinese understood it, did not contain any grammar, and it was taught in China without any grammatical instructions. Some European philologists, on the model of our Latin grammatical categories, have constructed a 'grammar' for the Chinese language. It does not fit particularly well and the Chinese continue to dispense with it. The Latin-style grammar, with its familiar categories, may, however, help some Europeans to learn the Chinese language more easily. In a similar way, an attempt to define Buddhist thought in the philosophical terminology current in Europe may facilitate the approach to it. Buddhism, as a 'philosophy', could then be described as a 'dialectical pragmatism' with a 'psychological' turn. Let us consider these three items one by one.

In its origin and intention a doctrine of salvation, Buddhism has always been marked by its intensely practical attitude. Speculation on matters irrelevant to salvation is discouraged. Suffering is the basic fact of life. If a man were struck by an arrow he would not refuse to have it extracted before he knew who shot the arrow, whether that man was married or not, tall or small, fair or dark. All he would want would be to be rid of the arrow. The Buddha's last injunction to his disciples ran: 'All conditioned things are impermanent. Work out your salvation with diligence.'* In their long history, the Buddhists have never lost this practical bent. Innumerable misunderstandings would have been avoided if one had seen that the statements of Buddhist writers are not meant to be propositions about the nature of reality, but advice on how to act, statements about modes of behaviour, and the experiences connected with them. 'If you want to get there, then you must do this.' 'If you do this, you will experience this.'

We can, therefore, say with some truth that Buddhist thinking tends in the direction of what we call *Pragmatism*. The value of a thought is to be judged by what you can do with it, by the quality of the life which results from it. Wherever one finds evidence of such qualities as detachment, kindness, serene self-confidence, etc., one would be inclined to believe that the philosophy behind such an attitude had much to say in its favour.

> Of whatever teachings you can assure yourself that they conduce to
> dispassion, and not to passions; to detachment and not to bondage;
> to decrease of frugality and not to covetousness; to content and not

* *Dīgha Nikāya* ii.156

to discontent; to solitude and not to company; to energy and not to sluggishness; to delight in good and not to delight in evil, of such teachings you may with certainty affirm: This is the Norm. This is the Discipline. This is the Master's Message.*

As Buddhism developed, its pragmatism became even more explicit. One came to see that anything one may say is ultimately false – false by the mere fact that one says it. 'Those who say do not know, those who know do not say.' The 'Āryan silence' alone did not violate the Truth. If one says something – and it is astonishing to find how much the supporters of the Āryan silence had to say – it is justified only by what they called 'skill in means'. In other words, one says it because it may help other people at a certain stage of their spiritual progress. The holy doctrine is primarily a medicine. The Buddha is like a physician. Just as a doctor must know the diagnosis of the different kinds of illness, must know their causes, the antidotes and remedies, and must be able to apply them, so also the Buddha has taught the Four Holy Truths, which indicate the range of suffering, its origin, its cessation, and the way that leads to its cessation (see pp.29 *et seq.*). If one, however, isolates the Buddha's statements from the task they intend to perform, they become quite meaningless, and lose all their force.

Meditation is in Buddhism easily the chief means of salvation. The stress is throughout far less on 'doing something' by overt action, than on contemplation and mental discipline. What one aims at is the control of mental processes by meditating on them. In consequence, Buddhist thought is impregnated with what we call *Psychology*. It mixes metaphysics and psychology in a way to which we have no parallel in the West.

In addition to pragmatism and psychological emphasis, Buddhist thought is inclined to what we may call *Dialectics*. Dialectics is a form of logic, associated in Europe with such names as Zenon of Elea and Hegel. It stands for the belief that if you think properly and deeply on anything you arrive at contradictions, i.e. statements which to some extent cancel each other out. Buddhist thinkers loved paradox and contradiction. I may illustrate this by two quotations from the *Diamond Sūtra*, a treatise probably written about 350AD, which has

* *Vinaya* ii.10

had more readers than any other metaphysical work. There the Buddha says:

> 'Beings,' 'beings,' O Subhūti, as 'no-beings' have they been taught by the Tathāgata. Therefore are they called 'beings.'

Or again:

> As many beings as there are in these world systems, of them I know, in my wisdom, the manifold trends of thought. And why? 'Trends of thought,' 'trends of thought,' O Subhūti, as 'no-trends' have they been taught by the Tathāgata. Therefore are they called 'trends of thought'. And why? Past thought is not got at; future thought is not got at; present thought is not got at.[*]

By defeating thought, contradictions are set free. Another fetter of existence has been cast off, and the vastness of the unlimited space of truth opens itself up. In a more secular way, some people get a similar feeling from reading nonsense literature. In Buddhism, the ordinary rules of logic are defied in the name of the freedom of the Spirit which transcends them. In addition, it is the introduction of the notion of the Absolute which here, as also with Zenon, Nicholas of Cues, and Hegel, makes self-contradictory statements appear permissible.

SELF-EXTINCTION, AND THE DOCTRINE OF NOT-SELF

The specific contribution of Buddhism to religious thought lies in its insistence on the doctrine of 'not-self' (*anattā* in Pāli, *anātman* in Sanskrit). The belief in a self is considered by all Buddhists as an indispensable condition to the emergence of suffering. We conjure up such ideas as 'I' and 'mine', and many most undesirable states result. We would be perfectly happy, quite blissfully happy, as happy as, according to some psychologists, the child is in the womb, if we could first get rid of our selves. The assertion that one can be really happy only after one is no longer there is one of the dialectical paradoxes which to the man in the street must appear as just plain nonsense. In any case, it is fairly obvious that unhappiness requires that I should identify myself with other things, in the sense that I

---

[*] *Vajracchedikā* 17f and 18b

think that what happens to them happens to me. If there is a tooth, and there is decay in that tooth, this is a process in the tooth, and in the nerve attached to it. If now my 'I' reaches out to the tooth, convinces itself that this is 'my' tooth – and it sometimes does not seem to need very much convincing – and believes that what happens to the tooth is bound to affect *me*, a certain disturbance of thought is likely to result. The Buddhist sees it like this: Here is the idea of 'I', a mere figment of the imagination, with nothing real to correspond to it. There are all sorts of processes going on in the world. Now I conjure up another figment of the imagination, the idea of 'belonging', and come to the conclusion that some, not particularly well-defined, portion of this world 'belongs' to that 'I', or to 'me'. In this approach Buddhism greatly differs from some of our traditions in the West. In the philosophy of Aristotle, for instance, this idea of 'belonging' (*hyparkhein*) is quite uncritically treated as an ultimate datum of experience, and the entire logic and ontology of Aristotle is built upon it.

This doctrine of anattā is very deep. One assumes that it will need more than one lifetime to get to the bottom of it. As it is handed down by Buddhist tradition, it really comprises two statements. The two propositions which we must distinguish are (1) It is claimed that nothing in reality corresponds to such words or ideas as 'I', 'mine', 'belonging', etc. In other words, the self is not a fact; (2) We are urged to consider that nothing in our empirical self is worthy of being regarded as the real self (see pp.89 *et seq*.).

The second of these propositions will become clearer in the course of this book. We must now have a look at the first one.

We are urged to struggle against the intellectual conviction that there is such a thing as a 'self', or a soul', or a 'substance', or such relations as 'belonging' or 'owning'. It is not denied that the self, etc. are data of the world as it appears to common sense. But as facts of ultimate reality, we must reject the 'self', and all kindred ideas. This step has an important corollary. If there is no such thing as a 'self', there is also no such thing as a 'person', for a 'person' is something which is organized round a supposed inner core, a central growing point, a 'self'.

In my book, *Contradiction and Reality*, I have attempted to restate in modern terms the Buddhist arguments against the objective validity of the notion of 'self'. Their repetition would lead us too far here. Whatever arguments there may be against the idea of 'self', it is obvious that we habitually speak of it, and find it difficult to dispense with the word. In England, Hume's denial of the existence of the ego, as an entity distinct from mental processes, comes very near the anattā doctrine. From the purely theoretical point of view Buddhism has in this respect little to teach that one cannot find as well, and probably in a more congenial form, in Hume and kindred thinkers, like William James. The difference between the Buddhist and the European and American philosophers lies in what they do with a philosophical proposition once they have arrived at it. In Europe, we have become accustomed to an almost complete gap between the theory of philosophers and their practice, between their views on the nature of the universe and their mode of life. Schopenhauer and Herbert Spencer, for instance, at once come to mind as particularly striking examples. If a philosopher here has proved that there is no ego, he is apt to leave it at that, and to behave very much as if there were one. His greed, hate, and attachment[2] remain practically untouched by his philosophical arguments. He is judged by the consistency of his views, not with his life, but with themselves, by his style, his erudition – in short, by purely intellectual standards. It just would not do to 'refute' a philosopher by pointing out that he is insufferably rude to his wife, envies his more fortunate colleagues, and gets flustered when contradicted. In Buddhism, on the contrary, the entire stress lies on the mode of living, on the saintliness of life, on the removal of attachment to this world. A merely theoretical proposition, such as 'there is no ego' would be regarded as utterly sterile, and useless. Thought is no more than a tool and its justification lies in its products.

Not content with the intellectual conviction that there is no ego, a Buddhist aims at an entirely new attitude to life. Day in, day out, in all the many functions and bothers of daily life, he must learn to behave as if there were no ego. Those who look to Buddhism for startlingly new and unheard-of ideas on the problem of self will find little. Those who look to it for advice on how to lead a selfless life may learn a great deal. The great contribution of Buddhist 'philosophy' lies in the methods it worked out to impress the truth of not-self on our reluctant minds, it lies in the discipline which the Buddhists imposed upon themselves in order to make this truth into a part of their own being.

'RADICAL PESSIMISM'

The other side of the anattā doctrine, which consists in the repudiation of everything that constitutes or attracts the empirical self, has earned for Buddhism the reputation of being a 'pessimistic' faith. It is true that this world, i.e. everything conditioned and impermanent, is emphatically regarded as wholly ill, as wholly pervaded with suffering, as something to be rejected totally, abandoned totally, for the one goal of Nirvāṇa. I am not quite sure, however, that 'radical pessimism' is really a good word for this attitude to the world. Observers of such Buddhist countries as Burma and Tibet record that their inhabitants are spontaneously cheerful, and even gay – laymen and monks alike. It is rather puzzling that the pessimistic gloom which one reads into the Buddhist doctrine of universal suffering should reflect itself in a cheerful countenance. This world may be a vale of tears, but there is joy in shedding its burden. It must be renounced. But if there is a kingdom of God to win by renouncing it, the gain infinitely outweighs the loss. In any case, the best thing we can do with such a word as 'pessimism' is to discard it and look the problem straight in the face.

The negative attitude of Buddhist thinkers to this world is obviously bound up with the question of the meaning of life, and the problem of the destiny of man. However difficult this problem may be, however unscientific it may be to concern ourselves with it, we must come to a decision on it, because the entire happiness and fruitfulness of our lives depends on the answer. The views on the nature and destiny of man, or the meaning of human existence, fall roughly into two classes. According to some, man is a product of the earth. The earth is his home. His task is to make himself at home on the earth. Self-preservation is the highest law, and even duty, of man. Others, however, believe that man is a spirit ill at ease, a soul fallen from heaven, a stranger on this Earth. His task is to regain the state of perfection which was his before he fell into this world. Self-denial is the highest law and duty of man.

Our modern civilization favours the first viewpoint, Buddhism the second. It would, of course, be futile to contend that such issues can be decided by argument alone. In all decisions on values one must be careful not to exalt one's own personal tastes, temperament, and preferences to the dignity of an objective and natural law. One should only define one's position, and not coerce others into it. The Buddhist point of view will appeal only to those people who are completely disillusioned with the world as it is, and with themselves, who are extremely sensitive to pain, suffering, and any kind of turmoil, who have an extreme desire for happiness, and a considerable capacity for renunciation. No Buddhist would assume that all men are either able or willing to understand his doctrine.

The Buddhist seeks a total happiness beyond this world. Why should he be so ambitious? Why not be content with getting as much happiness out of this world as we can, however little it may be? The answer is that in actual practice we are seen not to be content. If increase in physical comfort and earthly satisfactions would make us content, then the inhabitants of the suburbs of London should be immeasurably more radiant and contented than Chinese coolies or Spanish peasants. The exact opposite is the case. Our human nature, according to the Buddhist contention, is so constituted that we are content with nothing but complete permanence, complete ease, complete security. And none of that can we ever find in this shifting world.

The discoveries which philosophers and psychologists have made in recent years about the central importance of anxiety at the very core of our being, have quite a Buddhist ring about them. According to the views elaborated by Scheler, Freud, Heidegger, and Jaspers, there is in the core of our being a basic anxiety, a little empty hole from which all other forms of anxiety and unease draw their strength. In its pure form, this anxiety is experienced only by people with an introspective and philosophical turn of mind, and even then only rarely. If one has never felt it oneself, no amount of explanation will convince. If one has felt it, one will never forget, however much one may try. It may come upon you when you have been asleep, withdrawn from the world; you wake up in the middle of the night and feel a kind of astonishment at being there, which then gives way to a fear and horror at the mere fact of being there. It is then that you catch yourself by yourself, just for a moment, against the background of a kind of nothingness all around you, and with a gnawing sense of your powerlessness, your utter helplessness in the face of this astonishing fact that you are there at all. Usually, we avoid this experience as much as we possibly can, because it is so shattering and painful. Usually, I am very careful not to have myself by myself, but the I plus all sorts of other experiences. People who are busy all the time, who must always think of something, who must always be doing something, are incessantly running away from this experience of the *basic* or *original* anxiety. What we usually do is lean and rely on something other than this empty centre of ourselves. The Buddhist contention is that we will never be at ease before we have overcome this basic anxiety, and that we can do that only by relying on nothing at all.

IMMORTALITY

With their exalted view of the nature of man, Buddhists regard it as a reasonable and sensible thing for us to strive for immortality. The aim of Buddhism, like that of many other religions, is to gain immortality, a deathless life. The Buddha, after he had become enlightened, claimed to have opened up the 'doors to the Undying'.[*] It is obvious that there is a great difference between the perpetuation of this individuality on the one side and immortality on the other. Immortality is just the opposite of this life, which is bound up with death, and inseparable from it. We start dying the moment we are born. The rate of metabolism in our bodies begins to slow down immediately after conception. Birth is the cause of death. All the circumstances which may bring about actual death are but its occasions. The act of birth – or conception, to be more accurate – is the decisive cause which makes death inevitable. I sometimes believe that the English persist in the gentle habit of executing criminals by hanging because this form of execution affords such a close parallel to the course of human life. At the moment of conception we jump, as it were, off a board, with a noose round our necks. In due course, we will be strangled – it is only a matter of sooner or later. We are all the time aware of our perilous condition, whether we dare face it or not. How *can* one be at one's ease in the interval? Immortality is therefore not a desire to perpetuate an individuality which is bought at the price of inevitable decay, but a transcending of this individuality.

Now suppose that Mr John Smith is fed up with this state of affairs in which everything is just produced for a short time in order to be destroyed again. Suppose he wishes to become immortal. Then he

[*] *Dīgha Nikāya* ii.39

has no choice but to deny himself throughout the whole length and breadth of his being. Anything impermanent in himself he has to get rid of. Just try to think of what is left of Mr Smith after he has become immortal. His body would obviously be gone. With the body his instincts would have disappeared – since they are bound up with his glands, with the needs of his tissues, in short with the body. His mind also, as he knows it, would have to be sacrificed. Because this mind of ours is bound up with bodily processes, its operations are based on the data provided by the bodily organs of sense, and it reveals its impermanence by incessantly and restlessly jumping from one thing to another. With the mind would go his sense of logical consistency. As a matter of fact, Mr John Smith, turned immortal, would not recognize himself at all. He would have lost everything that made him recognizable to himself and to others. And he could be born anew only if he had learned to deny all that clutters up the immortal side of his being – which lies, as the Buddhists would put it, outside his five skandhas – if he would deny all that constitutes his dear little self. Buddhist training consists, indeed, in systematically weakening our hold on those things in us that keep us from regaining the immortality we lost when we were born. The body is subdued, the instincts are weakened, the mind is calmed, logical thinking is baffled and exhausted by absurdities, and sensory facts are thought little of, the eye of faith and the eye of wisdom replacing the eyes of the body. It comes really to the same as the precept of John Wesley, when he urged a disciple of his to 'kill himself by inches'.

But, as I have said, it all depends on one's view on the nature of man. Those who regard man as a creature of the earth only will be inclined to compare this Buddhist yearning for immortality with the snail that leaves its house in order to go on a flying expedition. Those who regard man as an essentially spiritual being will prefer the Buddhist simile of the mountain swans who, when they have left their mountain lake, go from puddle to puddle, without making their home anywhere, until they are back to their true home in the clear waters of the mountain lake.

SURVIVAL VALUES

However eloquent the sages may be on this issue, common sense cannot help feeling that this kind of unworldliness is all very well and noble, but certainly quite unsuitable for anyone who has to live in this world, and on this Earth. We are all of us nowadays unconscious Darwinians, and the survival value of an unworldly doctrine seems to be fearfully small. How could it ever keep its footing on the Earth? Historical facts, however, are rather disconcerting to common sense. The Buddhist community is the oldest institution of mankind. It has survived longer than any other institution, except the kindred sect of the Jains. Here you have the big bullying empires of history, guarded by hosts of soldiers, ships, and magistrates. Scarcely one of them lasted longer than perhaps three centuries. There you have a movement of deliberate beggars, who always prized poverty more than wealth; who were sworn not to harm or kill other beings; who spent their time in dreaming superb dreams, and inventing beautiful never-never-lands; who despised whatever the world valued; who valued whatever the world despises – meekness, generosity, idle contemplation. And yet, where these mighty empires, built on greed, hatred, and delusion, lasted just a few centuries, the impulse of self-denial carried the Buddhist community through 2,500 years.

I suppose that quite a number of conclusions could be drawn from this fact. The one that I would like to point out is that Darwinism, and the other philosophies behind the big empires, are very shallow; they have their day – it is really a very short day, and not a very restful one while it lasts. Whereas the great and universal wisdom tradition of mankind goes deep down to the very roots, the very breath and rhythm of life. It is the meek that will inherit the Earth, it is the meek that *have* inherited the Earth – because they alone are willing to live in contact with it. The Chinese philosopher Lao-tse expressed this very beautifully in the *Tao-Teh-King* (chapter 7):

> Heaven is lasting and earth enduring.
> The reason they are lasting and enduring is that they do not live for
>   themselves;
> Therefore they live long.
> In the same way the Sage keeps himself behind and he is in front;
> He forgets himself and he is preserved.
> Is it not because he is not self-interested
> That his self-interest is established?

1

COMMON GROUND

THE FLAVOUR OF DHARMA

The historian who wants to determine what the Buddha's doctrine actually was finds himself confronted with literally thousands of works, which all claim the authority of the Buddha, and yet contain the most diverse and conflicting teachings. Some influential writers, bred in a Nonconformist tradition, have recently contended that one must seek the true Buddhist doctrine only in what Gautama Buddha actually said about 500BC. This thesis has led to some acrimoniousness. The truth is that the oldest stratum of the existing scriptures can only be reached by uncertain inference and conjecture. One thing alone do all these attempts to reconstruct an 'original' Buddhism have in common. They all agree that the Buddha's doctrine was certainly not what the Buddhists understood it to be. Mrs Rhys Davids, for instance, purges Buddhism of the doctrine of 'not-self', and of monasticism. To her, some worship of 'The Man' is the original gospel of Buddhism. H.J. Jennings, in cold blood, removes all references to reincarnation from the scriptures, and claims thereby to have restored their original meaning. Dr P. Dahlke, again, ignores all the magic and mythology with which traditional Buddhism is replete, and reduces the doctrine of the Buddha to a quite reasonable, agnostic theory.

In this book I set out to describe the living tradition of Buddhism throughout the centuries, and I confess that I do not know what the 'original gospel' of Buddhism was. To regard all later Buddhist history as a record of the 'degeneration' of an 'original gospel' is like regarding an oak tree as a degeneration of an acorn. In this book I assume that the doctrine of the Buddha, conceived in its full breadth, width, majesty and grandeur, comprises all those teachings which are linked to the original teaching by historical continuity, and which work out methods leading to the extinction of individuality by eliminating the belief in it.

THE DOCUMENTS

Throughout the book we will have to refer to the scriptures as the essential documents of Buddhist history. A general survey of Buddhist literature must be inserted at this point, and we must briefly consider the various divisions of the scriptures, their age, and the collections in which they are preserved.

From early times onwards, the scriptures were divided into *Dharma* and *Vinaya*. *Vinaya* deals with monastic discipline, *Dharma* with doctrine. At a later time, we find a threefold division, into *Vinaya, Dharma* or *Sūtra*, and *Abhidharma*. The *Abhidharma* deals with more advanced doctrines (see pp.85 *et seq.*).

Another important division is that between *Sūtra* and *Śāstra*. A sūtra is a text that claims to have been spoken by the Buddha himself. It always begins with the words, 'Thus have I heard at one time. The Lord dwelt at ...' The 'I' here means the disciple Ānanda, who recited the entire Buddha-word immediately after the Buddha's death. Many sūtras were composed centuries after the death of the Buddha. The actual authors of the sūtras which were not spoken by the historical Buddha himself, are, of course, unknown. The Buddhists themselves were sharply divided as to the value of these later sūtras. One fraction, known as the *Hīnayāna*, or 'Lesser Vehicle', held that works composed a substantial time after 480BC and not recited at the First Council immediately after the Buddha's death, could not be authentic, could not be the Buddha's own words, could be no more than mere poetry and fairy-tale. The other section, however, known as the *Mahāyāna*, the 'Great Vehicle', asserted, in the face of all chronological difficulties, that even these later sūtras come from the Buddha's own mouth. The time lag in publication was accounted for in various ways. One well-known story, for instance, runs that the *Prajñāpāramitā sūtras*, the texts dealing with perfect wisdom, were revealed by the Buddha himself, but that they were too difficult to be understood by his contemporaries. In consequence, they were stored in the palace of the serpents, or dragons, called nāgas, in the Nether world. When the time was ripe, the great doctor Nāgārjuna went down into the Nether world and brought them up into the world of men. This tale is not meant to be believed by everyone. In their desire to adapt themselves to the various dispositions of different people, the Buddhists were ever ready to give a mythological explanation to people who thought in mythological terms, and at the same time a philosophical explanation for those used to philosophical ways of thinking. The philosophical justification of the later sūtras makes use of the doctrine of the three bodies of the Buddha, which we shall explain soon. It maintains that the old sūtras were taught by the Buddha's 'form body', and the later ones by his 'enjoyment body' (see p.144).

A *śāstra* is a treatise written by an author who is generally known by name, who endeavours to be more systematic than the sūtras usually are, and who quotes the sūtras as authorities. Many śāstras by the doctors of the Church, such as Nāgārjuna, Vasubandhu, and others, are preserved for us.

The total literary output of the Buddhists was enormous. Only fragments have reached us. Our history of Buddhism must therefore always remain fragmentary and tentative. For about 400 years the tradition was transmitted only orally, by schools of Reciters. Some features of the older scriptures are clearly those of an oral tradition, such as the many repetitions, and a fondness for verse and for numerical lists. Owing to this preference for oral transmission, many of the oldest documents are now lost.

About the *age* of the scriptures we are somewhat in the dark. Buddhism is a body of traditions in which few names stand out, and in which fewer dates are precisely known. It is indeed most exasperating when we try to apply our current ideas of historical criticism. Langlois and Seignobos, in their textbook of historical method, state that 'a document whose author, date and provenance cannot be determined, is just good for nothing'. Alas, that is the case with most of the documents on which we build a 'history' of Buddhism. Hindus have always shown an almost complete indifference to historical dates. Historical change is considered as quite unimportant compared with the unchanging Truth. The Indian Buddhists shared this attitude. Even with regard to a date as fundamental as that of the lifetime of the Buddha, their estimates varied substantially. Modern scholars generally place the death of the Buddha at 483BC. In India, Buddhist tradition put forward many other dates, for instance 852BC, or 652, or 552, or 353, or even 252. Without a firm framework of dates, a great deal of what we say about the temporal sequence of events in Buddhist history can be no more than plausible guesswork. We should, however, admit that the Buddhist attitude to dates, exasperating though it is to the historian, is not quite as wrong-headed as it seems. The Dharma itself has no history. What changes are only the external circumstances in which it operates. And much of what is really important from a spiritual and religious point of view has no place in a historical book at all. Most of the experiences of the sages and saints of old in their solitude elude the historian.

The Buddhists also preserved few names, because it was, in the best periods, bad form for a monk to make a name for himself by literary work. It did not matter to them *who* said something, but whether it was true, helpful, and in keeping with tradition. Originality and innovation were not encouraged, and anonymity was a concomitant of sanctity. This attitude has its compensations. If a persistent collective effort is made, over a long time, by a great number of people devoted singly to their emancipation, to work out a system of spiritual healing, the result after, say, ten centuries, is likely to be fairly imposing.

In addition, even where names are mentioned, they cannot be always taken at their face value. The great names of men like *Aśvaghoṣa, Nāgārjuna*, and *Vasubandhu*, often attracted to themselves so many works that later pious tradition sometimes extended the lifetime of their holders over many centuries, while modern historical criticism has had the greatest difficulties in distinguishing the different persons behind the one name.

Nevertheless, some rough dating of literary works is possible. The *Sutta Nipāta*, for instance, seems to contain some of the oldest texts we possess, partly because of its archaic language, and partly because a commentary of a part of it is included in the canon of the Theravādins. Our conjectures as to the relative dates of Buddhist writings may be based on linguistic or doctrinal grounds. With regard to the latter, one is faced with the danger – not often avoided in the past – that one forms some arbitrary conception of 'primitive' Buddhism, and then dates everything in reference to that. Chinese translations are a great help to us, because they always meticulously record the date, and allow us to infer that the book in question must have been composed in India some time before that date. But, even then, we find that the composition of just the most important works seems to have extended over a long period. Works like the *Mahāvastu* and the *Lalitavistara* contain materials which may range from 200BC to 600AD. In a book like the *Lotus of the Good Law*, or the *Perfection of Wisdom in 8,000 Lines*, the last chapters are centuries later than the first.

What has survived of the scriptures exists now in three great collections:

1. The Pāli Tripiṭaka

This contains the scriptures of one of the Hīnayāna schools, the Theravāda. The scriptures of other Hīnayāna schools are partly preserved in Sanskrit and Chinese, but the greater number of them is lost. For future reference I give a short survey of the chief divisions of the Hīnayāna canon.

2. The Chinese Tripiṭaka

Its composition is less rigidly fixed, and it has varied in the course of time. The oldest catalogue, of 518AD, mentions 2,113 works, of which 276 are still in existence. In 972 the canon was printed for the first time. The latest Japanese edition, the *Taishō Issaikyō*, 1924–9, gives 2,184 works in 55 volumes of about 1,000 pages each.[*]

3. The Tibetan Kanjur and Tanjur

The Kanjur is a collection of the sūtras, and it comprises either 108 or 100 volumes. Of these, 13 deal with Vinaya or monastic discipline; 21 with Prajñāpāramitā, or Perfect Wisdom; 45 with various sūtras, and 21 with Tantric texts. The Tanjur, in 225 volumes, gives the commentaries and the śāstras. The Tanjur falls into three parts. The first, of one volume only, gives 64 hymns; the second, 2,664 commentaries on Tantric texts, in 86 volumes. The third part is less homogeneous. It gives, first of all, 38 commentaries to the Prajñāpāramitā in 15 volumes; then the śāstras of the Madhyamaka School (vols. 1–33);

---

[*] The *Taishō Issaikyō* is composed as follows: 21 volumes of Sūtras, 3 of Vinaya, 8 of Abhidharma, 12 of Chinese commentaries, 4 of Chinese and Japanese schools, and 7 of histories, catalogues, dictionaries, and biographies.

then commentaries to a variety of sūtras (vols. 34–43) and the śāstras of the Yogācārins (vols. 44–61). This concludes the Mahāyāna texts. Then follow about 30 volumes of scientific works belonging to the Hīnayāna. With volume 94 of part 3, the distinctly Buddhist śāstras come to an end. They are followed by 30 volumes devoted to the translations of Sanskrit works dealing with accessory subjects, such as Logic, Grammar, Medicine, various arts and crafts and social economics, and, finally, by 13 volumes of Tibetan works on technical subjects.

Theravādins (Pāli)	Sarvastivādins (Chinese)	Mahāsaṅghikas
1. Vinaya Piṭaka (1564pp)	1. Vinaya (c.3000pp)	1. Vinaya (Chinese)
		Mahāvastu, from Vinaya (Sanskrit)
2. Sutta Piṭaka:	2. Sūtra:	2.
(a) Dīgha Nikāya (904pp)	(a) Dīrghāgama	(a) –
(b) Majjhima Nikāya (1092 pp)	(b) Madhyamāgama	(b) –
(c) Saṁyutta Nikāya (1686 pp)	(c) Saṁyuktāgama	(c) –
(d) Aṅguttara Nikāya (1840 pp)	(d) Ekottarāgama (only partly preserved)	(d) Ekottarāgama (Chinese)
(e) Khuddaka Nikāya: 15 works	(e) Kṣudraka	(e) –
e.g. Dhammapada (95 pp)	e.g. Dharmapada (Sanskrit)	
Sutta Nipāta (226pp)		
Jātaka	Jātakas	
Apadāna (613pp)	many avadānas	Lalitavistara (Sanskrit)
3. Abhidhamma Piṭaka: 7 works	3. Abhidharma: 7 works	3. –
e.g. Dhammasaṅgaṇī (264pp)	e.g. Dharmaskandhapada (232pp)	–
Vibhaṅga (436pp)	Jñānaprasthāna (554pp)	–
Paṭṭhāna (3120pp)		

A number of *Sanskrit* works are preserved, but there exists no collection or canon of them.

In this book all the treatises enumerated under these four headings are regarded as authentic sources of Buddhist thought. The choice has been made in the past by men wiser than myself, and I have no reason to dispute it.

The greater part of this book will be devoted to the discussion of beliefs and practices shared only by a section of the Buddhist community, which is divided into monks and laymen, Hīnayāna and Mahāyāna, and various schools of thought. A few beliefs have, however, been common ground for the whole Buddhist movement in all its forms and it is with them that we must now begin. We must, first of all, say a few words about the beliefs held concerning the Buddha, and in connection with that, discuss the supposed 'atheism' of the Buddhist faith. Secondly, a few points of doctrine are common to all Buddhists. They concern either the essence of the spiritual life and are laid down in the 'four holy truths', or they concern the structure and evolution of the world and are derived from Hinduism.

THE BUDDHA

As the beliefs concerning the Buddha do not form part of our cultural heritage, they are anything but obvious to most people, and require careful explanation. The Buddha can be considered from three points of view: as a human being, as a spiritual principle, or as something in between the two.

(1) *As a human being*, the Buddha Gautama lived probably between 560 and 480BC, in the north-east of India. The historical facts of his life cannot be isolated from the legend which all Buddhists accept. The existence of Gautama, or Śākyamuni ('the sage from the tribe of the Śākyas'), as an individual is, in any case, a matter of little importance to Buddhist faith. The Buddha is a type that has been embodied in this individual – and it is the type which interests the religious life. While it is possible, though by no means certain, that ordinary believers may have thought sometimes of the Buddha as a personal being, the official Buddhist theology does nothing to encourage such a belief. In the official theory, the Buddha, the 'Enlightened', is a kind of archetype which manifests itself in the world at different periods in different personalities, whose individual particularities are of no account whatsoever.

It is obvious to Buddhists, who believe in reincarnation,[3] that Gautama did not come into the world for the first time at 560BC. He had, like everyone else, undergone many births, had experienced the world as an animal, as a man, as a god. During his many rebirths, he would have shared the common fate of all that lives. A spiritual perfection like that of a Buddha cannot be the result of just one life. It must mature slowly throughout the ages. His had been a long journey, of a length which staggers the imagination. It took slightly more than three immense aeons (*kalpas*, see p.34) according to the usual reckoning. In terms of years that would be about 3×10^{51} years, or at least some number of that order of magnitude. During all that time, the future Buddha practised all virtues in all possible ways. The *earth-witnessing posture* of so many Buddha statues symbolizes the Buddha's long preparation for Buddhahood. The legend tells us of Śākyamuni's struggle with Māra, the Evil One, the Lord of this world, just before his enlightenment. Śākyamuni tells Māra that he proved his contempt for worldly power and grandeur when he sacrificed wealth, limbs, and life so many times in so many lives. He points to the earth as his witness, and the deity of the earth rises out of the ground to confirm his statement. She also bore witness to the fact that Śākyamuni had fulfilled the complete discipline and duty of a Bodhisattva. This parable hides a deep spiritual truth. Māra, who corresponds to Satan, is the Lord of this world and of this Earth. He claims therefore that the Bodhisattva, representing that which is beyond this world and irredeemably hostile to it, has no right even to the piece of ground on which he is seated in meditation. The Bodhisattva, on the other hand, claims that through his innumerable deeds of self-sacrifice in his former lives, he has won a right to this little bit of earth.

(2) If the doctrine of the Buddha had been just the saying of some person or individual, it would lack in compelling authority. As a matter of fact, it emanated from the *spiritual principle*, from the Buddha nature, which lay hidden in that individual Śākyamuni, and which as we might say 'inspired' him to understand and to teach the truth. When the Buddhists consider the Buddha as a spiritual principle, they call him the *Tathāgata*, or speak of his *Dharma body*. The original meaning of the word 'Tathāgata' is no longer known. Later commentaries explain the term as composed of the two words: *tatha-*, 'thus', and the past participle *agata*, 'come', or *gata*, 'gone'. In other words, the Tathāgata is one who has come or gone 'thus', i.e. as the other Tathāgatas have come or gone. This explanation stresses the fact that the 'historical Buddha' is not an isolated phenomenon, but just one in an endless series of innumerable Tathāgatas, who appear throughout the ages in the world and always proclaim the same

doctrine. The Tathāgata is, therefore, essentially one of a group. Sets of seven, or twenty-four, or a thousand, Tathāgatas were particularly popular. In Sanchi and Bharhut, for instance, the seven Tathāgatas, i.e. Śākyamuni and his six predecessors, are represented in art by the seven stupas which contained their relics, or by the seven trees under which they won enlightenment. In Gandhara, Mathura, and Ajanta, the seven Buddhas are shown in human form, one practically indistinguishable from the other.

(3) We must now consider the Buddha in his *glorified body*. When he walked about as a human being, Śākyamuni naturally looked like any other human being. But this ordinary human body of the Buddha was nothing but a kind of outer layer which both enveloped and hid his true personality, and which was quite accidental and almost negligible. It was not at all an adequate expression of the Buddha's own being. Hidden behind this outer shell was another kind of body, different in many ways from that of ordinary mortals, which could be seen only with the eye of faith. The Buddhists variously called it the 'enjoyment body', the 'unadulterated body', the 'body which expresses the Buddha's own true nature'. A list of thirty-two 'marks of a superman', often supplemented by a list of eighty 'subsidiary marks', described the most salient features of the Buddha's 'glorious body'. The list of the thirty-two marks is common to all schools, and it must be fairly old. The paintings and statues of the Buddha that we find in Buddhist art never depicted the human body visible to all, but always try to represent the 'glorious body' of the Buddha.

Far from being invented only in the later stages of Buddhist history, the idea that various signs on the body, known only to the wise, indicate a person's destiny, stature, and future, is very much older than Buddhism itself. The thrity-two signs of the superman are derived from a pre-Buddhistic manual of astrology. The Buddha's 'glorious body' did not suffer from the physical limitations of an ordinary body. It can move about in a space which is not bigger than a mustard grain, and, on one occasion, the Buddha rose in three steps to the heaven of Indra, which is very distant indeed.

It would lead us too far to discuss all the traditional signs of a superman in detail, although an understanding of Buddhist art is quite impossible without a thorough acquaintance with them. The Buddha's 'glorious body' was eighteen feet high, and many statues of the Buddha have attained that height. The body was golden in colour. 'Between the Lord's eyebrows there was a woolly curl (ūrṇā), soft like cotton, and similar to a jasmine flower, to the moon, to a conch-shell, to the filament of a lotus, to cow's milk, to a hoar-frost blossom.'* Many-coloured light radiates from this hair-tuft, which is as white as snow or silver. Sculptures usually represent the ūrṇā by a simple dot or by a jewel. In the later stages of Buddhism the Tantra, under the influence of Shivaism, interpreted the ūrṇā as a third eye, the 'eye of wisdom'. We have here to deal with a tradition which owes much to yoga practices. It is usual for yogis to concentrate on an invisible centre above and between the eyebrows, and the yoga doctrine has always assumed that some centre of psychic or spiritual force is located in that part of the forehead.

Two other features of the Buddha's 'glorious body' are particularly conspicuous and important. There is the uṣṇīṣa, literally 'turban', a kind of 'cowl on the head', which is shown on statues as a growth or protuberance on the top of the head. It is round in Gandhara, conic in Cambodia, pointed in Siam and on Bengal miniatures of the eleventh century, and of the shape of a flame in Laos. In addition, light emanates incessantly from the Buddha's body. Rays of light issue from him and illuminate a vast space. 'Around the body of the Buddha there is always a light, a fathom wide, on all sides, which shines constantly day and night, as brilliantly as a thousand suns, and resembling a mountain of jewels in movement.'† According to common Indian tradition, a kind of fiery energy radiates from the bodies of great men, and the habit of meditation increases it. Very often this magical power is represented by flames which emanate from a halo round the figure of the Buddha, and sometimes from his shoulders. In Java, the small flames which issue from the halo behind Buddha statues are in the shape of the sacred syllable oṁ, i.e. in the shape of an inverted question mark with a spiral tail. Round the head of the Buddha there is a nimbus which signifies divinity and sanctity. In the art of Gandhara the nimbus is also given to gods and kings, and Christian art adopted this symbol in the fourth century.

Whenever the word Buddha is used in the Buddhist tradition, one has this threefold aspect of the Buddha in view. To the Christian and

---

* Untraced at time of publication
† *Vibāṣā*

agnostic historian, only the human Buddha is real, and the spiritual and the magical Buddha are to him nothing but fictions. The perspective of the believer is quite different. The Buddha nature and the Buddha's 'glorious body' stand out most clearly, and the Buddha's human body and historical existence appear like a few rags thrown over this spiritual glory.

IS BUDDHISM ATHEISTIC?

It has often been suggested that Buddhism is an atheistic system of thought, and this assumption has given rise to quite a number of discussions. Some have claimed that since Buddhism knew no God, it could not be a religion; others that since Buddhism obviously was a religion which knew no God, the belief in God was not essential to religion. These discussions assume that 'God' is an unambiguous term, which is by no means the case. We can distinguish in this context at least three meanings of the term. There is firstly a personal God who created the universe; there is secondly the Godhead, either conceived as impersonal or as supra-personal; there are thirdly a number of gods, or of angels not clearly distinguished from gods.

(1) As for the first, Buddhist tradition does not exactly deny the existence of a creator,[4] but it is not really interested to know who created the universe. The purpose of Buddhist doctrine is to release beings from suffering, and speculations concerning the origin of the universe are held to be immaterial to that task. They are not merely a waste of time but they may also postpone deliverance from suffering by engendering ill will in oneself and in others. While thus the Buddhists adopt an attitude of agnosticism to the question of a personal creator, they have not hesitated to stress the superiority of the Buddha over Brahmā, the god who, according to Brahminic theology, created the universe. They represent the god Brahmā as seized by pride when he thought to himself: 'I am Brahmā, I am the great Brahmā, the King of the Gods; I am uncreated, I have created the world, I am the sovereign of the world, I can create, alter, and give birth; I am the Father of all things.'* The scriptures are not slow in pointing out that the Tathāgata is free from such childish conceit.

* *Dīrghāgama* T1.xxii, T24.i; *Vibhāṣā* T1545.iic

If indifference to a personal creator of the universe is atheism, then Buddhism is indeed atheistic.

(2) We are, however, nowadays, if only through the writings of Aldous Huxley, familiar with the difference between God and God-head as an essential feature of the *Perennial Philosophy*. When we compare the attributes of the Godhead as they are understood by the more mystical tradition of Christian thought with those of Nirvāṇa, we find almost no difference at all. It is indeed true that Nirvāṇa has no cosmological functions, that this is not God's world but a world made by our own greed and stupidity. It is indeed true that through their attitude the Buddhists express a more radical rejection of the world in all its aspects than we find among many Christians. At the same time, they are spared a number of awkward theological riddles and have not been under the necessity to combine, for instance, the assumption of an omnipotent and all-loving God with the existence of a great deal of suffering and muddle in this world. Buddhists also have never stated that God is Love, but that may be due to their preoccupation with intellectual precision, which must have perceived that the word 'Love' is one of the most unsatisfactory and ambiguous terms one could possibly use.

But, on the other hand, we are told that Nirvāṇa is permanent, stable, imperishable, immovable, ageless, deathless, unborn, and unbecome, that it is power, bliss and happiness, the secure refuge, the shelter, and the place of unassailable safety; that it is the real Truth and the supreme Reality, that it is the Good, the supreme goal, and the one and only consummation of our life, the eternal, hidden, and incomprehensible Peace.

Similarly, the Buddha who is, as it were, the personal embodiment of Nirvāṇa, becomes the object of all those emotions that we are wont to call religious.

There has existed throughout Buddhist history a tension between the bhaktic and the gnostic approach to religion, such as we find also in Christianity. There is, however, the difference that in Buddhism the gnostic vision has always been regarded as the more true one, while the bhaktic, devotion, type was regarded more or less as a concession to the common people (see pp.120 *et seq*.). It is generally found in philosophical thought that even philosophical abstractions are clothed with some kind of emotional warmth when they concern the Absolute. We have only to think of Aristotle's description of the

Prime Mover. In Buddhism, however, in addition, a whole system of ritual, and of religious elevation, is associated with an intellectually conceived Absolute in a manner which is not logically very plausible, but which stood the test of life for a long time.

(3) We now come to the thorny subject of polytheism. The Christian teaching which has to some extent pervaded our education, has made us believe that polytheism belongs to a past period of the human race, that it has been superseded by monotheism, and that it finds no response in the contemporary mind. In order to appreciate the Buddhists' toleration of polytheism, we must first of all under-stand that polytheism is very much alive even among us. But where formerly Athene, Baal, Astarte, Isis, Sarasvati, Kuan-Yin, etc., excited the popular imagination, it is nowadays inflamed by such words as democracy, progress, civilization, equality, liberty, reason, science, etc. A multitude of personal beings has given way to a multitude of abstract nouns. In Europe, the turning point came when the French deposed the Virgin Mary and transferred their affections to the Goddess of Reason. The reason for this change is not far to seek. Personal deities grow on the soil of a rural culture in which the majority of the population are illiterate, while abstract nouns find favour with the literate populations of modern towns. Medieval men went to war for Jesus Christ, Saint George, and San José. Modern crusades are in aid of such abstractions as Christianity, the Christian Way of Life, Democracy, and the Rights of Man.

Literacy, however, is not the only factor which differentiates our modern polytheism from that of ancient times. Another factor is our separation from the forces of Nature. Every tree, every well, lake, or river, almost every type of animal, could once bring forth a deity. We are now too remote from Nature to think that. In addition, our democratic predilections make us less inclined to deify great men. In India, kings were held to be gods and, ever since the days of Egypt, the despotism of a divine ruler has been a most efficient way of keeping vast empires together – in Rome, in China, in Iran, and in Japan. However much people may think of Hitler, Stalin, and Chur-chill, they are disinclined to grant them *full* divinity. The deification of great men is not confined to political figures. The inveterate polytheism of the human mind broke out in Islam and Christianity, through the crust of an official monotheism, in the form of the worship of saints. In Islam again the saints fused with the spirits which since ancient times had inhabited different localities. Finally, we must realize that religious people everywhere expect also immediate advantages from their religion. I saw, recently, in an Anglican shop window in Oxford, that at present Saint Christopher seems to be the only saint who appeals to those circles. His medals protect from car accidents. Similarly, the Buddhist expected from his religion that it would protect him from illnesses and fire, that it would give him children and other benefits. It is quite obvious that the one God, who soars above the stars and has the entire universe to look after, cannot really be bothered with such trifles. Special needs, therefore, engender special deities to provide for them. At present, we have developed a kind of confidence that science and industry will provide those needs, and our more superstitious inclinations are reserved for those activities which contain a large element of chance.

Among the populations which adopted Buddhism almost all activities contained a large element of chance, and a great number of deities were invoked for protection and help. The Buddhists would find no objection whatsoever in the cult of many gods because the idea of a jealous god is quite alien to them; and also because they are imbued with the conviction that everyone's intellectual insight is very limited, so that it is very difficult for us to know when we are right, but practically impossible to be sure that someone else is wrong. Like the Catholics, the Buddhists believe that a faith can be kept alive only if it can be adapted to the mental habits of the average person. In consequence, we find that, in the earlier scriptures, the deities of Brahmanism are taken for granted and that, later on, the Buddhists adopted the local gods of any district to which they came.

If atheism is the denial of the existence of a God, it would be quite misleading to describe Buddhism as atheistic. On the other hand, monotheism has never appealed to the Buddhist mind. There has never been any interest in the origin of the universe – with only one exception. About 1000AD Buddhists in the north-west of India came into contact with the victorious forces of Islam. In their desire to be all things to all men, some Buddhists in that district rounded off their theology with the notion of an Ādi-Buddha, a kind of omnipotent and omniscient primeval Buddha, who through his meditation originated the universe. This notion was adopted by a few sects in Nepal and Tibet (see pp.162 et seq.).

THE FOUR HOLY TRUTHS

Next to the Buddha, the Dharma. The essence of the doctrine, accepted by all schools, has been laid down in the Four Holy Truths, which the Buddha first preached at Benares immediately after his enlightenment. I will first give the formula of this basic teaching, and then comment on it.

> (1) What then is the Holy Truth of Ill? Birth is ill, decay is ill, sickness is ill, death is ill. To be conjoined with what one dislikes means suffering. To be disjoined from what one likes means suffering. Not to get what one wants, also that means suffering. In short, all grasping at (any of) the five skandhas (involves) suffering.
>
> (2) What then is the Holy Truth of the Origination of Ill? It is that craving which leads to rebirth, accompanied by delight and greed, seeking its delight now here, now there, i.e. craving for sensuous experience, craving to perpetuate oneself, craving for extinction.
>
> (3) What then is the Holy Truth of the Stopping of Ill? It is the complete stopping of that craving, the withdrawal from it, the renouncing of it, throwing it back, liberation from it, non-attachment to it.
>
> (4) What then is the Holy Truth of the steps which lead to the stopping of Ill? It is this Holy Eightfold Path, which consists of: right views, right intentions, right speech, right conduct, right livelihood, right effort, right mindfulness, right concentration.[*]

Systematic meditation on the four Holy Truths, as on the basic facts of life, is a central task of the Buddhist life. I must confine myself here to the first Truth. A survey of some of its implications will greatly help us to see the Buddhist doctrine in its proper perspective.

The first part presents little intellectual difficulty, and anybody can assent to it. It merely enumerates seven well-known aspects of life which are fraught with suffering. Our intellectual resistance will begin only with the second part, which infers the universality of suffering. We must, however, reckon with an emotional resistance which acts as a powerful obstacle to the full appreciation even of the first part. Most of us are inclined by nature to live in a fool's paradise,

[*] *Majjhima Nikāya* 141

to look on the brighter side of life, and to minimize its unpleasant sides. To dwell on suffering runs normally counter to our inclinations. Usually, we cover up suffering with all kinds of 'emotional curtains'. For most of us life would be intolerable if we could see it as it is, and if our mental perspective would emphasize its distasteful features as much as its gratifying ones. We like to keep distressing facts out of sight. This is illustrated by the widespread use of 'euphemisms', which is nothing but the avoidance of words that call up disagreeable associations. A vague or roundabout expression covers up a fact which is disagreeable or taboo. There are, in all languages, hundreds of euphemisms for death, deformity, disease, sex, the processes of digestion, and domestic troubles. A man does not 'die', but he 'passes away', 'breathes his last', 'goes to sleep', 'leaves the world behind', 'joins his Maker', etc. A special effort of meditation is needed to face the full reality of death. It is common practice to shut one's eyes to unpalatable facts, to pass over them, to minimize their importance, or to prettify them. Middle-aged women are not gladly reminded of their age. When people see a corpse, they often shudder and look away. As subjects of conversation, the distressing and disheartening aspects of life shock the 'nice people', and frighten the others. Again, special meditation is needed to bring to the fore that which is usually glossed over. I cannot show here in detail how this flight from displeasing reality is partly caused by concern for narcissistic self-love, and chiefly by fear, coupled with a desire to protect the personality from ideas which threaten its integrity. The overwhelming majority of people cannot live joyfully without adopting some kind of ostrich attitude to life. In this sense the first Truth is not self-evident. To understand it, we must do violence to our ingrained habits of thought. In the desire to impress the unattractive aspects of life on a reluctant mind, the Buddhist yogi will therefore repeatedly contemplate in great detail one by one the seven items of the formula.

At the end of the formula, the Buddha has stated that everything in this world is bound up with suffering. The 'skandhas' have been mentioned before (p.3). It is now said that it is impossible to 'grasp' at matter, or at feelings, perceptions, impulses, and acts of consciousness, without getting involved in suffering. Buddhaghosa explains the Buddha's meaning by a set of well-chosen similes.

As in the case of the fire and the fuel, of the weapons and the target, of gadflies, mosquitoes, etc., and a cow's body, of the reapers and the field, of the village robbers and a village – so here also birth, etc., trouble the five grasping skandhas, in which they are produced, just as grass and creepers grow on the earth, or as flowers and fruits sprout on trees. [*]

The universality of suffering does not immediately stand out as a self-evident fact. We tenaciously cling to the belief that some happiness can be found in this world. Only the accomplished saint, only the Arhant, can fully understand the first Truth. As the Buddha put it:

It is difficult to shoot from a distance arrow after arrow through a narrow keyhole, and miss not once. It is more difficult to shoot and penetrate with the tip of a hair split a hundred times a piece of hair similarly split. It is still more difficult to penetrate to the fact that 'all this is ill'. [†]

As a matter of fact, the insight into the universality of suffering gradually extends with our spiritual growth. There is much obvious suffering in the world. A great deal of it, however, is concealed, and can be perceived only by the wise. Obvious suffering is recognized by the unpleasant and painful feelings which are associated with it, and by reactions of avoidance and hate. Concealed suffering lies in what seems pleasant, but is ill underneath. It is sufficient to mention four kinds of concealed suffering, the understanding of which depends on the maturity of our spiritual insight.

(1) *Something, while pleasant, involves the suffering of others.* One is usually rather blind to this aspect of one's enjoyments. As our capacity for compassion grows, it widens the field of the sorrow which we feel as our own. Roast duck is pleasant as long as one ignores the feelings of the duck. Our unconscious mind has a greater sense of solidarity with other people than we often realize. When we buy pleasure by depriving someone else of happiness, we are apt to feel that pleasure as a kind of privilege which is coupled with an unconscious sense of guilt. This is well illustrated by the attitude of the wealthy to their wealth. Few of the wealthy people I have met

[*] *Visuddhimagga* xvi.58
[†] *Saṃyutta Nikāya* v.454

did not fear to become poor. They feel unworthy of their wealth, as is shown by the efforts they make to prove that they deserve it. Since they got their wealth at the expense of the poor, they wish to shut the poor out from their sight, or buy them off, or tread mentally upon them by contemplating their unworthiness. Repressed compassion results in an unconscious sense of guilt. One easily compares oneself with an afflicted person, poor or deformed, and often puts oneself in their place. Some of us feel that they did nothing to deserve being better off than their ill-fated fellow men. On the contrary, we may feel we richly deserve to be punished, and that there is really nothing that can protect us from a similar fate. Acute mental distress is avoided by shutting out the unpleasant experience. We also have to bear in mind that our social conscience is never quite extinct. Those who are better off are always inclined to blame themselves for the misery of the others. They therefore invent a picture of the social world in which misery is either minimized, or justified, or prettified. 'Nobody need go without food in England.' 'Everybody can find work if he only wants to.' 'Beggars are simply lazy, and often they are quite wealthy. Did you not see the case in the papers recently...?' 'The poor would be better off if they did not drink so much, or smoked fewer cigarettes.' All this may be quite true, but why this elaborate superstructure if there is no sense of guilt at the bottom of it?

(2) *Something, while pleasant, is tied up with anxiety, since one is afraid to lose it.* Buddhists call this 'suffering from reversal', and most, if not all, things are liable to it. Anxiety and worry are inseparable from attachment. This becomes fully obvious only when one dares to be free from attachment, and tastes the bliss and fearlessness which result.

(3) *Something, while pleasant, binds us still further to conditions which are the ground on which a great deal of suffering is inevitable.* What terrors are we not exposed to by the mere fact of having a body! Much pleasure is followed by bad karmic consequences (punishment), and by fresh craving which ties us to this world. There is suffering inherent in the mere fact that our existence is conditioned. We are usually quite unable to see that, and our eyes are only opened to the extent that we gain, through prolonged meditation, some understanding of the Unconditioned as our original home (see pp.90 *et seq.*).

(4) *The pleasures derived from anything included in the 'skandhas' are worthless to satisfy the inmost longings of our hearts.* They are short-

lived, riddled with anxiety, coarse, and vulgar. It is absurd to try and build any real ease on anything as shifting, trivial, and insignificant as this world has to offer. This becomes more and more obvious as one acquires an experience of spiritual bliss. Compared with that, sensory pleasures seem unsatisfying, even pernicious, because they shut out the calm which comes from the rejection and extinction of craving.

> The joy of pleasures in the world,
> And the great joy of heaven,
> Compared with the joy of the destruction of craving
> Are not worth a sixteenth part.

> Sorry is he whose burden is heavy,
> And happy is he who has cast it down;
> When once he has cast off his burden,
> He will seek to be burdened no more.[*]

As for the second and third Truths, their meaning is fairly obvious. They assert that craving is the cause of suffering, and that the abolition of craving will abolish suffering. The mechanism which inevitably links suffering to craving has been stated in an important corollary to the Four Holy Truths, which is known as the formula of *conditioned co-production*. Beginning with Ignorance, it enumerates a set of twelve conditions, with decay-and-death as the last, which comprise everything that happens in this world. The discovery of the twelve links of conditioned co-production was hailed as the greatest deed of the Tathāgata. One verse sums up the credo of all Buddhist schools, and it is found everywhere on temples, stones, statues, steles, and manuscripts throughout the whole world of Buddhist influence.

> The Tathāgata has expounded the cause of all those dharmas which spring from a cause, and also their cessation. That is the teaching of the Great Ascetic.[†]

The actual interpretation of the formula of the twelve links differs greatly, however, in the various schools. The details fall outside the

---

[*] *Tibetan Vinaya*, quoted in E.J. Thomas, *The Life of the Buddha*, 1927, p.79
[†] e.g. *Vinaya* i.41

scope of this book. The practices comprised in the Eightfold Path will be discussed in detail in the following chapters. Here it is sufficient to note that *Right Views* means the 'Four Holy Truths', *Right Intentions*, a desire for self-extinction and the welfare of others, paraphrased by Buddhaghosa in the three terms 'Renunciation, Absence of Ill Will, and Inoffensiveness', and that *Right Effort* refers to one's endeavours to abandon all unwholesome *dharmas*, and to gain, increase, and develop instead states which are wholesome.

COSMOLOGY

The Four Holy Truths state the essence of the specific religious doctrine of Buddhism. In their views on the structure and evolution of the universe, the Buddhists were, however, content to borrow from the traditions of contemporary Hinduism. Hindu cosmology is largely mythological, and differs greatly from our own. One must say a few words about some of its essential features. We will confine ourselves to explaining the notion of *aeons* and *world systems* on the one hand, and the six *conditions of living existence* on the other.

Before the Copernican revolution and the invention of the telescope the European mind was confined into a universe but tiny in its dimensions. Galilei, when he became blind in 1638, wrote to his friend Diodati:

> Alas, your friend and servant Galileo has for the last month been
> irremediably blind, so that this heaven, this earth, this universe
> which I, by my remarkable discoveries and clear demonstrations,
> have enlarged a hundred thousand times beyond what has been
> believed by wise men of past ages, for me is from this time forth
> shrunk into so small a space as to be filled by my own sensations.[*]

Europeans in the seventeenth century were quite unaware that 'the wise men of bygone ages' in India had for a long time already done justice to the immensity of time and space, not, however, through 'marvellous discoveries and clear demonstrations', but through the intuitions of their cosmic imagination.

First, as regards the extent of Time, they measured cosmic time not in years, but in *kalpas* or aeons. A kalpa is the duration of time that

---

[*] M. Allan-Olney, *The Private Life of Galileo*, Macmillan, London, p.283.

elapses between the origin and the destruction of a world system. The length of a kalpa is either suggested by way of simile, or reckoned by way of number. Suppose there is a mountain of a very hard rock, much bigger than the Himalayas; and suppose that a man, with a piece of the very finest cloth of Benares once every century should touch that mountain ever so slightly – then the time it would take him to wear away the entire mountain would be about the time of an aeon. As for numbers, some say that a kalpa lasts only 1,344,000 years, others reckon 1,280,000,000 years, and no general agreement has been arrived at. In any case, a very large and almost incomputable stretch of time is intended.

During the course of one kalpa, a world system completes its evolution, from its initial condensation to the final conflagration. One world system follows the other, without beginning and end, quite interminably. A world system is a conglomeration of many suns, moons, etc. Innumerable world systems reach out into space, immeasurably far. In a way, modern astronomy has an analogous idea when it speaks of 'island universes',5 billions of which are already known, many of them billions of light years away. Each such 'spiral nebula' consists of thousands of millions of stars rotating round a common centre. Their shape is often that of a mill-wheel, just as the Buddhists had asserted. The Earth forms part of the 'galactic system', which would correspond to what the Buddhists called 'this sahā-world'.

In regard to the size of the universe, Buddhist views are borne out by recent discoveries, and their vast cosmic perspective cannot fail to be salutary to spiritual growth. It would, however, be idle to pretend that the detailed description which the Buddhist scriptures give of the constitution and composition of a world system can be harmonized with the conclusions of modern science. Almost all the traditional assertions must appear fabulous to us. We hear, in particular, a great deal about the 'heavens' and 'hells' attached to each world system, and the account of the Earth's geography is quite at variance with the picture presented by a modern atlas. Buddhists assume, by the way, as a matter of course, that life is not confined to this Earth, that living beings dwell in many of the stars, and the later Buddhism of the Mahāyāna laid great stress on the Buddhas and Bodhisattvas who worked to release suffering beings in world systems other than our own (see p.129 *et seq.*).

Now to the classes of living beings. At present, we distinguish three kinds of life: men, animals, and plants. Buddhist tradition counts six: the six 'planes of life' are the gods, the asuras, men, ghosts, animals, and hells. Some authors count only five 'worlds', omitting the asuras. There was much disagreement on details, but the general scheme was accepted by all schools. All the innumerable beings in the world fall into one of those six, or five, classes. The merit one has acquired in the past decides on the place where one can choose one's rebirth.

The 'gods' (devas) are 'above' us in the sense that their material constitution is more refined than ours, that their emotions are less coarse, that their life-span is much longer, and that they are less subject to suffering than we are. They resemble the Olympian gods, but with the important difference that they are not 'immortal'. In some ways they are more 'angels' than 'gods'. Buddhist tradition gives an elaborate classification of the gods which we can omit here. The asuras are also celestial beings. They are furious spirits who continually fight with the gods. Some authors count them among the gods, and others again among the ghosts.

The animal world, the world of ghosts, and the hells, are the three 'Dismal Destinies', or 'States of Woe'. The term 'ghosts' (*preta*) referred originally to the 'Spirits of the Departed,' but the more developed Buddhist theory attempts to systematize under this heading a great deal of the folklore current in India. The 'hells' are very numerous, and usually divided into hot hells and cold hells. Since life in hell comes to an end some day, they are more like the Purgatory of the Catholics than like the Hell of orthodox Christianity.

Suffering is the common lot of life in all its forms. The gods suffer because they are bound in due course to fall from their exalted condition. Men have much sorrow and little joy, and they often fall into a worse rebirth. The pretas are incessantly tormented by hunger and thirst, and the pains of the beings in hell are almost unthinkable. Faced with this vast ocean of suffering, one trained in the doctrine will feel compassion, and he will reflect: 'Even if I would give the greatest happiness in the world to these beings, that happiness must end in suffering. It is only through the eternal bliss of Nirvāṇa that I can do good to all. I must therefore first win true wisdom, and then I can work the weal of other beings.' Rebirth as a *man* is, however, essential for the appreciation of the Dharma. Gods are too happy to feel dislike for conditioned things, and they live too long to appreciate impermanence. Animals, ghosts, and the damned lack in clarity of mind. Once he has gained a certain height of spirituality, a man can never again be reborn in the 'states of woe'. He may, however, in the view of all Buddhist schools, voluntarily seek rebirth in them, in order to help beings by the teaching of the Dharma. Thereby he gladdens and heartens those beings, and also increases both his disgust for existence, and his patience.

2

MONASTIC BUDDHISM

THE SANGHA

The first, and the most fundamental, division among Buddhists is that between monks and householders. In this chapter I intend to describe the essential virtues of the monastic life, proceed in the next chapter to a survey of popular Buddhism, and then devote the remainder of the book to an outline of the various schools of Buddhist thought.

The core of the Buddhist movement consisted of monks. A monastic life alone will normally provide the conditions favourable to a spiritual life bent on the highest goal. The monks lived either in communities or, as hermits, in solitude. The entire 'brotherhood' of monks and hermits is called the Sangha. The Sangha naturally always formed only a small minority of the Buddhist community. Its proportion to the householders varied greatly with social conditions at different times. China, for instance, knew 77,258 monks and nuns in 450AD, and 2,000,000 seventy-five years later, in 525. Ceylon, in 450AD had 50,000 monks, but only 2,500 in 1850, and again 7,300 in 1901. In Japan, in 1931, there were 58,400 priests to 40,000,000 laymen. In Tibet, one third of the entire male population lived at times in the monasteries.

The monks are the Buddhist élite. They are the only Buddhists in the proper sense of the word. The life of a householder is almost incompatible with the higher levels of the spiritual life. This has been a conviction common to all Buddhists at all times. They differed only in the strictness in which they adhered to it. The Hīnayāna was, on the whole, disinclined to grant any exceptions. The *Questions of King Milinda*, it is true, somewhat grudgingly admit (p.265) that also a layman can win Nirvāṇa, but add at once that he must then either enter the Order or die. In any case, a layman could attain Nirvāṇa in this life only if he had pursued a monastic life in some former existence (p.353). The Mahāyāna went further, and granted that householders could be Bodhisattvas, i.e. first-class Buddhists. Vimalakīrti is a famous example from literature. In order that he should not be contaminated by home and family, a Bodhisattva must preserve a correct and watchful attitude towards sense pleasures. He must feel disgust for them, and fear them, 'just as someone in the middle of a wilderness infested with robbers, would eat his food in trembling, and with the ever recurring hope of getting away from this dreadful place'.[*]

The continuity of the monastic organization has been the only constant factor in Buddhist history. Monastic life was regulated by the rules of the *Vinaya*. The term is derived from *vi-nayati*, 'to lead away (from evil) to discipline'. The monks were apt to attach extra-ordinary importance to the observance of the Vinaya rules. Monastic discipline was codified in the *prātimokṣa* rules. Different sects count between 227 and 253 of them. They are very similar in all sources, and must therefore be very old, older than the independent development of the schools. The word *prāti-mokṣa* either means to 'abandon sin', or it may mean 'equipment, armour'. The rules must be recited twice a month in an assembly of the chapter.

POVERTY

Poverty, celibacy, and inoffensiveness were the three essentials of monastic life. A monk possessed almost no private property at all. He was allowed to have his robes, an alms-bowl, a needle, a rosary, a razor with which to shave the head every fortnight, and a filter which served to remove little animals from his drinking water. Originally, the dress consisted of rags which were taken from the rubbish heaps in the villages, and which were stitched together and dyed a uniform saffron colour. Later on, the cloth for the robes was usually donated by the faithful.

---

[*] *Aṣṭasāhasrikā* xvii.332–3

In theory and intention a monk should be without a home or permanent shelter. The life of the monk is described as the homeless life, and in order to enter upon it he had to leave the home, filled with faith. The original rigour of the monastic rules seems to have demanded that a monk lived in the forest, in the open, at the foot of a tree. The Vinaya speaks of the dwelling in convents, sanctuaries, temples, houses, and grottos as of a luxury, permissible, but nevertheless full of dangers. Food should be obtained by begging.

As a matter of fact, a monk should really rely on begging for all his needs. A number of monks, who wanted to lead a particularly strict life, conformed to this rule. Others seem, from very early times onwards, to have accepted invitations into the houses of the faithful. The possession of money was forbidden for a very long time. About a hundred years after the foundation of the Order, some monks of Vaiśālī tried to break this rule, and their conduct led to the first real crisis in the Order. The Second Council of Vaiśālī settled the matter in favour of the strict observance of the rules, but in later times a great deal of laxity about the possession of money, land, and other property set in.

The begging-bowl was the Buddha's badge of sovereignty. Many statues show the Buddha holding his begging-bowl, indicating that he obtained it as the reward of rejecting the position of a world ruler. Teachers often gave their begging-bowl to their successor as a sign of the transmission of authority. It must, of course, be remembered that in Asiatic countries begging has always been an accepted mode of earning one's living. We are apt to forget that, during the Middle Ages, all through Europe monastic orders maintained themselves by begging, and it was really only the economic system of rising industrialism which found that begging was incompatible with its needs for industrial workers, and passed the vagrancy laws as one of its first measures. When we consider history, we find that all the more developed forms of society seem to have a great deal of surplus wealth to spend. The Egyptians used it for the building of pyramids. At present, only too much of it goes into wars, female vanity, and drugs, i.e. beer, tobacco, cinemas, fiction. In Buddhist countries it is spent on maintaining the Sangha, and on manufacturing innumerable objects of worship such as stupas and statues. The Buddhists considered the practice of begging as a breeding ground for many virtues. The monk had no sense of inferiority about this mode of livelihood. He felt that he was not idle by any means, but led a strenuous life, in curbing his desires and developing his meditations. Since generosity is one of the prime virtues, the monks felt that by accepting alms they gave the householder an opportunity for gaining merit. At present, society is inclined to regard contemplatives as parasites. From the Buddhist point of view, the existence of contemplatives is the only justification of human society.

On their begging rounds the monks often met with humiliating experiences. They were called 'bald-pate', and similar names, and the curbing of pride is counted among the advantages of begging. In addition, one learns to have few desires, to be easily contented, and to restrain the sentiments of anger and disappointment. The results of begging are uncertain and one trains oneself in doing, for a time, even without the necessities of life. The indifference of the begging monks to worldly advantages, their calm and dignified behaviour, helps to convert unbelievers and to strengthen the faith of the believers.

The practice of begging gives ample opportunities to watch well over the body, control the senses, and to repress[6] thoughts. The monk must go from house to house without making a distinction between those of the poor and those of the wealthy. He must pay no attention to what he gets, and must be neither pleased nor displeased. If a woman hands him his food he must not speak to her, or look at her, or observe her beauty or ugliness. The food which was given to the monks was not always either ample or dainty, or even wholesome. Gastric troubles were the professional disease of the monastic communities. The experiences of the Buddhist monks were to some extent paralleled by those of Saint Francis of Assisi, who had once been a prosperous man, and who had been 'dainty in his father's home'. After his great renunciation of all property, he took a bowl and begged scraps of food from door to door. As the legend says:

> When he would have eaten that medley of various meats, at first he
> shrank back, for that he had never been used willingly even to see,
> much less to eat, such scraps. At length, conquering himself he began
> to eat; and it seemed to him that in eating no rich syrup had he ever
> tasted aught so delightsome.[*]

* *Sūtra on the Twelve Ascetic Practices*, T783, p.720c

Finally, the absence of ties, the great independence, the ability to come and go freely, was one of the greatest advantages of begging. Compared with the life of the wandering monk, the home life of the householder seemed cramped and stuffy. Even the more settled life of monastic communities contained many afflictions and distractions, which distract the mind and impede the practice of the path. One must obey the rules of the monastery, interrupt one's meditations to receive guests, help to administrate the affairs of the community, accept duties, and fulfil functions.

The Hīnayāna treats begging chiefly as a school of self-discipline. The Mahāyāna, which largely abandoned the practice of begging, stressed its altruistic aspects. This instance confirms, I think, the general observation that the profession of altruistic sentiments is often a means to cover up some personal advantage. The Mahāyānist, in any case, should use his begging round as an opportunity to cultivate his love for his fellow beings.

In the course of time, particularly outside India, the practice of begging was discontinued. The reasons which Asaṅga in his *Yogaśāstra* gives for the abrogation of the ancient poverty are very noble and altruistic; they are, at present, heard frequently among well-to-do Christians. According to Asaṅga, monks may possess wealth and property, even gold, silver, and silken clothes, because such possessions allow them to be more useful to others and to help them. At present the habit of begging has totally disappeared from China, Korea, and Annam.7 In China, under the T'ang dynasty, a special sect, the Vinaya sect, was founded for the purpose of reviving the old practice of begging, and enforcing the strict rules of the Vinaya in general. Under the Sung dynasty, the Ch'an monks practised begging and this practice persists among the Zen monks in Japan. It is in Japan, however, not the chief source of livelihood but only a disciplinary exercise for novices, or a mode of collection on special occasions and for charitable purposes.

MONASTIC CELIBACY

Celibacy was another cornerstone of the monastic life. Innumerable and meticulous rules hedged in the conduct of a monk towards the women he met on his alms rounds, or whom as nuns he had to instruct. Unchastity was an offence which automatically led to expulsion from the Order. Chastity, called *brahmacarya*, or 'conduct worthy of a Brahmin or a holy man', was a great ideal from which the monk must not swerve even at the cost of his life. The orthodox decried sexual intercourse as the 'bovine or bestial' habit, and they cultivated a certain contempt for women. This contempt is, of course, easily understood as a defence mechanism, since women must be a source of perpetual danger to all celibate ascetics – especially in a hot climate. The monk was warned to be perpetually on his guard, and a short dialogue admirably sums up the attitude of the early Buddhists:

> Ānanda: 'How should we behave to women?' Lord: 'Not see them!'
> Ānanda: 'And if we have to see them?' Lord: 'Not speak to them.'
> Ānanda: 'And if we have to speak to them?' Lord: 'Keep your
> thoughts tightly controlled!'[*]

The reasons for this rejection of the sexual impulse are not far to seek. A philosophy which sees the source of all evil in craving for sensuous pleasure would not wish to multiply the occasions for indulgence in sensual pleasure.

> As long as even the slightest thought of lust of a man towards
> women remains undestroyed, so long is his mind tied, even as the
> sucking calf is bound to its mother.[†]

It is very difficult to have sexual relations with women without becoming fond of one or the other of them. Such attachment would be fatal to a man's freedom. In its later development, in the Tantra, the initiate was bidden to expose himself to this danger, and to indulge in sex without polluting his mind thereby. For more than 1,000 years such audacity would have seemed an almost blasphemous foolhardiness to the monks. Furthermore, sexual relations may lead to children, and children would be a terrible tie to one who wished to live outside society in carefree independence. There is, however, a much deeper reason why the saints of all ages have viewed the sexual impulse with particular suspicion. Sexual intercourse is apt to produce a certain rapturous calm and relaxation. Neurotics are known to use it for the purpose of warding off their mental conflicts for the time being. In this respect, the better is the

[*] Dīgha Nikāya ii.141
[†] *Dhammapada* 284

foe of the good. In his practice of trance the monk possessed a far more efficacious method for inducing inward quietude. Meditation and sexual intercourse have in common the goal and the force which they use. For the simple reason that one cannot use the same force twice, complete suppression of sexual behaviour is indispensable to success in meditation.

Psychologists have often observed the similarity between mystical states and the experiences of our sexual life. The sexual imagery in some mystical writers has been widely discussed. On the whole, psychologists are inclined to derive the spiritual from the sexual, and to regard meditation as a kind of sublimated or attenuated sexuality, as an aim-inhibited and object-inhibited sexuality, or, in other words, as a lesser version of something else. A practising mystic, on the other hand, would be inclined to say that we are as true to ourselves in meditation as in sexual intercourse, if not much more so. He would agree to the considerable similarity between enlightenment and sexual union, but he would, with Plotinus, regard the spiritual activity as primary, and the sexual as secondary and derived. It is illuminating to quote Plotinus in this context, when he says

> There is in ecstatic union no space between the soul and the highest.
> There are no longer two, but both are united in one. They cannot be
> separated from each other as long as one is there. This union is
> imitated in our world by lovers and loved when they wish to unite in
> one being.[*]

Following this line of argument, the transfer of the meditational force to sexual activity would amount to a fall, a degradation, a dulling of that energy. By indulging in sex one would make an absurd and unworthy use of it. Sex would be a 'bovine' and abortive attempt to gain the union of enlightenment and its emotional satisfaction, but in its essence it would be a miscarriage or misuse of the longing for reunion with the Absolute.

For more than a thousand years, these views remained predominant in the Order. After that, a section of the community, swayed by other considerations, came to believe that sexual life was not incompatible with monkhood. Married monks are reported for Kashmir about 500AD, and from about 800AD onward the Tantra sanctioned

* Untraced at time of publication

the marriage of monks in the districts that came under its influence. In the left-handed Tantra, as we shall see later on (Chapter 8), there was nothing shameful about sexual intercourse, but it was, on the contrary, one of the means of winning enlightenment. Padmasambhava, the Lotus-born, who about 770 established Buddhism in Tibet and who is considered as a second Buddha, accepted from the Tibetan king the gift of one of his five wives, and many paintings represent Padmasambhava flanked by his two chief wives, Mandāravā and Yeshe Tsogyal. Marpa the translator (1012–97), one of the greatest teachers of Tibet, married when 42 years old, and he also had 'eight other female disciples, who were his spiritual consorts.'[*] Quite different is the motivation of the Shin School in Japan (founded about 1200). Its adherents claim that they are so 'low and inferior' that they cannot be expected to follow the Buddha's precepts. They thus habitually lead a married life and eat meat. The bonze Kenryo Kawasaki has succinctly expressed the motives of this School:

> It is not at all necessary to withdraw from the world and to practise special austerities in order to become a perfect Buddhist. Our founder, the Shonin Shinran, was married and lived as the world does. It is our duty to live according to the moral code of our environment, of our family, profession, or nation, and not to distinguish ourselves from other people by external acts or manifestations.[†]

We will have occasion to return to this argumentation. It is sufficient here to have explained the attitude which the majority of the monks adopted towards celibacy, and at the same time to have illustrated the fact, astonishing to the Western mind, that on some questions the Buddhist religion does not speak with one voice. When facing this, or any other vital issue, Buddhism has, like a proper Janus' head, consistently looked in the two opposite directions. It has attempted to arrive at the truth, not by excluding opposite as falsehood, but by including it as another arm of the same truth.

---

[*] Quoted in Ch. Bell, *The Religion of Tibet*, 1931, p.63

[†] E. Steinilber-Oberlin, *Les sectes bouddhiques japonaises*, 1930, p.216

INOFFENSIVENESS

About 500BC two religions came to the fore in India which placed 'no harming' into the very centre of their doctrine – the one being Jainism and the other Buddhism. This special emphasis on the prohibition of doing harm to any living being was presumably a reaction against the increase in violence that marked human relationships as a consequence of the invention of bronze and iron. It was directed in India not only against the massacres that marked tribal warfare, but also against the enormous slaughter of animals that accompanied the Vedic sacrifice, and to some extent against the cruelty that marks the attitude of peasants to animals. The doctrine of Jains and Buddhists is based on two principles: (1) The belief in the kinship of everything that lives, which is further strengthened by the doctrine of reincarnation, according to which the same being is today a man, tomorrow a rabbit, after that a moth, and then again a horse. By ill-treating an animal one might thus find oneself in the invidious position of ill-treating one's deceased mother or one's best friend. (2) The second principle is expressed in the *Udāna*, where the Buddha says: 'My thought has wandered in all directions throughout the world. I have never yet met with anything that was dearer to anyone than his own self. Since to others, to each one for himself, the self is dear, therefore let him who desires his own advantage not harm another.'* In other words, we should cultivate our emotions so that we feel with others as if they were ourselves. If we allow the virtue of compassion to grow in us, it will not occur to us to harm anyone else, any more than we willingly harm ourselves. It will be seen that in this way we diminish our sentiment and love of self by widening the boundaries of what we regard as ours. By inviting, as it were, everybody's self to enter our own personality, we break down the barriers that separate us from others.

Through this attitude, Buddhism can be said to have had an immense humanizing effect on the entire history of Asia. It is the kindness of everyone which strikes the observers in countries saturated by Buddhism, such as Burma. King Aśoka was converted to Buddhist faith repenting the slaughter which had won him his empire. It was he who made Buddhism into a world religion. Sir Charles Bell's book on *The Religion of Tibet* shows again and again

* *Udāna* v.1

how Buddhism softened the rough warrior races of Tibet and Mongolia, and nearly effaced all traces of their original brutality.

In this context, we must consider two kindred problems, the attitude of Buddhism to vegetarianism and its attitude to religious persecution. Since it is impossible to eat animals without harming them, a Buddhist should be a vegetarian. But if he is a monk, who begs his food by going round a village from house to house, and if this village is inhabited by non-vegetarians, he comes up against a serious difficulty. In order that he should have no attachment to food, he is bidden to eat everything and anything which is thrown into his bowl; and the Venerable Pindola has been held up to the reverence of posterity for calmly eating a leper's thumb which had fallen into his bowl. Monastic discipline would be undermined if monks would start to pick and choose their food. In consequence, a compromise has been arrived at, and in actual practice Buddhists who take their religion seriously avoid eating meat unless compelled to do so.

One often argues against Buddhist vegetarianism, that it is quite futile because, while a few hens and cows might be kept alive who otherwise would have been killed, nevertheless the normal pursuit of our ordinary life involves a considerable amount of destruction of life which cannot be avoided while we live. By merely washing our hands, we kill as many living creatures as there are human beings in the whole of Spain. So we are faced with the alternative of either killing ourselves to save others, or of killing others to save ourselves. The taking of life seems to be inseparable from life itself. The Buddhists have always been fully aware of the gravity of this objection. They advise us, at least, to diminish the involuntary slaughter, for instance, by being careful about what we tread on when walking in the woods. In addition, the Buddhists believe that it is very salutary for us to realize what a calamity there is involved in the mere fact of our being alive, and a contemplation of the extent of this calamity should induce us to be more energetic in our efforts to escape from a condition in which our own suffering can be perpetuated only by inflicting a great deal of suffering on other creatures also. When Calderón once said that the greatest sin of all is that we were born, he expressed a typically Buddhist thought. Some people only see what they call pessimism in such a thought, but it also involves a recollection of the more noble side of our nature which deplores the thoughtless way in which we crush other beings all the time in order to perpetuate our own miserable existence.

It goes without saying that there would be little room in Buddhism for religious persecution – for Crusades, or Inquisitions. If the Buddha were insulted, a Buddhist would see little reason to torture or kill the person who 'insulted' him. 'Why become indignant when the Buddhas are insulted? The Buddhas are not touched by blasphemies.' It would appear incongruous to a Buddhist to convince someone of the superior quality of his great benevolence by burning him alive. It would, of course, be an exaggeration to claim that Buddhist writings are entirely free from invective and vituperation. Even in some of the most sacred writings, such as the *Prajñāpāramitā* and the *Lotus of the Good Law*, we find a somewhat deplorable inclination on the part of the writers to consign fellow Buddhists, who think differently from them, to hell for long periods of time. What has, however, prevented this natural exuberance of theological spite from hardening itself into deliberate intolerance, has been the strong sense of individual and temperamental differences with which the Buddhists are normally strongly imbued. The Dharma is not really a dogma, but it is essentially a path. If dogma is placed into the centre of religion, and if one believes that a statement is either true or false, and that a man's salvation depends on his acceptance of a true statement as true, then one's benevolence may easily come to destroy the bodies of others in order to save their souls. According to the Buddhists, however, it is very difficult, if not impossible, to make any positive statement at all which is not false and inadequate owing to the mere fact of its being made (see p.110). All statements made in words are at the best half-truths, and their only value lies in inducing one to adopt a certain path of action. Just as we are told in the Bible that in Our Father's House there are many mansions, so it is not unlikely that more than one path leads to the heavenly city. According to their dispositions, different people have different needs – what is food for one is poison for another; and it would be coming near to an almost insensate presumption if one were to be quite certain about the needs of others. As a result of this conviction, the history of Buddhist thought is marked by a bold and almost boundless experimentation with spiritual methods which were tested merely pragmatically, merely by the results attained. In Tibet, there is a proverb that every lama has his own religion, and that there are as many Buddhisms as there are lamas. It has been said that this boundless tolerance has been responsible for the decline of Buddhism. As a matter of fact, Buddhism has lasted longer than most historical institutions. In any case, little would be gained by perpetuating the forms of its worship at the expense of its spirit.

We shall see that royal patronage has been one of the chief causes for the spread of Buddhism. Royal power is obviously based on brutality and violence, and equally obviously the conversion of the rulers has sometimes been incomplete. It would therefore be an exaggeration to say that Buddhist rulers have never used violence for furthering the cause of religion. As soon as the monks became, through the friendship of emperors and kings, invested with social and political power, they were also open to some contamination from power. Finally, we would expect that in a country in which Buddhism provides all the terminology of culture, popular rebellions would avail themselves of its ideas to express their social aspirations, just as the Lollards and German peasants did with Christianity.

In their desire to express disapproval of Christianity, many authors have painted the record of Buddhism too white, and it will be necessary to admit that on occasion the Buddhists were capable of behaviour which we usually regard as Christian. In Tibet, for instance, there was a bad king Langdarma, who about 900AD persecuted the monks. A Buddhist monk murdered him. The official Tibetan history praised him for his 'compassion for the king who was accumulating sins by persecuting Buddhism',* and later generations, far from disapproving, have canonized the monk. Nearly all European histories praise the Yellow Church, which has dominated Tibet for the last 300 years. They suggest that the ascendancy of this sect over the older Red sects was due to the great learning of Tsongkhapa, to the purer morality of its adherents, and to their comparative freedom from magic and superstition. This may be true to some extent, but some of the success of the Gelugpa was due to the military support of the Mongols, who, during the seventeenth century, frequently devastated the monasteries of the rival Red sects, and who throughout supported the Dalai Lama, the head of the Yellow Church. In Burma, King Anuruddha, in the eleventh century, made

* Quoted in Ch. Bell, *The Religion of Tibet*, 1931, pp. 47–8

war on the neighbouring kingdom Thaton in order to seize a copy of the Holy Scriptures, which the king of Thaton refused to have copied. In a warlike country like Japan, the monasteries during the Middle Ages were a source of constant turmoil, and the monks were in the habit of invading Kyoto in vast armed hordes from their mountain retreats. The Boxers were an example of a popular movement resorting to violence and employing Buddhist terminology. This fusion of popular discontent with Buddhist beliefs is fairly old in China, and the predecessors of the Boxers, such as the White Lotus sect, have had a powerful influence on Chinese history. In Burma, the English offended the religious feelings of the Burmese, for instance by licensing and promoting the sale of liquor. They also destroyed monastic discipline by suppressing the hierarchy of the Church. In consequence, a kind of political Buddhism spread more and more, since there was nothing to check it. Saya San, a popular leader, for instance, issued in 1030 a proclamation which, according to M. Collis,* read 'In the name of Our Lord and for the Church's greater glory, I, Thupannaka Galon Raja, declare war upon the heathen English who have enslaved us.'

These examples could be mulitplied indefinitely. On the whole, the Buddhists would deplore such incidents as lapses from grace and as due to the inherent corruption of human nature. In India itself the monks offered no resistance when the Hephtalitic Huns, and later on the Muhammadans, sacked the monasteries, killed their inhabitants, burned the libraries, and destroyed the sacred images. Organized Buddhism, as a consequence of this persecution, was extinguished first in Gandhara, and then in the whole north of India. But the essence of the doctrine, as expressed in the Prajñāpāramitā and Nāgārjuna, has lived in India until today and, under the name of Vedanta, it is still the official doctrine of Hinduism on its highest level.

THE MAIN CURRENTS OF MONASTIC THOUGHT

The development of monastic thought, or of the metaphysics of spirituality, will be described later on in Chapters 4–9. The main lines

---

* M. Collis, *Trials in Burma*, p.206

of division are shown on the diagram on the next page, in explanation of which I will say a few words here.

The basic division is that between Hīnayāna and Mahāyāna. In the Hīnayāna there is, first of all, the Old Wisdom School, which, about 200 years after the Buddha's Nirvāṇa, split into two branches. In the east of India the Theravādins, who at present still dominate Ceylon, Burma, and Siam;[8] and in the west the Sarvastivādins, who flourished for 1,500 years, with Mathura, Gandhara, and Kashmir as their centres. In addition, there were a number of other schools, of which almost no record is preserved. The Mahāsaṅghikas, in Magadha and in the south round Amarāvatī, organized from c. 250BC onward, the dissenters from the Old Wisdom School into a separate sect, which perished only when Buddhism was destroyed in India.

The more liberal Mahāsaṅghika version of the Buddhist tradition soon developed into a new trend, called the Mahāyāna. The Mahāyāna divided itself into different schools, not immediately, but after about 400 years. Each of the schools stressed one of the many means of emanicipation. The Mādhyamikas, founded about 150AD by Nāgārjuna, expected salvation from the exercise of wisdom understood as the contemplation of emptiness. Because they formulated their doctrines in deliberate contrast to those of the Old Wisdom School, we speak of a New Wisdom School. Another school of thought, closely connected with the Mādhyamikas, placed its trust in faith in the Buddhas and Bodhisattvas, and in devotion to them. The systematization carried out by the Mādhyamikas neglected, however, some of the ideas current in the early Mahāyāna, which later on received greater weight from parallel developments in Hinduism. The influence of the Sāṃkhya-Yoga philosophy shows itself in the Yogācāra School, founded about 400AD by Asaṅga, which relied for salvation on introspective meditation known as yoga. Finally, after about 500AD, the development of the Tantra in Hinduism furthered the growth of a magical form of Buddhism, called the Tantra, which expected full enlightenment from magical practices. The Tantra became very influential in Nepal, Tibet, China, Japan, Java, and Sumatra. Outside India, few genuinely new schools developed from the fusion of the Mahāyāna with indigenous elements. Noteworthy among them are, in China and Japan, the Ch'an (meditation) School, and Amidism, and in Tibet the Nyingma, who absorbed much of the Shamanism native to Tibet.

The creative impulse of Buddhist thought came to a halt about 1,500 years after the Buddha's Nirvāṇa. During the last 1,000 years no new school of any importance has sprung up, and the Buddhists have merely preserved, as best they could, the great heritage of the past. It is possible to believe that the lotus of the doctrine has, after 1,500 years, fully unfolded itself. Perhaps there is no more to come. The conditions of our industrial civilization, however, offer a challenge which may lead to a new synthesis. Unless our present civilization perishes soon from its own violence, Buddhism will have to seek some accommodation with it. The Dharma cannot be heard in a world dominated by modern science and technical progress. A great deal of adaptation is needed, and a great change is bound to take place in the exposition of the doctrine. So far, the vague beginnings of such a change are discernible in various parts of the world, but they are not yet sufficiently definite to merit inclusion in this historical treatise.

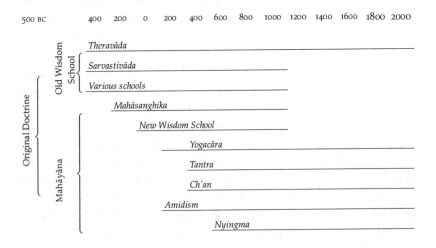

3

POPULAR BUDDHISM

THE PLACE OF THE LAITY

In its essence and inner core, Buddhism was and is a movement of monastic ascetics. A laity is, however, indispensable to it. As Buddhism grew from a sect into a widespread church, the lay followers became increasingly important. The monks and ascetics who constituted the core of the Buddhist movement did not, as we saw, earn their own living. For their material support they depended on the good will of laymen. In addition, from the beginning, the Buddha and the monks felt responsibility for the welfare of the people at large. The Jātakas tell the story of how Sumedha – the Buddha Śākyamuni in a past life – renounced the possibility of winning freedom from passion, and Nirvāṇa. Dīpaṃkara was then the Tathāgata. When Dīpaṃkara came to the city of Ramna, 'Sumedha joyfully threw himself in the mire before him to serve as a bridge.' When, as he lay in the mire, he beheld the Buddha-majesty of Dīpaṃkara, he resolved to win 'the supreme knowledge of the truth, thereby enabling mankind to enter the ship of Dharma, and so carry them across the ocean of existence, and when this was done, afterwards to attain Nirvāṇa.'* The Dharma was something to be shared. The missionary urge was ever strong in Buddhism. King Aśoka is a fine example of a monarch who strove to make his people happy through Dharma, and who sent out missionaries to make it known to neighbouring countries. When a self-centred monasticism

---

* *Jātaka* i.10

developed in some quarters, it was at once corrected by the development of the Bodhisattva ideal (see chapter 5).

The zeal with which the Buddhists of all schools carried their gospel all over Asia, and the qualities that enabled them to do so, is well exemplified by the story of Pūrṇa, one of the earliest apostles of the Dharma. He asked permission of the Buddha to go as a missionary to a barbarous country, called Śroṇāparānta. The Buddha tried to dissuade him, and the following dialogue developed:

Buddha: 'The people of Śroṇāparānta are fierce, violent, and cruel. They are given to abusing, reviling, and annoying others. If they abuse, revile, and annoy you with evil, harsh, and false words, what would you think?'

Pūrṇa: 'In that case I would think that the people of Śroṇāparānta are really good and gentle folk, as they do not strike me with their hands or with stones.'

Buddha: 'But if they strike you with their hands or with stones, what would you think?'

Pūrṇa: 'In that case I should think that they are good and gentle folk, as they do not strike me with a cudgel or a weapon.'

Buddha: 'But if they would strike you with a cudgel or a weapon, what would you think?'

Pūrṇa: 'In that case, I would think that they are good and gentle folk, as they do not take my life.'

Buddha: 'But if they kill you, Pūrṇa, what would you think?'

Pūrṇa: 'In that case, I would still think that they are good and gentle folk, as they release me from this rotten carcass of the body without much difficulty. I know that there are monks who are ashamed of the body, and distressed and disgusted with it, and who slay themselves with weapons, take poison, hang themselves with ropes, or throw themselves down from precipices.'

Buddha: 'Pūrṇa, you are endowed with the greatest gentleness and forbearance. You can live and stay in that country of the Śroṇāparāntas. Go and teach them how to be free, as you yourself are free.'[*]

It is often asserted that the Hīnayāna had less missionary zeal than the Mahāyāna. This is not the case. The Hīnayāna, like the

---

[*] *Divyāvadāna* 38–9

Mahāyāna, was carried to Ceylon, Burma, Tibet, China, Java, and Sumatra. If the Mahāyāna alone survived in Tibet and China, it was because it was more adapted to non-Indian populations than the Hīnayāna. The king of Tibet, for instance, about 750 invited the Hīnayāna sect of the Sarvāstivādins – flourishing at that time in Kashmir and Central Asia – to establish themselves in Tibet. The masses of the people, however, wanted a religion that was impregnated with magic, and for that reason the Sarvāstivādins soon died out in Tibet. Thus, Buddhists of all shades of belief were ever ready to spread the good news about the Dharma.

At the same time, wherever the Dharma has been a living, social reality, Buddhist theory has combined lofty metaphysics with a willing acceptance of the magical and mythological beliefs of the peasants, warriors, and merchants among whom it took roots. If they wanted to be true to their ideals of compassion, the monks had to win followers. If they wanted to exist, they needed alms from their lay followers, or from rulers. Two questions must therefore be considered. (1) What did the monks do for the masses of their adherents, or for their royal patrons? (2) How did the concern for the needs of the laity in its turn influence Buddhist thought?

BUDDHISM AND THE TEMPORAL POWER

Without the support of kings and emperors, the triumphant spread of the Dharma throughout Asia would have been impossible. It was one of the greatest rulers of India, King Aśoka (274–236BC), who first made Buddhism into a world religion, spread it through the length and breadth of India, brought it to Ceylon, Kashmir, and Gandhara, and even sent missions to the Greek princes of his time – Antiochos II of Syria, Ptolemy Philadelphos, and Antigonos Gonatas of Macedonia. After Aśoka, the Buddhists were favoured by another great conqueror, the Scyth Kanishka (78–103AD), who ruled over the north of India, by Harshavardhana (606–647), and by the Pāla dynasty (750–1150) which ruled over Bengal. Outside India, Chinese emperors and empresses were often converted to Buddhism, so were Mongol Khans, so in Japan a statesman of the calibre of Shōtoku Taishi (572–621). In Further India,[9] we find an abundance of Buddhist dynasties at various times.

Only very few of the monarchs just mentioned were Buddhists to the exclusion of other religious leanings. The Pālas and the rulers of Ceylon and Burma were the exceptions. Buddhism does not require the exclusive allegiance of its adherents. Kadphises I – a Kuchana king (25–60AD) – calls himself 'constant adept of the true Dharma'. The money which he issued shows, on the one side, a seated Buddha, on the other the Zeus of the city of Kāpisa. Kanishka adorned his money with gods from Iran – Verethraghna, Ardokhcho, Pharso – with the Hindu Shiva, and with the Buddha – shown either standing or in the lotus seat, with his name in Greek characters as Boddo, or Boudo. Gupta kings favoured both Vishnuism and Buddhism, the kings of Valabhī (490 onwards) – though 'devotees of Shiva' – protected Buddhism, Harshavardhana combined Buddhist piety with a cult of the Sun, etc., etc. Similarly, outside India. The great Khan Mongka (c. 1250) favoured Nestorians, Buddhists, and Taoists, in the belief that, as he said to the Franciscan William of Rubrouck, 'all religions are like the fingers of one hand' – although to the Buddhists he said that Buddhism was like the palm of the hand, the other religions being the fingers. Kublai Khan combined leanings towards Buddhism with a partiality for Nestorianism.

Since it is the purpose of rulers to rule, it is unlikely that their conviction of the spiritual value of the Buddhist doctrine would be the only, or even the chief, motive for the protection which they extended to the Buddhist religion. In what manner, then, could the seemingly other-worldly and anarchic doctrine of Buddhism increase the security of a ruler's power over his people? It does not only bring peace of mind to the other-worldly, but it also hands over the world to those who wish to grab it. In addition, the belief that this world is ineradicably bad, and that no true happiness can be found in it, would tend to stifle criticism of the government. Oppression by government officials would appear partly as a necessary concomitant of this world of birth-and-death, and partly as a punishment for one's own past sins. The stress which Buddhism lays on non-violence would tend to pacify a country and to make the position of its rulers more secure. In addition, if the people regard this world as none too important, their cheerfulness will not be impaired by lack of possessions, and it is preferable to rule over a cheerful rather than a sullen people. In Buddhist society, a simple life would be held most in keeping with the religious doctrine, and people would want to be 'poor' in the sense in which Burmans were poor. M. Collis makes the following apt comment on the British contempt for the Burmans on account of their poverty:

> A Burman who had, as many of the villagers had, his own house and his own farmland, a wife, and lots of children, a pony and a favourite actress, a bottle of wine and a book of verse, racing bullocks and a carved teak-cart, a set of chess and a set of dice, felt himself at the summit of felicity, and ignored the English view that he was a poor man because his cash income was about ten pounds a year.[*]

Buddhism would everywhere discourage the accumulation of material wealth in the hands of individuals, and encourage people rather to give away any material wealth, and to invest it in works of piety, as has been the case in Burma and Tibet for so many centuries. If we consider that the encouragement of a desire for material possessions and for a higher 'standard of living' among the European masses has not only destroyed all despotic forms of government, but has undermined all steady and permanent governmental authority in Europe, we can understand why Buddhism should appear as a blessing to the habitually despotic rulers of Asia.

Ever since the Neolithic Age, rulers, particularly where they had to cope with large and heterogeneous empires, were to some extent deified. This idea of the divinity of kings is quite familiar from Egypt, China, and Japan. It played its role in Rome and Byzantium, has been superseded by democratic ideas only quite recently, and still shows a surprising vigour in the attitude which a number of Germans adopted to Hitler, or in some of the pronouncements made about Josef Stalin in the Soviet Union. In India the divinity of the rajas, however small their domain, has always been a commonplace of popular belief. The moral authority of a king would grow immensely if and when his will could appear as the will of God. It was particularly among the great conquerors that Buddhism found favour. The Buddhists actively increased the prestige of such a monarch by their theory of the 'wheel-turning King', in Sanskrit *cakravartin*. The scriptures give a somewhat idealized portrait of such a ruler. Here is the description from the *Divyāvadāna* (548–9):

[*] M. Collis, *Trials in Burma*, p.214

He is victorious at the head of his troops, just (*dharmiko = dikaios*), a king of Dharma, endowed with the seven treasures, i.e. a chariot, an elephant, a horse, a jewel, a wife, a minister, and a general. He will have a hundred sons, brave and beautiful heroes, destroyers of the enemies' armies. He shall conquer the whole wide Earth to the limits of the ocean, and then he will remove from it all the causes of tyranny and misery. He will rule without punishing, without using the sword, through Dharma and peacefulness.

It has been a fiction among Buddhists that the rulers who favoured them more or less lived up to this ideal conception. When later on the Mahāyāna elaborated a new pantheon of deities, Buddhist kings received some of the reflected glory. Rulers in Java, Cambodia, and also in Ceylon in the tenth century, were regarded as Bodhisattvas. In Cambodia, at the end of the twelfth century, Jayavarman VII consecrated a statue of his mother as Prajñāpāramitā, Mother of Buddha. In the twentieth century, the King of Siam is still the 'Holy Master Buddha' (*Phra Phutticchao*). In an Uigur inscription of 1326, Genghis Khan is called a Bodhisattva in his last birth. Kublai Khan became in Mongol tradition a *cakravartin*, a sage, and a saint (*hutuktu*). Travellers often refer to the rulers of Mongolia and Tibet as 'living Buddhas'. This is a misnomer and does not express the sense in which the Dalai Lama is regarded as an incarnation of the Bodhisattva Avalokiteśvara, or the Hutuktu of Urga as a manifestation of Amitāyus. The Buddhist idea is that the Buddhas and the Bodhisattvas conjure up phantom bodies which they send to different parts of the world, and that those dignitaries are such phantom bodies. Whatever the exact connotation, the prestige value of such suggestions is obvious. It will not only increase the docility of the population, but it will also induce the monks to act as spiritual policemen for the government. It is one of the curiosities of history that, outside India, under Buddhist influence, real theocracies on the Egyptian model were built up in Indo-China, in Java, and in Tibet.

In all pre-industrial societies one believed that the prosperity and welfare of the state depended on the harmony with the invisible and celestial forces which were the true rulers of the universe. At every step in the Odyssey the fate of Odysseus is decided by a decision made on Olympus. By being friendly with the Buddhist monks a ruler would try to keep on good terms with the invisible forces, and a monk who could claim particular familiarity with them might rise to high office as a responsible adviser. So we read in Wei Shou's (c. 550AD) account of Buddhism in China of a Kashmirean monk of c. 400AD, who was 'clever in fortune-telling, in preventive magic, and spoke in detail of the fortunes of other states, much of which came true. Mêng-Hsün often consulted him on affairs of state'.[*]

The motives which we have explained so far would, of course, induce rulers to support not only Buddhism, but any other religion which would support their authority. There were, however, two factors that favoured Buddhism in particular. In many cases it was not Buddhism alone that was introduced into countries like Japan or Tibet, but the new religion was coupled with many advantages of a superior civilization. In the case of Japan, for instance, the entire apparatus of Chinese civilization was carried across the sea at the time when Shōtoku Taishi decided to adopt the Buddhist faith. The Tibetans, together with the Buddhist Dharma, also took over the secular sciences of India – such as grammar, medicine, astronomy, and astrology. Secondly, there is something cosmopolitan and international about Buddhism which would recommend it to monarchs who wished to unify large areas. There is nothing, or almost nothing, in the Buddhist interpretation of spiritual truth that ties it to any soil or any climate, to any race or tribe. Hinduism as compared with it is full of tribal taboos. In Buddhism there is nothing that cannot easily be transported from one part of the world to another. It can adapt itself as easily to the snowy heights of the Himalayas as to the parched plains of India, to the tropical climate of Java, the moderate warmth of Japan, and the bleak cold of outer Mongolia. Indians, Mongols, and the blue-eyed Nordics of Central Asia could all adjust it to their own needs. Although it is essentially hostile to industrialism, in Japan it managed during the last forty years to adjust itself even to the highly uncongenial industrial conditions. A creed as flexible and adaptable as that would be valuable to men who have to rule vast empires, because it would help to unify heterogeneous populations through giving them common beliefs and practices, and through the mutual contact which monks of different regions would cultivate. As far as the spread of Buddhism from Indian to non-Indian countries was concerned, merchants and traders played a

[*] *T'oung Pao* 1933, p.133

prominent part. The strict caste rules of Hinduism made it difficult for orthodox Hindus to leave the country; special sea-voyages were frowned upon and held to pollute so that travellers on their return had to be purified. In consequence, a great deal of the external trade of India during the Middle Ages was in the hands of Buddhists who carried their religion wherever they went.

Having considered the problem of the services Buddhism rendered to the temporal power, we can now ask what it did for the masses and its lay followers.

THE SERVICES OF THE SANGHA

The accounts which we have of the early years of the Order indicate that the Buddha showed great sagacity in his dealings with the laity, and was ever ready to meet their needs and their legitimate grievances. In order to keep the religion alive for more than 2,500 years, the small élite of the monks must have done something for the lay followers which they could appreciate. The needs of the laity that Buddhism catered for were, I think, threefold: spiritual, mythological, and magical.

(1) Even those who in general pay no attention to spiritual values are intermittently afflicted by a sense of the futility of the life they lead. They feel that their present condition does not allow them an adequate expression of their true self, and that escape from the world might bring them into their own. To the world-weary, the monks could offer a coherent account of the origin and destiny of man, of his place in the world, of the meaning of his life, and of the means by which a better life could be obtained. In this way, the doctrine as preached was a window out of the world. And in their lives, many of the monks gave examples of that kindliness, self-possession, and detachment from circumstance which people feel they need to pull themselves out of the world. They were happy, although they treated as nothing the things other people worry about all the time.

(2) In chapter 1 (p.27 *et seq.*) we showed why mythology seems to satisfy some deep-rooted need of the human soul. The world, as we see it, is too small to hold all the love and faith that are in the heart of man. According to Buddhist theory, faith is the step in the direction of Buddhism, and for the laymen faith is bound to cover more or less the sum total of their religious aspirations. Faith would in this

context not be an acceptance of definite dogmas, but its essence would consist in some measure of detachment from this world, and a partial turning-away from the visible to the invisible, without, however, quite reaching it. What then would the faith of a Buddhist layman consist in?

He would have respect for the Buddha, for his doctrine (the Dharma), and for the community of monks. He would be convinced that these 'Three Treasures' were helpful to him, that a person's good or bad fortune depends on his deeds, and that to acquire merit matters more than anything else. It appears, indeed, that the acquisitive instincts of men were deliberately canalized into the acquiring of merit. Merit is gained, for instance, by giving gifts, particularly to priests and holy men, by leading a pure life, by remaining patient when insulted, and by being friendly to others.

Westerners seem often to have difficulties in understanding what the Buddhists mean by 'merit'. The advantage of merit is supposed to lie in that it either gives you a more happy or comfortable life in the future, or, what is more important, a life that is more abundant in spiritual opportunities and in spiritual achievements. To be reborn in a better world could be regarded as either a good thing in itself, or as a means of obtaining more favourable conditions for attaining enlightenment in a future life. For instance, a very wicked person would be reborn as a fish, and among the fish the religion of the Buddha would be completely unknown. In the perspective of a householder, Nirvāṇa was too remote to aim at in this life. The burden of his past deeds was too heavy for him to climb so high. No one who believes in a separate individuality – and who would be a householder if he did not? – could win Nirvāṇa; but the belief in individuality does not, it is taught expressly, hinder rebirth in heaven. Our records show that a hope to be reborn in the heavens as a reward for a life of purity and devotion animated large numbers of Buddhist laymen during many centuries.

Faith is a longing for things not of this world, and it expresses itself in worship. Buddhists are in the habit of worshipping the relics and footprints which were the visible traces of the Buddha's presence on Earth. They also worship what are technically known as *caityas*. A caitya is a general name for any sanctuary or shrine. It is always connected with the person of the Buddha himself, although the connection may be a very indirect one. The caitya may contain a relic of the Buddha's physical body, a tooth, or other bone; it may contain something which the Buddha had worn on himself or used, like his robe, which was preserved at Haḍḍa, or his alms-bowl, which was shown at Peshawar; or it may contain portions of the Dharma body of the Buddha, in other words, of the scriptures. Some years ago some very ancient Buddhist manuscripts were found in Gilgit in Kashmir, where they had lain in a stone mound or stupa for 1,500 years. In some cases, however, the caitya just commemorates an incident in the life of the Buddha. Bodh Gaya, the most sacred place of world Buddhism, for instance, centres round the tree under which the Buddha obtained enlightenment.

By what actions, and in what spirit, then, were sacred objects worshipped by the Buddhists? Worship (*pūjā*) requires that one should make offerings of food, garlands of flowers, umbrellas (which are the symbols of royalty), and sometimes of money. At the same time a reverential attitude is indicated by circumambulation – one goes round the image or temple, always keeping it to one's right.

Images were important objects of contemplation and fruitful sources of merit. To produce and to multiply sacred images was held to be highly meritorious, and in periods of exalted faith, the manufacture of images almost assumed the profusion of a natural force. At the same time it is believed that the prosperity of a nation depends on honouring those images. It would, of course, never have occurred to a Buddhist that an image was the deity himself. Protestant missionaries often believe that the heathen mistake their idols for gods, but among the heathen no support has been found for this assumption. The image is: (a) a very imperfect symbol of a divine force, and an inadequate support to one's contemplation of it, (b) an object charged with magical power. The image is meant to call to mind the spiritual force represented by a Buddha or Bodhisattva, but it does not claim to possess a material or sensory similarity to them. For 500 years, the Buddhists refrained from representing the Buddha after his enlightenment in human form, because he had, strictly speaking, outgrown all humanity. They were content, in the scenes from his life which were carved in stone, to remind the onlooker of his presence by means of a tree, of a wheel (a symbol of the Dharma), a throne, a stupa containing his relics. We do not yet know the motives which induced them to change this convention, and to carve and paint the Buddha in a human form.

While on the one hand images symbolized spiritual forces, they were also regarded as a kind of magical power station. The magical force inherent in them became manifest to the faithful by the miracles that habitually occurred in connection with caityas, stupas, or images. The theory was, according to the Hīnayāna, that these miracles were not produced by the Buddha or by the relics, but that they were the result either of the grace of Arhants and deities, or of the resolute faith of the devotee. So *The Questions of King Milinda* (p.309). The Mahāyāna, on the other hand, assumes that the supernatural power of the Buddha's grace continues to work in his relics and in the places where they are deposited. But both Hīnayāna and Mahāyāna believe that the sanctity of any object was to a great extent generated by the faith and worship bestowed upon it. A well-known story may illustrate this. An old woman in China heard that a friend of hers was going on a trade journey to India, and she asked him to bring her back one of the Buddha's teeth. The trader went to India, but forgot all about the old woman's request, which he remembered only when he was nearly back home again. He saw a dead dog lying by the wayside, took out one of the teeth, and gave it to the old woman as his present from India. The old woman was overjoyed, built a shrine for the tooth, and she and her friends worshipped it daily. After a time the tooth became radiant, and emitted a strange light. Even after the merchant had explained that it was only a dog's tooth, the halo round the tooth persisted, so strong was the faith and devotion of this old woman.

It would, incidentally, never have occurred to the Buddhists that they could in any way please the Buddha by worshipping his relics. The Gods of Olympus insisted on their hecatombs, and Jehovah on being treated with respect. The Buddha, however, does not desire to be worshipped, 'in the same way as an extinct fire does not require or desire any fuel'.* The purpose of worship consisted in promoting in the worshipper a mental disposition favourable to spiritual progress. For 'Faith is the seed, Faith is the wealth here best for man.'†

(3) We now must say a few words about the magical functions of Buddhism. It is not quite easy for us at present to see the magical convictions of our forefathers in the light in which they did. A

---

* *Milindapañha* 95
† *Sutta Nipāta* 77.182

complete historical revolution separates the reader, and to some extent also the historian, from the ideas about magic which have dominated human thought for at least 20,000 – and for perhaps 200,000 – years. Urbanization and the startling practical success of scientific methods in industry and medicine have destroyed the belief in magic among most educated people. Science in every way appears to us as much more plausible because it is so much more successful than magic. Wherever the practical results of magic can be accurately assessed and compared with those of science – be it in raising crops or cattle, in warfare, in fighting disease, in chemistry, or even in weather-making – magic seems to compare most un-favourably with science. To the educated public, for which this book is intended, the value of magic seems to be once and for all symbol-ized in the efforts of the Burmese peasants, who in 1930 'advanced upon machine guns chanting formulas. With amulets in their hands, they ran upon regular troops. They pointed their fingers at aero-planes and expected to see them fall.'[*] To us it seems just ludicrous to believe that one could be made invulnerable to bullets by the use of pills and oils, or by chanted formulas and letters tattooed on the body.

This contempt for magic may act as a serious obstacle to our historical understanding of the past. In order to live, in order to keep its feet on the earth, a religion must to some extent serve the material preoccupations of the average man. It must be able to insert itself into the rhythm of communal life which in the past was everywhere permeated and dominated by magic. Then, as now, the average man was deeply absorbed in the problems of everyday life which con-cerned his crops or cattle, and the cycle of birth, marriage, and death in the family. To some extent he expected from a religion the peace of mind which results from a firm faith and a pure life, and which is the reward of a life of renunciation. But with a strange absence of logical consistency, he also expected that same religion, which was based on the renunciation of all things of the world, to provide him with that control over the unseen magical forces all around him which would guarantee or at least assist the secure possession of the things of the world.

Like all the other religions of the past, Buddhism provided magical protection and magical power. The success of crops depended, in

[*] M. Collis, *Trials in Burma*, p.209

popular belief, to a great extent on the ceremonies which Buddhist priests performed; and one assumed that some evil force would destroy the crops if those ceremonies were omitted. The fertility of the soil and the health of the community depended on the monks. At the same time the private desires of individuals were not neglected. In Mahāyāna countries the Bodhisattvas were believed to be concerned also with the earthly fortunes of the faithful. They might deliver from fire and water, protect ships and cattle, or give children. The scriptures of the later Tantric school give detailed advice on how one can, by propitiation of the unseen powers, fulfil all one's desires. It is a testimony to the all-embracing compassion of the Buddhist religion that it considers really everything which man can desire – from full enlightenment to the gift of eloquence and the seduction of a particular woman who has taken one's fancy. In countries like China and Japan, Buddhism acquired a great deal of social stability by acquiring a kind of monopoly in everything connected with death. In China, death and funerals are the prerogatives of Buddhist priests who, however, would never think of officiating at a marriage. In Japan, Buddhism found it easy to fuse with the native Shinto system of magic, with its reverence for the ancestors.

We shall hear more about the magical side of Buddhism (Chapter 8). This is a historical work, and it is sufficient for me to stress the importance of magic in the actual practice of historical Buddhism. Any attempt to make these beliefs plausible would consume too much space. Readers who regard magic, miracles, and the occult as so much superannuated superstition, must, however, be warned against assuming that the more enlightened Buddhists participated in magical practices as a kind of time-serving gesture, and as a materially necessary concession to beliefs which they did not share. Protestant readers, in particular, are faced here with the same difficulty which confronts them in the life of the Catholic church, where the belief in the occult, in magic, and in miracle, has always been shared by all, from the most intellectual to the least instructed. In Buddhism we have, for instance, the example of Hsüan Tsang, one of the masterminds of Chinese Buddhism. Superbly educated, widely travelled, deeply versed in philosophy, he nevertheless found himself continually confronted by miraculous events on his journey in India. Historically, the display of supernatural powers and the working of miracles were among the most potent causes of the conversion of tribes and individuals to Buddhism. To a Buddhist, however refined and intellectual he may be, the impossibility of miracles is not obvious. He does not see why the spiritual must be necessarily impotent in the material world. As a matter of fact, he would be inclined to think that a belief in miracles is indispensable to the survival of any spiritual life. In Europe, from the eighteenth century onwards, the conviction that spiritual forces can act effectively on material events has given way to a belief in the inexorable rule of natural law. The result has been that the experience of the spiritual has become more and more inaccessible to modern society. No known religion has become mature without embracing both the spiritual and the magical. If it rejects the spiritual, religion becomes a mere weapon to dominate the world, unable to reform or even restrain the men who dominate it. Such was the case in Nazism and in modern Japan. If, however, religion rejects the magical side of life, it cuts itself off from the living forces of the world to such an extent that it cannot even bring the spiritual side of man to maturity.

It has, therefore, been essential to Buddhism to combine lofty metaphysics with an adherence to the most commonly accepted superstitions of mankind. Even in a scripture as exalted and other-worldly as the Prajñāpāramitā, the traces of this synthesis are clearly visible. The chief message of the Prajñāpāramitā books is that perfect wisdom can be attained only by the complete and total extinction of all self-interest, and only in an emptiness in which everything that we see around us has disappeared like an insignificant dream. But side by side with this extreme spiritual teaching, we find the same perfection of wisdom recommended as a sort of magical talisman or lucky amulet, and the tangible and visible advantages which perfect wisdom confers in this very life here and now are set out in loving detail. The perfection of wisdom protects from the attacks of others, from illness, from violent death, and from all 'worldly ills'. Beneficial deities will guard the believer, and the evil spirits will have no chance against him. 'When one bears this perfection of wisdom in mind and goes into battle, one will not lose one's life therein. Swords and sticks will be unable to touch the body of the believer.'* Among all the paradoxes with which the history of Buddhism presents us, this combination of spiritual negation of self-interest with magical

---

* *Aṣṭasāhasrikā* iii.54

subservience to self-interest is perhaps one of the most striking. Illogical though it may seem, a great deal of the actual life of the Buddhist religion has been due to it.

THE INFLUENCE OF THE LAITY

We have just considered the services – spiritual, mythological, and magical – which the Sangha rendered to the laity. Our account of popular Buddhism would be incomplete without a sketch of the effect that Aśoka's patronage (c. 250BC) seems to have had on the attitude of the monks to the laity.

Originally, the monks seem to have given very little scope to the laity. There were, of course, discourses and advice on spiritual problems. There was some outlet for devotional needs by worship of caityas and stupas,[10] and by pilgrimage to the holy places. There was almost no ritual or ceremony in which laymen could participate. Contact with the magical properties of the relics of the Buddha and of his foremost disciples gave a sense of strength to laymen, for whom the relic worship was reserved, since for the monks it was held to be a waste of time and effort. For the rest, the Buddhists worshipped the Hindu deities like everybody else, and used the spells of the Hindu environment to further their aims. Since on the whole the average man finds it easier to worship his gods than to do their will, the monks continually remind the laymen that the Buddha is best honoured not by worship, but by doing the duties enjoined. The minimum duties of a householder are summed up in what was traditionally known as the Three Treasures, or Jewels, and the observance of the Five Precepts. The formula of the Three Jewels, which has been recited for more than 2,500 years, runs like this:

> To the Buddha for refuge I go.
> To the Dharma for refuge I go.
> To the Sangha for refuge I go.
> For the second time to the Buddha for refuge I go.
> For the second time to the Dharma for refuge I go.
> For the second time to the Sangha for refuge I go.
> For the third time to the Buddha for refuge I go.
> For the third time to the Dharma for refuge I go.
> For the third time to the Sangha for refuge I go.

As for the five commandments,[11] the accepted formula is:

(1) To abstain from taking life.
(2) To abstain from taking what is not given.
(3) To abstain from going wrong about sensual pleasures.
(4) To abstain from false speech.
(5) To abstain from intoxicants as tending to cloud the mind.*

These commandments are capable of much interpretation, but their essential meaning is perfectly clear.

The patronage of Aśoka seems to have brought about a considerable change in the attitude to the laity. Some sections of the Order appear from then onwards to have made a greater bid for popularity. We must particularly mention the sect of the Mahāsaṅghikas, who from the beginning of their separate existence had tried to make the order of monks more comprehensive by relaxing the Vinaya rules which, by their very strictness, excluded many potential members. Engaged as they were for about a century in combating the somewhat stiff exclusiveness of some of the other sects, they strove, after Aśoka, to find a bigger place for the laity; and the other sects collaborated more or less wholeheartedly in the new approach. As a result, Buddhism became more of an all-round religion than it had been before. The Buddha became a kind of God, the highest God of all. The adoration of the Buddha was rendered more concrete by the representation of the Buddha in human form, which developed one or two centuries after Aśoka. The teaching, instead of being chiefly concerned with Nirvāṇa, 'dharmas', 'concentrations', and similar subjects, unattractive to laymen, lays greater stress on the doctrines of karma and rebirth, which seem to concern the average man much more closely. A large popular literature for the edification of the laity was produced. This literature consists of stories of the former lives of the Buddha, which are preserved for us either as Jātakas (birth stories), or as avadānas (see p.20). In many temples sculptures illustrated those stories. This new literature contains nothing about the monks and their life in the monasteries. It has little to do with the fundamental teachings of Buddhism. It is concerned just with the general moral virtues, and the inexorable law of karma, according to which we reap as we sow, however many lives it may take for the

---

* *Khuddaka-pāṭha* i and ii

reward or the punishment to come to fruition. We have here to do with a new gospel – a gospel for the busy householder – which strives to stimulate his imagination and devotion and to bind him in loyalty to the Buddhist order.

This concern for the needs of the laity gained in momentum as time went on, and it resulted in the development of the Mahāyāna (see Chapter 5).[12] It is here sufficient to give some of the reasons why the patronage of Aśoka should have created a kind of crisis in the Order. The royal patronage had been lavish but short-lived. It had meant that a part of the crown revenue was used for the upkeep of the monks. Many persons would have joined the Order without any real vocation just because it offered a fairly easy life. Much of the primitive simplicity of monastic life had gone. The monks lived no longer content with any old rags for their dress, but had come to rely on gifts of robes. Many of them would no longer beg for food, but have regular meals cooked in their monasteries. As the scriptures were written down, the monks would become accustomed to the accessories of learning, and learning proved itself here as detrimental to the vows of poverty as in the case of the early Dominicans and Franciscans. In all these ways the monks had given hostages to fortune and become more dependent on outside support than ever before.

At the same time, it must be remembered that a certain aloofness from mundane matters as a result of Buddhist practices may easily militate against the survival of the religion. It is, indeed, remarkable how closely interwoven the monastic community was with the life of the clans in Magadha in the first decades òf Buddhist history. This intimate contact with the villagers would in many cases have been dissolved when the Royal Treasury took over the responsibility for the upkeep of monks. When Aśoka's support was withdrawn, a great need arose to strengthen the bonds of the monks with the outside world, and to win the good will of the householders. The Mahāyāna, with its greater solicitude for the salvation of the many, had its origin in these circumstances; and it was a successful way of meeting the crisis.

4

THE OLD WISDOM SCHOOL

SECTS

In c. 480BC, when the Buddha died, a number of Buddhist monastic communities seem to have been in existence in the north-east of India. The loss of the Buddha's physical presence and of his guidance were felt as a severe blow. No successor was appointed. In the words of the scriptures, only the Buddha's doctrine (Dharma) remained to guide his community. This doctrine did not, of course, exist in a written form. For four centuries the scriptures were not written down, and existed only in the memory of the monks. Like the Brahmins, the Buddhists had a strong aversion to writing down religious knowledge. In ancient times we find such an attitude as far west as Gaul, where, according to Julius Caesar the Druids

> did not think it proper to commit these utterances (on philosophy) to
> writing. I believe they have adopted the practice for two reasons –
> they do not wish the rule (discipline) to become common property,
> nor those who learn the rule to rely on writing and so neglect the
> cultivation of the memory; and, in fact, it does usually happen that
> the assistance of writing tends to relax the diligence of the student
> and the action of the memory.*

It is incidentally due to this aversion to written records that our knowledge of the early history of Buddhism is so scrappy and unsatisfactory. It is, however, obvious that during those centuries,

---

* *De Bello Gallico* vi.14

when the sacred texts were kept alive by being recited or chanted communally, a great variety of traditions was bound to develop in different localities, particularly as the religion spread. It is commonly believed that immediately after the decease of the Buddha a council of 500 Arhants rehearsed the scriptures as Ānanda remembered them. But even at that time there was another monk, who said that the sayings of the Lord as he remembered them were quite different, and he was allowed to go in peace.

Of the schools and sects which developed as a result of differences in scriptural tradition, in the philosophical interpretation of the scriptures and in local customs (see pp.62 *et seq.*), we must first of all consider those sects which we can group together as the Old Wisdom School.

ŚĀRIPUTRA

It has often been observed that it is not the founder himself but one of his followers who shapes the policy of religious and monastic movements in the first generation of their existence. The specific shape of the organization of the Franciscan Order owed more to Elias of Cortona than to Saint Francis himself, that of the Jesuit Order to Laynez than to Saint Ignatius of Loyola. As Saint Paul stands to Jesus, as Abū-Bekr to Muhammed, as Xenocrates to Plato, as Stalin to Lenin, so does Śāriputra stand to the Buddha.

It is easy to see why a comparatively subordinate follower should exert a more decisive influence than the founder himself. The founder would be, of course, the living source of the life-giving inspiration which initiates the movement, but a great deal of his teachings and insight would be beyond the range of more ordinary people. With less genius the successor produces a kind of portable edition of the Gospel which accords more with the needs of the average man and his capacity for comprehension. Robin's remark covers all the cases referred to above when he says about Xenocrates, Plato's successor, that he 'enclosed Plato's living thought in the rigid framework of a bookish doctrine, mechanized in response to the daily needs of teaching'.[*] It is true that Śāriputra died six months before the Buddha, and therefore could not take over the organization after his death. The influence Śāriputra exerted was due to the shape

* L. Robin, *Pyrrhon et le scepticisme grec*, 1944

which he gave to the teaching, and which determined not only the training of the monks for a long time, but also decided which aspects of the Buddha's doctrine should be emphasized, and which should be relegated into the background.

As a matter of fact, Śāriputra's version and understanding of the Buddha's doctrine dominated the Buddhist community for about fifteen to twenty generations. He dominated it in the sense that one section of the community adopted his interpretation, and that another section formed their opinions in conscious and direct opposition to it.

Śāriputra, 'Son of Śāri', was born in Magadha of a Brahmin family. He early took up the religious life under Sañjaya, a thoroughgoing sceptic. Within a fortnight of entering the Buddhist order he attained full enlightenment, and from then onwards until his death spent his time teaching and instructing the younger monks. His was a predominantly analytical intellect. He liked to arrange knowledge so that it could be easily learned and remembered, studied and taught, and there is a certain soberness and dryness about him.

To the Theravādins and Sarvāstivādins, Śāriputra appeared as a kind of second founder of the religion. Just as the Buddha is the King of Dharma, so Śāriputra is its Field Marshal. He excelled all other disciples in 'Wisdom' and learning. 'If we except the Saviour of the world, no one posesses even one-sixteenth part of Śāriputra's Wisdom.'[*] We must bear in mind that the word 'Wisdom' here is taken in a quite special sense, as a kind of methodical contemplation based on the rules of the Abhidharma (see pp.85 *et seq.*).

There were, however, other currents in the Order. Many monks may not have found the Abhidharma very much to their liking. In their memory, other disciples stood out as more important than Śāriputra – for instance, Maudgalyāyana, who excelled in psychic power, or Ānanda, the Buddha's personal attendant for twenty years – the most lovable of the great disciples, but, to the orthodox Abhidharmists, a constant object of adverse comment and a kind of scapegoat for all the misfortunes which befell the Church. Among the opponents of Śāriputra's interpretation the Sautrāntikas were the most influential group.

About four hundred years after the death of the Buddha, the literature of the Mahāyāna (see Chapter 5) began to develop.

---

[*] *Visuddhimagga* viii.21

Śāriputra's name continued to represent a programme. In works like the Prajñāpāramitā sūtras, the *Lotus of the Good Law*, and the *Avataṁsaka Sūtra*, Śāriputra perpetually occurs as the representative of an inferior kind of wisdom, who has still a great deal to learn, and as a person of slow and dull intellect, who was unable to understand the real teaching of the Buddha – so that for his sake the Buddha taught an inferior form of his doctrine, known as the Hīnayāna.

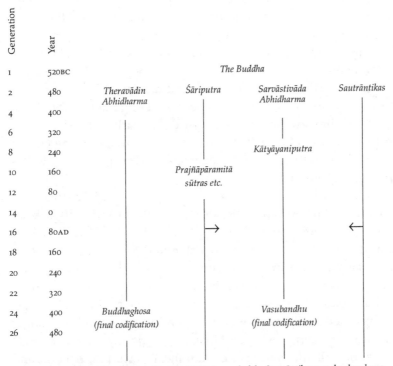

The two arrows indicate that the thought of the Mahāyāna and of the Sautrāntikas was developed as a reaction to the Abhidharma of the Sarvāstivādins.

Before I set out the main tenets of the school which derives from Śāriputra, I must say a few words in explanation of the term Old Wisdom School, by which I refer to it throughout this book. It is called Wisdom School because Wisdom is, in the scriptures of Śāriputra's school, held to be the highest of the five cardinal virtues, which are Faith, Vigour, Mindfulness, Concentration, and Wisdom. Among these the development of Wisdom alone can assure final salvation. Śāriputra's school is called the 'Old' as distinct from the

'New' Wisdom School which developed in reaction to it after about 100BC (see Chapter 5).

ARHANTS

There is no better way of understanding the spirit of the Old Wisdom School than by considering the type of man it wished to produce, and the idea of perfection it set up for the emulation of its disciples. The ideal man, the saint or sage at the highest stage of development, is called an Arhant. The Buddhists themselves derived the word Arhant from the two words *ari*, which means 'enemy', and *han*, which means 'to kill', so that an Arhant would be 'a slayer of the foe', the foe being the passions. Modern scholars prefer to derive the word from *arhati*, 'to be worthy of', and meaning 'deserving, worthy', i.e. of worship and gifts. It appears that originally, at the rise of Buddhism, the term Arhant was applied popularly to all ascetics. As a technical term in Buddhism, however, it is restricted to the perfect saints who are fully and finally emancipated. The Buddha himself is habitually called an Arhant.

Through Buddhist art many idealized portraits of Arhants have come down to us. An Arhant is normally depicted as dignified, bald, and with a certain severity. The scriptures of the Old Wisdom School define or describe an Arhant by a standard formula, which is repeated very frequently. An Arhant is a person 'in whom the "outflows" [i.e. sense desire, becoming, ignorance, wrong views] have dried up, who has greatly lived, who has done what had to be done, who has shed the burden, who has won his aim, who is no longer bound to "becoming", who is set free, having rightly come to know.'[*] He has shed all attachment to I and mine, is secluded, zealous, and earnest, inwardly free, fully controlled, master of himself, self-restrained, dispassionate, and austere.

The *Avadāna-śataka* gives a slightly fuller description of an Arhant:

> He exerted himself, he strove and struggled, and thus he realized that this circle of 'birth and death', with its 'five constituents' (skandhas) is in constant flux. He rejected all the conditions of existence which are brought about by a compound of conditions, since it is their nature to decay and crumble away, to change and to be destroyed. He

---

[*] e.g. *Saṁyutta Nikāya* i.140, *Divyāvadāna* 37

abandoned all the 'defilements' and won Arhantship. On becoming an Arhant, be lost all his attachment to the 'Triple World' [i.e. the world of sense desire, the world of form, and the formless world]. Gold and a clod of earth were the same to him. The sky and the palm of his hand were to his mind the same. He remained cool (in danger) like the fragrant sandalwood to the axe which cuts it down. By his Gnosis he had torn the 'eggshell of ignorance'. He had obtained Gnosis, the 'super-knowledges' [i.e. the heavenly eye, the heavenly ear, the cognition of others' thoughts, the ability to recollect former lives, wonder-working powers, the knowledge that his outflows are dried up], and the 'Powers of analytical Insight'. He became averse to worldly gain and honour, and he became worthy of being honoured, saluted, and revered by the devas (gods), including Indra, Vishnu, and Krishna.[*]

Except for the Buddhas, no being could be as perfect as an Arhant. It was logical to assume that a Buddha would possess a number of additional perfections as compared with an Arhant.[†] In the early days, however, little attention was paid to that question, which seemed to be devoid of any practical importance. It was only after three or four centuries, when the Arhant ideal lost its hold over a section of the Buddhist community (see p.93 *et seq.*), that the question of the difference between Arhants and Buddhas began to exercise the curiosity of Buddhist thinkers.

Mystics of all ages have never tired of mapping out the steps of the spiritual ladder. Before a man could become an Arhant a number of recognized stages had to be passed through. It is not necessary here to give all the details, but some understanding of the turning point in a man's career is essential for all that follows. All people are said to belong to one of two classes: they are either ordinary people or they are saints. The saints are called *āryas*.

In Sanskrit *āryan* means 'noble', 'right' or 'good'. The ordinary, common people live entirely in the world of their senses and the spiritual world beyond is to them either a matter of indifference, or of mere vague and impotent longing. The supra-sensory world of abiding reality is known in Buddhist theory either by the name of

[*] *Avadāna-śataka* ii.34

[†] *Dīgha Nikāya* ii.1–3, iii.7

Nirvāṇa – which is the final and ultimate state of quietude – or as the Path. The Path is the same as Nirvāṇa, considered as it manifests itself to us during certain stages of our spiritual progress. As a result of the spiritual practices which will be described soon, we reach, in the course of time, an experience which transforms us from 'common people' into 'saints'. It is technically known as the 'entrance into the stream'. To some extent it corresponds to what Christians call 'conversion'. On that occasion, the vision of the Supramundane Path bursts in upon us, and in the words of Buddhaghosa we see the 'Path' as we see the bright full moon through a rent in the clouds – the clouds symbolizing our sensory attachments. Once the stream is won, a long struggle is still ahead. It sometimes takes many lives to wear down our attachments to sensory objects and the love of ourselves. But the corner has been turned.

PRACTICES

In Buddhism the meditational practices are the well from which springs all that is alive in it. The historical development of Buddhism is essentially an elaboration of ever new means of salvation. It is, however, not so easy to give an intelligible account of these practices, because they are all of them methods which have the renunciation of the world as their aim, and most people today are not really interested in such an aim. It is only at two points that these methods hit the ken of the average man – at the beginning and at the end. The starting-point of all Buddhist endeavours is discontent with the world as it is found; many people feel such discontent fairly often, although they rarely know what to do with it. At the end the Buddhist struggles bring forth the fruit of even-mindedness that everybody would very much like to have, if he only knew how to get it. But in between the beginning and the end of the way there is a great deal of toil which people usually prefer to avoid.

It is in the nature of things that intimate knowledge of the Path is given only to those who walk on it. Nevertheless, we shall now try to explain the methods which were used by the Old Wisdom School to train Arhants. These methods traditionally fall under three headings, namely, Moral Discipline, Trance, and Wisdom. We are fortunate in possessing an excellent textbook dealing with these practices in Buddhaghosa's *Visuddhimagga*, which has been translated, though very imperfectly, as *The Path of Purity*.

MORAL DISCIPLINE

We spoke above about the monastic side of Buddhist discipline (see Chapter 2). The Buddhists believe that knowledge or insight is not mastered when we know about it as verbal expression, but only when we have impressed it upon our reluctant body. Little is gained by having an abstract conviction of the unimportance of sensory pleasures, or of the inherent repulsiveness and unloveliness of that which excites it, if this conviction of one's tongue and brain is contradicted by one's muscles, or one's glands, or one's skin. These parts of one's body act as the embodiments of desires which have become almost automatic. If we are greedy for food, look at all the girls we meet in the street, and become miserable when we are cold, hungry, and uncomfortable, then our intellectual convictions about the unimportance of worldly things possess only a fraction of our personality and are refuted in action by the remainder of it. This is well illustrated by the Hindu story about the teacher who asks his disciple what he values most of all. The disciple dutifully replies: 'Brahmā, or the supreme Spirit.' The teacher thereupon takes his disciple to a pond, ducks his head under the water for two minutes, and then asks his disciple what he desired most at the end of these two minutes. The disciple could not help replying that it was air he desired most of all, and that the supreme Spirit appeared curiously irrelevant at that moment. While we are in the frame of mind of that disciple, what use is the Holy Doctrine to us?

A mindful and disciplined attitude to the body is the very basis of Buddhist training. The step that frees us more decisively than any other from the illusions of individuality is the rejection of our self-infatuated and narcissistic attachment to the body. The physical body has always stood in the very centre of attention:

> Within this very body, mortal as it is and only six feet in length, I do
> declare to you, are the world and the origin of the world, and the
> ceasing of the world, and likewise the Path that leads to the cessation
> thereof.[*]

[*] *Saṁyutta Nikāya* i.62, *Anguttara Nikāya* ii.48

The human mind is wont to operate through contrasts. When we look at Buddhist works of art, either sculptures or paintings, we find that the human form is treated with great sensuousness in Amarāvatī and Ajanta, and that it is idealized into an ethereal refinement in the art of China and Tibet. A great deal of the training of the monk, however, consisted in the exact opposite. Again and again he is taught to view this material body as repulsive, disgusting, and most offensive:

> And further, the disciple contemplates this body, from the sole of the foot upwards, and from the top of the hair downwards, with a skin stretched over it, and filled with manifold impurities. There are in this body hairs of the head, hairs of the body, nails, teeth, skin; muscles, sinews, bones, marrow, kidneys; heart, liver, serous membranes, spleen, lungs; intestines, mesentery, stomach, excrement, brain; bile, digestive juices, pus, blood, grease, fat; tears, sweat, spittle, snot, fluid of the joints, urine.[*]

When such a vision or image of the 'thirty-two parts of the body' is superimposed on the sight of an attractive woman, it is sure to have some disintegrating effect on any sexual passions there may be. In addition, the Buddhists, like the Jains, are taught to concentrate their attention on the 'nine apertures', from which filthy and repulsive substances flow unceasingly: the two eyes, the two ears, the two nostrils, the mouth, the urethra, and the anus. Not content with this, the monk is urged to visit cemeteries or burial grounds in order to see what his body is really like in the varying stages of decomposition. In all this, Buddhist practice goes deliberately against the habits of civilized society which taboos the very aspects of life the Buddhist dwells upon. The aim of civilized society is the very opposite to that of the Dharma, and its average member is put off by any consideration which might endanger his somewhat precarious joy of life.

Like so many Christians the Buddhist is not supposed to take pride in his body, but to feel shame and disgust towards it. We must never forget that in this system of thought it was due to an act of will on our part that we joined ourselves to such a body, because it is such an admirable tool for preferences and desires. When we see how precarious our body is, how exposed to all sorts of dangers and

[*] *Dīgha Nikāya* ii.293

frailties, how repulsive in its essential function, then we should feel shame and horror at the conditions in which our divine Self has landed itself precariously placed between the two skins which, as we would say in modern jargon, have developed from the ectoderm and the entoderm respectively. Certainly in such conditions our Self is not at its best. Certainly it cannot be free and at its ease in such conditions which are created by greed, and which induce more greed. In this the Buddhist tradition agrees with the well-known poem by Andrew Marvell, when he says:

> Oh who shall, from this dungeon, raise
> A soul enslav'd so many ways?
> With bolts of bone, that fetter'd stands
> In feet, and manacled in hands;
> Here blinded with an eye, and there
> Deaf with the drumming of an ear;...*

It is nice to find words with which to convince others of the emptiness of all conditioned things. It is held to be more essential to teach one's own body this lesson. The sense organs are singled out for special attention, and they are subjected to rigid control. The technical term is *indriya-gutti*, literally 'guarding the sense organs'. When a monk walks along he should look straight ahead in front of him, and not look at everything right and left the whole time.

> Let not the eye wander like forest ape
> Or trembling wood-deer, or affrighted child.
> The eyes should be cast downward, they should look
> The distance of a yoke, he shall not serve
> His thoughts' dominion, like a restless ape.†

Then there is what is called 'guarding the doors of the senses'. We may distinguish two components in sensory experience. The one is the mere sensory apprehension of a stimulus, the other is our volitional reaction to it. The contact of our sense organs with their specific stimuli is an occasion for, to use the Buddhist formula, 'covetous, sad, evil, and unwholesome states to flow in over us, so

---

* Andrew Marvell, 'A Dialogue Between the Soul and the Body', 1681
† *Visuddhimagga* i.108

long as we dwell unrestrained'* with regard to the sense organs. We must therefore learn to check our insatiable desire for sights, sounds, etc., which really estrange us from ourselves; we must learn to prevent our mind or thoughts or heart from becoming entranced with the objects that our senses meet. We must learn to examine each stimulus as it enters the citadel of our mind so that our unwholesome passions should not cluster round it and be fortified by finding again and again a new centre. Anyone who has tried to carry out the Buddha's instructions for guarding his senses knows what an enormous degree of violence he must inflict on his mind, even to keep it still for one or two minutes. How can we find out what is the true nature of our mind if we cannot protect it from perpetual invasion by what is external to it and view it as it is in its own pure self?

TRANCE

The second group of Buddhist methods is traditionally referred to as 'concentration'. The Sanskrit word is *samādhi*, a word which etymologically corresponds to the Greek 'synthesis'. To 'concentrate' consists in narrowing the field of attention in a manner and for a time determined by the will. The result is that the mind becomes steady, like the flame of an oil lamp in the absence of the wind. Emotionally speaking, concentration results in a state of quiet calm, because one has withdrawn for the time being from everything which can cause turmoil. Three kinds of practices are traditionally comprised under 'concentration': (1) the eight *dhyānas*, (2) the four Unlimited, (3) occult powers.

These three items were the germ of much that unfolded itself in the later development of Buddhism. The practice of the dhyānas became of decisive importance in the Yogācāra system; the Unlimited were one of the seeds of the early Mahāyāna; and the occult powers were destined to become the core of the Tantra. We now have to explain each of these items one by one.

(1) The *dhyānas*, in Pāli *jhānas*, are means for transcending the impact of sensory stimuli and our normal reactions to it. One begins the exercise by concentrating on a sense stimulus – such as a circle made of light red sand, or a circle made of blue flowers, or a bowl of

* *Dīgha Nikāya* i.79

water, or an image of the Buddha. The first stage of trance is achieved when one can suppress for the time being one's unwholesome tendencies – i.e. sense-desire, ill will, sloth and torpor, excitedness, and perplexity. One learns to become detached from them and is able to direct all one's thoughts onto the chosen object. At the second stage one goes beyond the thoughts which went towards and round the object. One ceases to be discursive and adopts a more unified, peaceful, and assured attitude of confidence, which the texts call faith. This attitude of groping or stretching oneself out towards something which one does not know discursively, but which one knows would be more satisfying than anything known discursively, results in elation and rapturous delight. In a manner of speaking, this elation is still a blot and a pollution, and in its turn it has to be overcome. This task is achieved in the next two stages, so that in the fourth dhyāna one ceases to be conscious of ease and dis-ease, well-fare and ill-fare, elation and dejection, promotion or hindrance as applied to oneself. Personal preferences have become so uninteresting as to be imperceptible. What remains is a condition of limpid, translucent and alert receptiveness in utter purity of mindfulness and even-mindedness. Above this, there are four 'formless' dhyānas, which represent stages of overcoming the vestiges of the object. As long as we suck ourselves on to any object, however refined, we cannot drop into Nirvāna. One first sees everything as boundless space, then as unlimited consciousness, then as emptiness, then by giving up even the act which grasped the nothingness, one reaches a station where there is neither perception nor non-perception. Consciousness and self-consciousness are here at the very margin of disappearance.

Above this there is the cessation of perception and feelings, where one is said to touch Nirvāna with one's body. Outwardly this state appears as one of coma. Motion, speech, and thought are absent. Only life and warmth remain. Even the unconscious impulses are said to be asleep. Inwardly it seems to correspond to what other mystical traditions knew as the ineffable awareness of naked contemplation, a naked intent stretching into Reality, the union of nothing with nothing, or of the One with the One, a dwelling in the Divine Abyss, or the Desert of the Godhead.

According to the doctrine of the orthodox, these states, however exalted they may be, do not guarantee final salvation. That requires the complete obliteration of the individual self, whereas these ecstatic experiences cannot achieve more than a temporary self-extinction. The mind becomes progressively more simple, more renounced, more calm, but it is only for the duration of dhyāna that this self is forgotten. Wisdom alone can enter the Great Emptiness. It alone can enter the Nirvāṇa that permanently and for all time replaces the impact of sensory stimuli as the force which directs our mind, as long as there is a mind to direct.

(2) The Unlimited (apramāṇa) are methods of cultivating the emotions. They proceed by four stages: friendliness (maitrī), compassion, sympathetic joy, and even-mindedness. The essential purpose of these exercises consists in reducing the boundary lines between oneself and other people – be they very dear, indifferent, or hostile. One attempts to feel equally friendly towards oneself, friends, strangers, and enemies. Friendliness is regarded as a virtue. It is defined as an attitude in which one wishes well to others, desires to promote their welfare, and tries to discover behind an often unpleasing or forbidding exterior the lovable sides of their nature. It is not the place here to expound technical details of these meditations. Their spirit may become evident from this short passage from the Mettā Sutta:

> May all beings be happy and at their ease! May they be joyous and live in safety! All beings, whether weak or strong – omitting none – in high, middle, or low realms of existence, small or great, visible or invisible, near or far away, born or to be born – may all beings be happy and at their ease! Let none deceive another, or despise any being in any state; let none by anger or ill will wish harm to another! Even as a mother watches over and protects her child, her only child, so with a boundless mind should one cherish all living beings, radiating friendliness over the entire world, above, below, and all around without limit; so let him cultivate a boundless good will towards the entire world, uncramped, free from ill will or enmity.[*]

Next in order is compassion, far more difficult to develop. It is an attitude in which one concentrates on the sufferings of others, suffers with them, and desires to remove that suffering. Thirdly, after having learned to call forth compassion at will, one should practise

[*] *Sutta Nipāta* 146–50

sympathetic joy. Here one concentrates on the prosperous condition of others, is glad about it, and enters into joyous sympathy with their happiness. Last of all is even-mindedness, to which we may, according to tradition, successfully aspire only after we have repeatedly attained the third dhyāna with regard to the first three emotional states. It is, therefore, but rarely attained and we need only mention it here.

One is not only told to develop these emotional attitudes, but to make them Unlimited in the sense that one should learn to treat all people alike, and to steadily diminish one's personal preferences and antipathies. Anyone who has tried to carry out Buddhaghosa's prescriptions for doing these exercises will have noticed that, in our normal state of scatter-brainedness, we are unable to get very far with them. It is assumed that the mind must acquire the refinement and detachment that only the practice of the dhyānas can give it, to carry the Unlimited forward to anything like a successful conclusion.

(3) There is so much that is eminently rational in Buddhism that the importance of the occult in it has often been underestimated, especially by modern European authors. Such a view ignores two decisive factors, the historical circumstances in which the Buddhist religion has developed, and the laws of the spiritual life. It also makes nonsense of the later stages of Buddhist thought which appear as a degeneration, as a fall from the original heights. Buddhism has had its life among populations who believed as sincerely in magic as modern town-dwellers believe in science. The relics of the Buddha were prized for their magical potency. The heavens, the rivers, the forests with their trees, the wells, almost the whole of nature was filled with spirits. Thaumaturgical miracle-working is a commonplace of Indian life, and it was regularly used by all religious bodies for the conversion of outsiders. Throughout the Buddhist world, representations of miracles are favourite subjects of art. Even if the occult had not formed a part of the Holy Doctrine itself, it would have been impressed upon the church by its social environment.

There is, however, an additional point. Experience in all countries of the Earth has shown that one cannot possibly cultivate a spiritual life without at the same time calling forth psychic powers and sharpening one's psychic senses. This fact can arouse astonishment only where spiritual practices are virtually unknown. As a result of practising the trances the Buddha and his disciples came into the possession of all kinds of miraculous or magical powers called *ṛddhi*, or *iddhi*. Some of these are what we now call psychic – clairvoyance, clairaudience, recollection of former births, and knowledge of the thoughts of others. Others were more physical. The disciples could 'pass at will through wall or fence or hill as if through air, pass in and out of the solid earth, walk on the water's surface, or glide through the air'.* By magical action, they could prolong life in this body. Or they could project or conjure up a double of themselves, and make it endure. They could give their body the form of a boy, of a snake, etc.

The Christian gospels have to some extent been influenced by Buddhist doctrines, which were known in Alexandria and other parts of the Mediterranean world. The miraculous side of Buddhism in particular seems to have appealed to the early Christians. Saint Peter, walking on the water, trod in the footsteps of many Buddhist saints. One of the favourite miracles of the Buddhists was the 'twin miracle'. Fire streamed forth from the upper part of the body of the Tathāgata, and 'from his lower body proceeds a torrent of water'. In John 7:38 we find the curious statement: 'He that believes in me as the scripture has said, out of his belly shall flow rivers of living water.' As a third example, we may mention that the Tathāgata could, if he should so wish, remain for the aeon just as the Christ 'abideth for the aeon'.

Although psychic abilities are inseparable from a certain stage of spiritual development, they are not in all cases beneficial to the character or the spirituality of the person in whom they manifest themselves. There is much danger in psychic manifestations: conceit may be further increased; one may search for the power and lose the kingdom and the glory; one may expose oneself to contact with forces which demoralize. On the whole, the attitude of the Buddhist church during the first millennium of its existence seems to have been that the occult and the psychic are all right as long as one does not take too much notice of them, and exhibit them as a kind of cheap stunt to the populace. One day the Buddha came across an ascetic who sat by the bank of a river, and who had practised austerities for twenty-five years. The Buddha asked him what he had got out of all his labour. The ascetic proudly replied that now at last he could cross the river by walking on the water. The Buddha tried

* e.g. *Dīgha Nikāya* i.78

to point out that this was little gain for so much labour, since for one penny the ferry would take him across.

WISDOM

Wisdom is the highest virtue of all. It is usual to translate the Sanskrit term *prajñā* (Pāli, *paññā*) by 'wisdom', and that is not positively inaccurate. When we are dealing with the Buddhist tradition, however, we must always bear in mind that there Wisdom is taken in a special sense that is truly unique in the history of human thought. 'Wisdom' is understood by Buddhists as the methodical contemplation of dharmas. This is clearly shown by Buddhaghosa's formal and academic definition of the term:

> Wisdom has the characteristic of penetrating into dharmas as they
> are themselves. It has the function of destroying the darkness of
> delusion which covers the own-being of dharmas. It has the
> manifestation of not being deluded. Because of the statement 'he
> who is concentrated knows, sees what really is,' concentration is its
> proximate cause.[*]

The methods by which Wisdom should be developed have been set out in the Abhidharma books. These books are obviously later than the other parts of the canon (see p.20). Some schools, like the Sautrāntikas, insisted that they were not the authentic Buddha word, and should therefore be rejected. The meaning of the word *Abhidharma* is not quite certain. *Abhidharma* may mean Further Dharma, or Supreme Dharma. It is difficult to know at what time the Abhidharma books were composed. One does not, perhaps, go far wrong when assigning them to the first two centuries after the death of the Buddha.

Two recensions of the Abhidharma books have come down to us: a set of seven in Pāli and another set of seven, preserved in Chinese, but originally composed in Sanskrit. The Pāli texts represent the tradition of the Theravādins, the Sanskrit texts that of the Sarvāstivādins. About seven centuries after the original composition of the Abhidharma books, the teachings of both Abhidharma traditions were finally codified, probably between 400 and 450AD. This

[*] *Visuddhimagga* xiv.7

work was carried out for the Theravādins in Ceylon by Buddha-ghosa, and for the Sarvāstivādins by Vasubandhu in the north of India. After 450AD there has been little, if any, further development in the Abhidharma doctrines.

It must be admitted that the style of the Abhidharma books is extremely dry and unattractive. The treatment of the various topics resembles that which one would expect in a treatise on accountancy, or a manual of engineering, or a handbook of physics. Allurements of style are not altogether absent from Buddhist literature when it was destined for propaganda and attempted to win the consent of the unconverted, or to edify the sentiments of the faithful. The Abhidharma books, however, were meant for the very core of the Buddhist élite, and it was assumed that the Wisdom acquired from their perusal would be a sufficient reward and incentive of study.

The chief purpose of Buddhism is the extinction of separate individuality, which is brought about when we cease to *identify* anything with ourselves. From long habit it has become quite natural to us to think of our own experiences in the terms of 'I' and 'mine'. Even when we are convinced that strictly speaking such words are too nebulous to be tenable and that their unthinking use leads to unhappiness in our daily lives, even then do we go on using them. The reasons for this are manifold. One of them is that we see no alternative way of explaining our experiences to ourselves except by way of statements which include such words as 'I' and 'mine'. It is the great merit of the Abhidharma that it has attempted to construct an alternative method of accounting for our experiences, a method in which the 'I' and 'mine' are completely omitted, and in which all the agents invoked are impersonal dharmas. The Abhidharma is the oldest recorded psychology, and it is, I think, still sound for the purpose for which it was designed.

What then is our individuality in terms of dharmas? A person with all his possible belongings, can, according to Buddhist tradition, be analysed into five heaps, technically called skandhas. Anything a person may think of as his own, anything he may appropriate or lean on, must fall within those five groups. It must be either (1) material (our physical body and material possession), (2) a feeling, (3) a perception, (4) an impulse, (5) an act of consciousness.

The false belief in individuality or personality is said to arise from the invention of a 'Self' over and above those five heaps. In the form of a diagram:

REALITY   FICTION

FORM
  (= *matter*)
FEELING
  (*pleasant, unpleasant, neutral*)
PERCEPTIONS   'SELF'
  (*sight, etc.*)
IMPULSES
  (*greed, hate, faith, wisdom, etc.*)
CONSCIOUSNESS

The insertion of a fictitious self into the actuality of our experience can be recognized wherever I assume that anything is mine, or that I am anything, or that anything is myself. In order to make this teaching slightly more tangible, I will return to our example of the toothache (p.8). Normally, one simply says 'I have a toothache.' To Śāriputra this would have appeared as a very unscientific way of speaking. Neither 'I', nor 'have', nor 'toothache' are counted among the ultimate facts of existence (dharmas). In the Abhidharma, personal expressions are replaced by impersonal ones. Impersonally, in terms of ultimate events, this experience is divided up into: (1) this here is the *form*, i.e. the tooth as matter; (2) there is a painful *feeling*; (3) there is a sight-, touch-, and pain- *perception* of the tooth; (4) there is by way of *volitional reactions*: resentment at pain, fear of possible consequences for future well-being, greed for physical well-being, etc; (5) there is *consciousness* – an awareness of all this.

The 'I' of common-sense parlance has disappeared: it forms no part of this analysis. It is not one of the ultimate events. One might reply, of course: an imagined 'I' is a part of the actual experience. In that case, it would be booked either under the skandha of consciousness (corresponding to the self as the subject), or as one of the fifty-four items included among the skandha of volitional reactions which is called 'a wrong belief in self'.

This analysis is offered as an example of Abhidharma teaching, and it is not claimed that by itself it will appreciably reduce the woes we may feel about aching teeth. The analysis can be applied to any item of our experience whatsoever. The Abhidharma books supply us with a list of between 79 and 174 factors which they claim as *Ultimates*, and as more real than the *things* of the common-sense world which can be analysed into them. At the same time, they give us some rules for combining those factors in the form of a classified list of the possible relations between *Ultimates*. The five skandhas are merely the first five of those factors. The reader should remember that in order to make this method work, a great deal of technical knowledge about the contents of the Abhidharma textbooks must be combined with great mental discipline and prolonged perseverance in strenuous introspection. Otherwise, neither skill in the meditation nor benefit from it can be expected.

The central idea, however, is clear. Experiences should be analysed into an interplay of impersonal forces. When one has shown up the ultimate events behind the surface appearance of any datum that may present itself inside or outside our so-called personality, then, if we can believe the Abhidharma, one has accounted for it as it really is, or one has seen it as Wisdom sees it. The Western mind must, however, beware of assuming that the dharma theory is offered as a metaphysical explanation of the world, to be discussed and argued about. It is, on the contrary, presented as a practical method of destroying, through meditation, those aspects of the common-sense world which tie down our spirit. Its value is meant to be therapeutical, not theoretical. Properly applied, the method must have a tremendous power to disintegrate unwholesome experience. The meditation on dharmas by itself alone can obviously not uproot all the evil in our hearts. It is not a panacea, a cure-all, but just one of the medicines in the chest of the Great Physician. It is, however, bound to contribute to our mental health to the extent that, when it is repeated often enough, it may set up the habit of viewing all things impersonally. The burden of the world should be correspondingly diminished. Sri Aurobindo, in his *Bases of Yoga*, has well set out the effect which meditation on dharmas may have on our perspective:

> In the calm mind, it is the substance of the mental being that is still,
> so still that nothing disturbs it. If thoughts or activities come, they do

not arise at all out of the mind, but they come from outside and cross the mind as a flight of birds crosses the sky in a windless air. It passes, disturbs nothing, leaving no trace. Even if a thousand images or the most violent events pass across it, the calm stillness remains as if the very texture of the mind were a substance of eternal and indestructible peace. A mind that has achieved this calmness can begin to act, even intensely and powerfully, but it will keep its fundamental stillness – originating nothing from itself but receiving from Above and giving it a mental form without adding anything of its own, calmly, dispassionately, though with the joy of the Truth and the happy power and light of its passage. [*]

We saw that our mental ill-health goes back to the habit of identifying ourselves with what we are not. Our personality appropriates all sorts of pieces of the universe in things one can see or touch. In these *belongings* our true self gets estranged from itself, and for each and every attachment which we may form we pay the penalty of a corresponding fear, of which we are more or less aware. The Buddha teaches that we can get well – that we can escape this terrible round of birth-and-death only by getting rid of these accretions.

To some extent the hold which belongings have upon us is weakened by the practice of sound rules of moral conduct. The Buddhist is advised to possess as little as possible, to give up home and family, to cherish poverty rather than wealth, to prefer giving to getting, etc. In addition, the experience of trance works in the same direction. Although the state of trance itself is comparatively short-lived, nevertheless the memory of it must continue to shake the belief in the ultimate reality of the sensory world. It is the inevitable result of the habitual practice of trance that the things of our common-sense world appear delusive, deceptive, remote, and dreamlike, and that they are deprived of the character of solidity and reliability which is usually attributed to them. It is, however, believed that morality and trance cannot by themselves completely uproot and destroy the foundation of our belief in individuality. According to the doctrine of the Old Wisdom School, wisdom alone is able to chase the illusion of individuality from our thoughts where it has persisted from

---

[*] Sri Aurobindo, *Bases of Yoga*, 1981, pp.2–3

age-old habit. Not action, not trance, but only thought can kill the illusion which resides in thought.

If all our sufferings are attributed to the fact that we identify ourselves with spurious belongings which are not really our own, we imply that we would be really much better off without those belongings. This simple and perfectly obvious inference can also be stated in a more metaphysical way by saying that what we really are is identical with the Absolute. It is assumed first of all that there is an ultimate reality, and secondly that there is a point in ourselves at which we touch that ultimate reality. The ultimate reality, also called Dharma by the Buddhists, or Nirvāṇa, is defined as that which stands completely outside the sensory world of illusion and igno-rance, a world inextricably interwoven with craving and greed. To get somehow to that ultimate reality is the supremely worthwhile goal of the Buddhist life. The Buddhist idea of ultimate reality is very much akin to the philosophical notion of the 'Absolute,' and not easily distinguished from the notion of God among the more mysti-cal theologians, like Dionysius Areopagita and Eckart. Nirvāṇa is said to be *absolutely* good, and the Dharma *absolutely* true in the sense that they are good and true unquestionably, without any argument, and in all circumstances.

These convictions form the basis of a great deal of Buddhist medi-tation and contemplation. One distinguishes an unconditional world from the world of conditioned things. We suffer because we identify ourselves with conditioned things and act as if what hap-pens to them happened to us. By persistent meditation and mortifi-cation, we must reject and renounce everything but the highest, which is the Unconditioned alone. In other words, we de-identify ourselves from all conditioned things. The assumption is that if and when we manage to do so habitually and completely, our individual self becomes extinct, and Nirvāṇa automatically takes its place. This approach requires, of course, that we should take a very exalted view of ourselves. In a sense we should be ashamed that our actual being falls short of the Unconditioned. It also involves a high degree of audacity because we must be willing to throw away everything we value in the conviction that it hinders us from regaining our original unconditioned nature. As Buddhaghosa puts it:

The monk reviews all his conditioned experiences as perilous, he is repelled by them, he frets against them, he takes no delight in them. Just as a golden swan which delights in a fair lake at the foot of Mount Splendid Spur in the Himalayas is loath to dwell in a filthy muddy puddle at the gate of an outcaste village, so the yogi does not delight in complex and conditioned things, but only in the tranquil path.[*]

Our ability to recollect the godlike stature we had before we fell into this world is regarded as one of the first steps which lead on to the path of perfect wisdom.

By its very definition, the Absolute has no relation to anything. At the same time the idea of salvation implies that there is some kind of contact or fusion between the Unconditioned and the Conditioned. This idea is logically untenable, and when they thought about it, the Buddhists discovered a great number of paradoxes and contradictions (see Chapter 5). If the Absolute as such has no relation to this world, it is neither correct to say that it is transcendent nor that it is immanent. The Ch'an School of Buddhists made this fact into a basis for meditation, by asking the disciple to answer the question 'Is the Buddha nature in this dog?' The Buddha nature is, of course, the Unconditioned, and the dog is taken as a not particularly exalted example of a conditioned object. The correct answer to this question is 'Nyes,' i.e. 'Either yes and no,' or 'Neither yes nor no.'[†]

As far as the Absolute itself is concerned, nothing can be said about it at all, nor can anything be done about it. Any exertion put forward in favour of the Unconditioned results only in useless toil. Any idea we form of the Absolute is *ipso facto* false. Nevertheless, during a considerable part of the way to salvation, some idea of the Absolute is valuable when used as a form or standard by which one measures the value and width of our experiences. This 'Absolute', which forms the object of a provisional and ultimately untrue thought, is then, in religious practice, seen side by side with the conditioned world, considered to be either inside it or outside it. It is characteristic of the Old Wisdom School that it everywhere stresses the transcendence of

* *Visuddhimagga* xxi.43
† *Mumon kwan* no.1

the Absolute, its complete difference from anything that we do or can experience in or around us. Later Buddhists, of the Mahāyāna, corrected this somewhat one-sided emphasis, by making more of the immanence of the Unconditioned. The Old Wisdom School approaches ultimate reality by the *via negativa*, which in India was expounded by the great Yājñavalka in the Upanishads (c. 600BC), and which Dionysius Areopagita later on introduced into the West. We must, however, never lose sight of the fact that, ultimately, Nirvāṇa is unthinkable and incomprehensible. It is only as a therapeutically valuable, though basically false, concept that, during certain phases of our spiritual progress, it can be of use to our thoughts, and enter into the practice of contemplation.

In actual practice, this conviction of the transcendence of the Unconditioned meant that it was approached as the total negation of the things of this world as we know them. I must refer the reader to the textbooks on Buddhist meditation for the actual details, but a general outline of this approach cannot be omitted here: Assuming that we are displeased with the world as it appears to us, we ask what it is that displeases us. Three 'marks' are said to sum up all the irksome features of this world: impermanence, suffering, and not-self. Everything here is impermanent, ever-changing, doomed to destruction, quite unreliable, crumbling away, however much we may try to hold it. As for the mark of suffering, I must refer to the discussion of the first Truth in Chapter 1. It is a fundamental thesis of Buddhism that there is nothing which is not either directly experienced as ill, or in some way bound up with ill – past or future, one's own or another's. Finally, everything is not-self, for we never possess it quite surely, we never control it completely, and we do not really possess the possessor, nor control the controller. It is not asserted that this analysis of worldly experience is self-evident. On the contrary, the Buddhists repeat again and again that it can be accepted only after strenuous and prolonged exercise in methodical contemplation. Our normal inclinations induce us to dwell on the relative permanence of things, on what happiness there is in the world, and on the power, however slight, that we exert over our circumstances and ourselves. Only those people would be naturally inclined to agree with the Buddhist analysis who are extremely sensitive to pain and suffering, and possess a considerable capacity for renunciation. In order to do full justice to the Buddhist point of view, and to see the world as they did, we must, however, be willing to go through the prescribed meditations, which alone are said to foster and mature the conviction that this world is completely and utterly worthless. In this argument we must take the meditations and their result for granted.

So we would have on the one hand ultimate reality, which at a certain stage of the Path would appear as the unceasing, undisturbed, self-controlled bliss of peace. On the other hand we have conditioned events, which would all turn out to be impermanent, bound up with suffering, and not our own. As we repeat the comparison between the two, we end up by becoming thoroughly disgusted with anything that may have those three marks. None of it can give our Self the security it looks for. None of it can dispel our anxiety. The revulsion from all conditioned things is supposed to open our eyes more and more to the true nature of the Unconditioned. The Self becomes extinct and the Absolute remains. All the ideas about the Absolute which form the basis of meditation turn out to be a provisional framework which is discarded once the house is completed.

DECLINE

The Buddhists, who dwell so constantly on the impermanence of all things in this world, could not expect their own institutions to be an exception to the general rule. Like everything else, so the Law must decay – at least in so far as it has gained a precarious foothold in this world. In its full vigour and purity, it remains only for a short time; then follows a long period of decay, and finally total disappearance, until a new revelation takes place. Accounts vary as regards the exact duration of the Law. At first, one spoke of a period of 500 years. Later on, that was extended to 1,000, 1,500, or 2,500 years. The scriptures composed between 200BC and 400AD contain, in the form of prophecies, many descriptions of the stages of the decline of the Good Law. According to one account, preserved in Pāli, the monks are capable of attaining to the Path and of becoming Arhants only during the first period. From then onward the full fruit of the holy life is no longer attainable. Purity of conduct persists into the second period, a learned knowledge of the scriptures into the third, but in the fourth only the outward symbols, like the uniform of the clergy, remain; in the fifth the relics alone are left, and the religion disappears from the Earth. Another sūtra predicts that in the first 500 years after the Nirvāṇa,[13] the monks and other faithful will be strong in attaining union with Dharma; in the second 500 years they will be strong in meditation; in the third 500 years they will be strong in erudition; in the fourth 500 years they will be strong in founding monasteries; and in the last 500 years they will be strong in fighting and reproving. The pure Law will then become invisible. In China, it became usual to distinguish three periods. First, 500 years during which the Law was correctly practised and its fruits realized. Then 1,000 years of counterfeit Law, followed by a final period of 1,000 or 3,000 years in which the Law just decays. Through all the differences in the accounts we notice that there was a strong conviction that after 500 years some crisis would arise, some decisive change for the worse would take place.

The whole of later Buddhism proceeds under the shadow of this sense of decline. The literature bears witness to it everywhere. About 400AD, when Buddhism was outwardly still very vigorous in India, Vasubandhu concludes his famous *Treasure of the Abhidharma* with the melancholy observation that 'the religion of the Sage is at its last breath; this is an age in which the vices are powerful; those who want to be delivered must be diligent.'* Centuries later, about 1200AD, Hōnen in Japan justifies his abrogation of the old Buddhist practices by the assertion that his age was too far away from the Buddha, that times had become so degenerate that nobody could any longer properly understand the depth of Buddhist wisdom, and a simple act of faith in the Buddha was all that people were still capable of. In the nineteenth century again, Sri Weligama of Ceylon assured Sir Edwin Arnold that men had fallen from the old wisdom, and that today nobody was so advanced as the Sages of the past.

Unfavourable historical conditions were only in part to blame for the sense of despondency which came over the Order as the beginning of our era approached.[14] The difficulty went much deeper than that. The very methods which the Old Wisdom School had advocated began, about 300 years after the Buddha's Nirvāṇa, to lose much of their efficacy. In the beginning of the Order, we hear of many who became Arhants, some of them with astonishing ease.

* *Abhidharmakośa* viii.40

Fewer and fewer cases are recorded in later writings. In the end, as shown by the prophecies quoted above, the conviction spread that the time for Arhants was over. The cream had been taken off the milk. The scholars ousted the saints, and erudition took the place of attainment. One of the scriptures of the Sarvāstivādins relates the terrible and sad story of the death of the last Arhant by the hands of one of the scholars. The story well illustrates the mood of the times.

The community reacted in two ways to this failure. One section turned away from the interpretation which Śāriputra had given to the original doctrine, and built a new gospel (chapters 5–9). Another section remained faithful to the old views, but effected one or two minor adjustments. Owing to the decline in their vigour, which they interpreted as a decline in faith, the members of the conservative section began to change over from an oral to a written tradition. In Ceylon the Pāli scriptures were first committed to writing in the first century BC. Another change was the lowering of the goal. In the first centuries many of the monks had aspired directly for Nirvāṇa. Only the laity and the less ambitious monks were content with the hope of winning a better rebirth. But from c. 200BC onward, almost everybody felt that conditions were too unfavourable for winning enlightenment in this life. It is natural that about this time a tradition about the coming Buddha, Maitreya, came to the fore. Maitreya (from *maitrī*) personifies friendliness. His legend was to some extent stimulated by Persian eschatology, but it met the needs of the new situation. The Theravādins, it is true, accepted it without much enthusiasm, and Metteya[15] never held a great place among them. But for the Sarvāstivādins, and the followers of the Great Vehicle, it assumed an increasing importance. According to Buddhist cosmology, the Earth goes through periodic cycles. In some of the cycles it improves, in others it degenerates. The average age of man is an index of the quality of the period in which he lives. It may vary between ten years and many hundreds of thousands of years. At the time of Śākyamuni, the average life-span was a hundred years. After him, the world becomes more depraved, and the life of man shortens. The peak of sin and misery will be reached when the average length of life has fallen to ten years. The Dharma of Śākyamuni will then be completely forgotten. But after that the upward swing begins again. When the life of man reaches 80,000 years, Maitreya, at present in the Heaven of the Satisfied Gods (*Tuṣita*), will appear on Earth, which will then be in a particularly fruitful and exuberant state. It will be bigger than it is now. A fertile golden sand will cover its surface. Everywhere there will be trees and flowers, pure lakes and jewel heaps. All men will be moral and decent, prosperous and joyous. The population will be very dense, and the fields will yield sevenfold. Those people who at present do meritorious deeds, make images of the Buddha, build stupas, offer gifts, will be reborn as men in the time of Maitreya, and will obtain Nirvāṇa through the influence of his teaching, which will be identical with that of the Buddha Śākyamuni. In this way, salvation became a hope of the remote future not only for the laity, but for the monks as well.

In the first period of its decline, the Old Wisdom School still gave evidence of a vigorous intellectual life. Between 100BC and 400AD the monks codified the doctrine, and composed many commentaries and treatises on Abhidharma. After that time they were content to defend the gains of the past. During the last 1,500 years, the Old Wisdom School has been dying slowly, like a magnificent old tree, one branch breaking off after the other, until the trunk alone remains. Between 1000 and 1200 Buddhism disappeared from India, through the combined effects of its own weaknesses, a revived Hinduism, and Muhammedan persecution. The Sarvāstivādins had possessed outposts in Central Asia and in Sumatra, but those also were lost at about 800, when the Tantric Vajrayāna replaced the Hīnayāna in Sumatra, and about 900, when Islam conquered Central Asia. The Theravādins, on the other hand, have continued to exist in Ceylon, Burma, and Siam. Buddhism was brought by Aśoka to Ceylon about 250BC. In the Middle Ages the Mahāyāna had many adherents there. At the present time the Theravāda School has ousted all the others. Buddhism had been introduced into Burma in the fifth century, in the form of the Mahāyāna, but from 1050 onwards the Theravādins have dominated the intellectual and social life of the country. Similarly in Siam, Hīnayāna and Mahāyāna co-existed at first, but after 1150 Theravādins became more and more preponderant, with Pāli as the sacred language.

5

THE MAHĀYĀNA AND
THE NEW WISDOM SCHOOL

THE MAHĀSAṄGHIKAS

In the early history of the Order, divergencies were chiefly due to
geographical causes. The Dharma had begun in Magadha, and from
there it spread to the west and to the south. About 100 to 200 years
after the Nirvāṇa some separation and rivalry seems to have developed between east and west. About the time of Aśoka the dissensions
in the Order seem to have led to the first schism. The Sthaviravāda
seceded from the Mahāsaṅghikas, or vice versa. The Sthaviravāda
were the conservatives who followed the doctrine of the Elders,
while the more democratic Mahāsaṅghikas, the 'Great-Assemblists',
stood for the Great Assembly, which included monks of lesser attain-
ments and householders, in contrast to the exclusive and aristocratic
Assembly of the Arhants.

It is not easy to get at the true facts about this schism. The writings
of one of the parties concerned, the Mahāsaṅghikas, have nearly all
been lost. A great deal of sectarian pride and spite enter into all the
accounts which we possess. All that seems certain is that this split
occurred about the time of Aśoka, and that it was connected with the
'five points' of a monk called Mahādeva. This Mahādeva succeeded
in arousing the indignation of his opponents, who described him as
the son of a merchant who committed incest with his mother, poi-
soned his father, and then killed his mother and several Arhants.
Having done all this, he felt remorse, left family life, ordained himself – quite irregularly – and then tried to fasten his five points on

the Order. Two of these points are directed against the Arhants, and imputed to them some deficiency, both moral and intellectual. The one claimed that the Arhants could still have seminal emissions at night. This seemed to suggest that their passions were not quite exhausted, because they could be tempted and remained open to the molestations of Māra. In addition to a residue of passion, they also had some remainder of ignorance in them. They were not fully omniscient, so there was still something which obstructed their thoughts. This second point became very important for the development of the ideal of omniscience in the Mahāyāna (see pp.112 *et seq.*). Mahādeva's five points were only the occasion for the separate emergence of the Mahāsaṅghikas. In spite of what their opponents say about them, we have no reason to believe that their doctrines were any less old than those we have described in Chapter 4. If we do not speak about them here in greater detail it is because we have very little to go by.

The Mahāsaṅghikas became the starting point of the development of the Mahāyāna by their more liberal attitude, and by some of their special theories. In every way, the Mahāsaṅghikas were more liberal than their opponents. They were less strict in interpreting the disciplinary rules, less exclusive with regard to householders, they looked more kindly on the spiritual possibilities of women and of the less gifted monks, and were more willing to consider as authentic those additions to the scriptures that were composed at a later date. Among them, several of the distinctive features of the Bodhisattva ideal of the Mahāyāna were worked out for the first time, and in addition, some of their tenets had the historically very important effect of cutting the Buddhist tradition loose from the historical Buddha, making exclusive adherence to his sayings no longer imperative. 'With one single sound the Buddha has expounded all his doctrines.' 'He understands all things in one moment.' 'The form-body of the Tathāgata is boundless; so is his power, and the length of his life.' 'The Buddha is never tired of enlightening sentient beings and of awakening pure faith in them.' 'The Buddha neither sleeps nor dreams.' 'The Buddha is always in trance.'* Such sayings do not fit at all the man Gautama who lived in Magadha many years ago.

---

* cf. Vasumitra, *Treatise on the Origin and doctrines of early Indian Buddhist schools*, trans. J. Masuda, 1925, p.19

By placing all the emphasis on the supernatural, or supramundane, qualities of the Buddha, in which he differed from all other men, they led the believer away from the fortuitous historical circumstances of his appearance. Some Mahāsaṅghikas even went so far as to maintain that Śākyamuni had been no more than a magical creation who, on behalf of the Supramundane Buddha, had preached the Dharma. If the Buddha existed only about 500BC, then he could teach only at that time, and the body of his teachings would be completed at his death. If, however, the true Buddha exists at all times, then there is no reason why he should not at all times find instruments to do his teaching. A free and unfettered development of the doctrine was thus assured, and innovations, even if untraceable in the existing body of scriptures, could be justified as revelations of the real principle of Buddhahood.

HĪNAYĀNA AND MAHĀYĀNA

From the Mahāsaṅghikas developed a new gospel. Its adherents first called it the Bodhisattva career (Bodhisattvayāna), and, later on, the Mahāyāna, the Great Career, or the Great Vehicle. By contrast, the followers of the Old Wisdom School were occasionally referred to as Hīnayāna, or the Lesser, the Inferior, the Low Vehicle. The Mahāyāna seemed great for many reasons, chiefly because of the all-embracing nature of the sympathy, and emptiness which it taught, and because of the greatness of the goal it advocated, which was no other than Buddhahood itself.

In its original meaning, Hīnayāna is a term of abuse, and the Mahāyānists used it but rarely. They usually referred to their opponents as the 'disciples and pratyekabuddhas'. At present, when its original connotation is but dimly felt, the term Hīnayāna can be used for purposes of description, just as in art history words like baroque or rococo are nowadays descriptive terms, although originally they expressed a disapproval of the art in question.

We do not have any clear idea about the numerical proportions between Hīnayānists and Mahāyānists in India at different times. It seems probable that the Mahāyānists began to outnumber the Hīnayānists only from c. 800AD onwards, when Buddhism definitely declined in India. When the Buddhist faith spread to China, Japan, and Tibet, the Great Vehicle ousted and almost completely obliterated the Hīnayāna, which is now preserved in Ceylon, Burma, Cambodia, and Siam only.

Mahāyānists and Hīnayānists lived together in the same monasteries, and for a very long time they adhered to the same Vinaya rules. As I-tsing (c. 700) reports:

> The adherents of the Mahāyāna and Hīnayāna both practise the same Vinaya, recognize the same five categories of faults, are attached to the same four truths. Those who worship the Bodhisattvas and who read the Mahāyāna sūtras get the name of Mahāyānists; those who do not are Hīnayānists. [*]

How did Mahāyānists and Hīnayānists define their relations to each other? Hīnayāna literature simply ignores the Mahāyāna innovators. Rarely, if ever, are Mahāyāna authors or doctrines named in controversy. Nevertheless, a certain amount of Mahāyāna teaching was tacitly absorbed.

The Mahāyāna, in its turn, seems never to have reached a definite conclusion about its relation to the Hīnayāna. In the first centuries, up to about 400AD, we hear a great deal about the disciples and pratyekabuddhas. After that time, they are more and more lost sight of, as the Mahāyāna becomes more and more independent in doctrine, terminology, and mythology. In their views on the relative value of the two 'vehicles', the Mahāyānists were actuated by two conflicting sets of emotions. Sectarian bias, together with concern for self-justification and desire for superiority, struggled with tolerance, loving kindness, and modesty. This conflict led to all kinds of contradictory statements, which were never really resolved.

At some times the Buddha-vehicle is said to exclude the vehicle of the disciples, while at other times it is said to be identical with it. Occasionally, the Hīnayānists are treated with the utmost contempt, threatened with hell fire, and described as 'chaff', or worse. On other occasions, one adopts a more broad-minded attitude. One would 'break faith with the Tathāgata' if one were to 'show contempt to those who walk in the way of the disciples or the pratyekabuddhas, saying, "We are more distinguished than they."' [†]

---

[*] I-Tsing, *A record of the Buddhist religion*, trans. J. Takakusu, 1896, pp.14–15

[†] *Śikṣāsamuccaya* 98

The Sarvāstivādins had recognized three different families (*gotra*), or ways to salvation. There are the disciples, who attain Nirvāṇa through Arhantship. There is the pratyekabuddha, who is 'one enlightened by himself, i.e. one who has attained full enlightenment, but who dies without proclaiming the truth to the world.'[*] There are the Supreme Buddhas, who win perfect enlightenment, and teach the Dharma to others. Each individual, by his past, by character and temperament, belongs to one of those three groups, and he must use the means that suit his make-up. Some Mahāyānists agreed to leave it at that. Others, however, insisted that there is but one way to final salvation – the Buddha-vehicle, or the Great Vehicle, while the other vehicles do not get very far. The *Lotus Sūtra*, for instance, says

> All disciples fancy they have attained Nirvāṇa. But the Jina instructs
> them, and says, 'This is a temporary repose, no final rest.' It is a
> device of the Buddha when he taught this method. There is no real
> Nirvāṇa without omniscience. Strive to reach this![†]

The Arhants are told that, contrary to their belief, they had not 'accomplished their tasks', they had not 'finished what they had to do.' They had to strive on, until they gained the Buddha-knowledge. The hesitations of the Mahāyānists concerning the relative value of the two vehicles seem to indicate that a sense of sectarian superiority cannot be organically incorporated into the Buddhist doctrine.

LITERARY DEVELOPMENT

Between 100BC and 200AD the Mahāyāna burst out into a profusion of sūtras. If one wants to catch its spirit, one will find it expressed with particular force in the *Lotus of the Good Law*, and in the *Exposition of Vimalakīrti*, both of which are available in English translations. The core of the new doctrine is set forth in the voluminous sūtras dealing with Perfection of Wisdom. The Sanskrit word is *prajñāpāramitā*, literally wisdom-gone-beyond, or, as we might say, transcendental wisdom. Buddhists at all times have compared this world of suffering, of birth-and-death, with a river in full spate. On the hither shore we are erring about, tormented by all kinds of unease and distress.

[*] Har Dayal, *The Bodhisattva Doctrine*, 1932, p.3
[†] *Saddharmapuṇḍarīka* V vv.73–4

On the yonder shore lies the Beyond, the Paradise, Nirvāṇa, where all ills have, together with separate individuality, come to an end. These writings on Prajñāpāramitā are very elusive, and not easily understood. Whereas the original Buddhism came from northern India, from the region between Nepal and the Ganges, the Prajñāpāramitā originated in south-eastern India, in the Deccan, between the Godavari River and the Kistna River, near Amarāvatī and Nāgārjunakoṇḍa.

The doctrine of the Mahāyāna sūtras, and of the Prajñāpāramitā in particular, was developed in a systematic and philosophical form by the Mādhyamikas. *Madhyama* means middle, and the Mādhyamikas are those who take the Middle Way, between affirming and denying. The school was founded, probably about 150AD, by Nāgārjuna and Āryadeva. Nāgārjuna was one of the most subtle dialecticians of all times. Of Brahmin family, he came from Berar in South India, and was active in Nāgārjunakoṇḍa near Amarāvatī, and in northern India. His name is explained by the legend that he was born under an Arjuna tree, and that *nāgas*, i.e. serpent-kings, or dragons, had instructed him in secret lore in the Dragons' Palace under the sea. His theory is called Śūnyavāda, or emptiness-doctrine. He supplemented with a logical apparatus the views expounded in the sūtras on perfect wisdom, which he is said to have rescued from the Nether world of the Nāgas. While Śākyamuni, so the story goes, taught to men the doctrine of the disciples, in heaven he taught at the same time a deeper doctrine, which was first preserved by the Dragons, and then brought to Earth by Nāgārjuna.

The Madhyamaka School flourished in India for well over 800 years. About 450AD it split into two subdivisions: one side, the Prāsaṅgika, interpreted Nāgārjuna's doctrine as a universal scepticism, and claimed that their argumentations had the exclusive purpose of refuting the opinions of others; the other side, the Svātantrika, maintained that argument could also establish some positive truths. Together with Buddhism the Mādhyamikas disappeared from India after 1000AD. Their leading ideas have survived up to the present day in the Vedanta system of Hinduism into which they were incorporated by Gaudapāda and Śaṁkara, its founders.

Translations of the Prajñāpāramitā sūtras have exerted a profound influence in China from 180AD onwards. The Mādhyamikas existed for a few centuries, from 400 or 600 to 900, as a separate school called San loen t'sung. In 625 the school came to Japan, as Sanron, but it has been extinct there for a long time. Adapted to the Chinese and Japanese outlook on life, the doctrine lives on as Ch'an or Zen.

THE BODHISATTVA

The two key words which occur on almost each page of the Mahā-yāna writings are the words Bodhisattva and emptiness. What then is first of all a Bodhisattva? A Buddha is one who is enlightened. A Bodhisattva is literally an enlightenment-being. He is a Buddha-to-be, one who wishes to become a Buddha, that is to say, an Enlightened One. So far for the literal meaning.

It would be a mistake to assume that the conception of a Bodhisattva was a creation of the Mahāyāna. For all Buddhists each Buddha had been, for a long period before his enlightenment, a Bodhisattva. The Sarvāstivādins, in particular, had given much thought to the career of a Bodhisattva. The *Abhidharmakośa* gives a fine description of the mentality of a Bodhisattva:

> But why do the Bodhisattvas, once they have taken the vow to obtain the supreme enlightenment, take such a long time to obtain it?
>
> Because the supreme enlightenment is very difficult to obtain: one needs a vast accumulation of knowledge and merit, innumerable heroic deeds in the course of three immeasurable kalpas.
>
> One could understand that the Bodhisattva seeks this enlightenment, which is so difficult to obtain, if this enlightenment were his only means of arriving at deliverance. But this is not the case. Why then do they undertake such infinite labour?
>
> For the good of others, because they want to become capable of pulling others out of this great flood of suffering. But what personal benefit do they find in the benefit of others? The benefit of others is their own benefit, because they desire it.
>
> Who could believe that?
>
> It is true that men devoid of pity, and who think only of themselves, find it hard to believe in the altruism of the Bodhisattva. But compassionate men do so easily. Do we not see that certain people, confirmed in the absence of pity, find pleasure in the suffering of others, even when it is not useful to them? As well one

must admit that the Bodhisattvas, confirmed in pity, find pleasure in doing good to others without any egoistic preoccupation. Do we not see that certain people, ignorant of the true nature of the conditioned dharmas which constitute their so-called 'self', attach themselves to these dharmas by force of habit – however completely these dharmas may be devoid of personality – and suffer a thousand pains because of this attachment? Likewise, one must admit that the Bodhisattvas, by the force of habit, detach themselves from the dharmas which constitute their so-called 'self', do no longer consider these dharmas as 'I' or 'mine', growing in pitying solicitude for others, and are ready to suffer a thousand pains for this solicitude.*

This is the idea of the Mahāyāna, fully formed within the Hīnayāna schools. The innovation of the Mahāyāna is that it elaborated this idea into an ideal valid for all. It compared the Arhant unfavourably with the Bodhisattva, and it claimed that all should emulate the Bodhisattvas, and not the Arhants.

As to the Arhant, the Mahāyānists maintained that he had not completely shaken off all attachment to 'I' and 'mine.' He set out to obtain Nirvāṇa for himself, and he won Nirvāṇa for himself, but others were left out of it. In this way, the Arhant could be said to make a difference between himself and others, and thereby to retain, by implication, some notion of himself as different from others – thus showing his inability to realize the truth of 'not-self' to the full. Two passages from the Prajñāpāramitā put this criticism rather forcibly. The first contrasts the career of a Bodhisattva with the Hīnayāna career of a disciple, who aims at Arhantship, and of a pratyeka-buddha, who wins a fuller enlightenment, but, solitary like a rhinoceros, does not preach the doctrine to others.

> How do the persons belonging to the vehicle of the disciples and pratyekabuddhas train themselves? They think 'One single self we will tame, one single self we will pacify, one single self we will lead into Nirvāṇa.' Then they undertake exercises which bring about wholesome roots for the sake of taming themselves, pacifying themselves, nirvanizing themselves. Certainly, the Bodhisattva should not train himself like that. He should undertake exercises for bringing about wholesome roots with the idea: 'My self I will place in

* *Abhidharmakoṣa* iii.94, ii.191–2

Suchness (Nirvāṇa), and, for the sake of helping all the world, I will also place all beings in Suchness, the immeasurable world of beings I will lead to Nirvāṇa.[*]

In Tibetan, Bodhisattva is translated as 'Heroic Being'. The Christians also canonize only those saints who have exhibited virtues in *gradu heroico*. The heroic quality of the Bodhisattva is brought out by the Prajñāpāramitā in another place by way of a parable:

Suppose a hero, endowed with great accomplishments, had gone out with his mother, father, sons, and daughters. By some set of circumstances they would get into a huge wild forest. The foolish among them would be greatly frightened. The hero would, however, fearlessly say to them, 'Do not be afraid! I will speedily take you out of this great and terrible jungle and bring you to safety.' Since he is fearless, vigorous, exceedingly tender, compassionate, courageous, and resourceful, it does not occur to him to take himself alone out of the jungle, leaving his relatives behind. Against the Arhant it is claimed that we must take the whole of the creation with us to enlightenment, that we cannot just abandon it to its fate, as all beings are as near to us as our relatives.

What a man should do is make no discrimination between himself and others, and wait until he had helped everybody into Nirvāṇa before losing himself into it. The Mahāyānists thus claimed that the Arhant had not aimed high enough. The ideal man, the aim of the Buddhist effort, was, according to them, not the rather self-centred, cold, and narrow-minded Arhant, but the all-compassionate Bodhisattva, who abandoned the world but not the beings in it. Whereas wisdom had been taught as the highest, and compassion as a subsidiary virtue, compassion now came to rank as equal with wisdom. While the wisdom of the Arhant had been fruitful in setting free in himself what there was to be set free, it was rather sterile in ways and means of helping ordinary people. The Bodhisattva would be a man who does not only set himself free, but who is also skilful in devising means for bringing out and maturing the latent seeds of enlightenment in others. As again the *Prajñāpāramitā* puts it:

Doers of what is hard are the Bodhisattvas, the great beings who have set out to win supreme enlightenment. They do not wish to

[*] *Aṣṭasāhasrikā* xi.234–5

attain their own private Nirvāṇa. On the contrary, they have surveyed the highly painful world of being, and yet, desirous to win supreme enlightenment, they do not tremble at birth-and-death. They have set out for the benefit of the world, for the ease of the world, out of pity for the world. They have resolved: 'We will become a shelter for the world, a refuge for the world, the world's place of rest, the final relief of the world, islands of the world, lights of the world, leaders of the world, the world's means of salvation.'[*]

The ideal of the Bodhisattva was partly due to social pressure on the Order (cf. p.67 *et seq.*), but to a great extent it was inherent in the practice of the Unlimited, which had trained the monks not to discriminate between themselves and others. As we saw, Buddhism has at its disposal two methods by which it reduces the sense of separateness on the part of individuals. The one is the culture of the social emotions, or sentiments, such as friendliness and compassion. The other consists in acquiring the habit of regarding whatever one thinks, feels, or does as an interplay of impersonal forces called dharmas – weaning oneself slowly from such ideas as 'I' or 'mine' or 'self'. There is a logical contradiction between the method of wisdom, which sees no persons at all, but only dharmas, and the method of the Unlimited, which cultivates relations to people as persons. The meditation on dharmas dissolves other people, as well as oneself, into a conglomeration of impersonal and instantaneous dharmas. It reduces our manhood into five heaps, or pieces, plus a label. If there is nothing in the world except bundles of dharmas – as cold and as impersonal as atoms – instantaneously perishing all the time, there is nothing which friendliness and compassion could work on. One cannot wish well to a dharma which is gone by the time one has come to wish it well, nor can one pity a dharma – say a 'mind-object', or a 'sight-organ', or a 'sound-consciousness.' In those Buddhist circles where the method of dharmas was practised to a greater extent than the Unlimited, it led to a certain dryness of mind, to aloofness, and to lack of human warmth. The true task of the Buddhist is to carry on with both contradictory methods at the same time. As the method of dharmas leads to boundless contraction of the self – because everything is emptied out of it – so the method of the Unlimited leads

[*] *Aṣṭasāhasrikā* xv.293

to a boundless expansion of the self – because one identifies oneself with more and more living beings. As the method of wisdom explodes the idea that there are any persons at all in the world, so the method of the Unlimited increases the awareness of the personal problems of more and more persons.

How then does the Mahāyāna resolve this contradiction? The Buddhist philosophers differ from philosophers bred in the Aristotelean tradition in that they are not frightened but delighted by a contradiction. They deal with this, as with other contradictions, by merely stating it in an uncompromising form, and then they leave it at that. Here is a very famous passage from the *Diamond Sūtra* to illustrate this point:

> Here, O Subhūti, a Bodhisattva should think thus: 'As many beings as there are in the universe of beings – be they egg-born, or born from a womb, or moisture-born, or miraculously born; be they with form, or without; be they with perception, without perception, or with neither perception nor no-perception – as far as any conceivable universe of beings is conceived; all these should be led by me into Nirvāṇa, into that realm of Nirvāṇa which leaves nothing behind. And yet, although innumerable beings have thus been led to Nirvāṇa, no being at all has been led to Nirvāṇa. And why? If in a Bodhisattva the perception of a "being" should take place, he would not be called an "enlightenment-being" (bodhisattva).'[*]

A Bodhisattva is a being compounded of the two contradictory forces of wisdom and compassion. In his wisdom, he sees no persons; in his compassion he is resolved to save them. His ability to combine these contradictory attitudes is the source of his greatness, and of his ability to save himself and others.

EMPTINESS

Two things, the sūtra tells us, are most needful to the Bodhisattva, and to his practice of wisdom: 'Never to abandon all beings and to see into the truth that all things are empty.' We must now make an effort to understand this all-important idea of Emptiness.

---

[*] *Vajracchedikā* 3

Here again the Sanskrit root helps. It shows how easily the word 'empty' could become a synonym for 'not-self'. What we call 'emptiness' in English is *śūnyatā* in Sanskrit. The Sanskrit word *śūnya* is derived from the root *śvi*, 'to swell'. *Śūnya* means literally 'relating to the swollen'. In the remote past, our ancestors, with a fine instinct for the dialectical nature of reality, frequently used the same verbal root to denote the two opposite aspects of a situation. They were as distinctly aware of the unity of opposites as of their opposition. Thus the root *śvi*, Greek *ky*, seems to have expressed the idea that something which looks 'swollen' from the outside is 'hollow' inside. This is easily shown by the facts of comparative philology. You have the meaning 'swollen' in such words as Latin *cumulus* (pile, heap) and *caulis* (stalk). You have the meaning 'hollow', from the same root, in Greek *koilos*, Latin *cavus*. Thus our personality is swollen in so far as constituted by the five skandhas, but it is also hollow inside, because devoid of a central self. Furthermore 'swollen' may mean 'filled with something foreign'. When a woman is 'swollen' in pregnancy – and here again the Greeks use the same root in *kyo* – she is full of a foreign body, of something not herself. Similarly in this view, the personality contains nothing that really belongs to it. It is swollen with foreign matter. Like the child the foreign body must be expelled.

It is a great pity that these connotations of the word *śūnyatā* are lost when we speak of emptiness. The door is opened to innumerable misunderstandings. Particularly to the uninitiated, this emptiness will appear as a mere nothingness, just as Nirvāṇa did.[*]

Although in Buddhist art emptiness is usually symbolized by an empty circle, one must not regard the Buddhist emptiness as a mere nought, or a blank. It is a term for the absence of self, or for self-effacement. In Buddhist thought some ideas belong together which we do not usually associate. I set them out here in a diagram:

---

[*] It is one of the ironies of history that Buddhism, this most uncommercial and even anticommercial system, should have been responsible for the elaboration of a tool without which modern commercialism could scarcely have been developed. Without the invention of a zero, or nought, our shopkeepers, bankers, and statisticians would still be hampered right and left by the clumsiness of the abacus. The little circle which we know as zero was known to the Arabs about 950AD as *shifr*, empty. This became *cifra* in Latin, when about 1150 the nought came to Europe. In English we had originally 'cypher' as the name for zero, and cypher is nothing but the Sanskrit word *śūnya*.

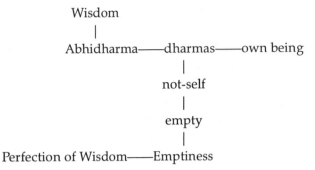

Wisdom
|
Abhidharma——dharmas——own being
|
not-self
|
empty
|
Perfection of Wisdom——Emptiness

Bodhidharma, an Indian or Persian, who went to China about 500AD, expressed the meaning of the term concisely when he said: 'All things are empty, and there is nothing desirable or to be sought after.'

Used as technical terms, the words empty and emptiness express in Buddhist tradition the complete negation of this world by the exercise of wisdom. The central idea is the complete denial and renunciation of, the complete withdrawal and liberation from, the world around us, in all its aspects and along its entire breadth.

The Abhidharmists knew the term 'empty', but used it very sparingly. In the Pāli canon it occurs only on a few occasions. The New Wisdom School treats the term as the sesame which opens all doors, and Nāgārjuna worked out its epistemological implications. Emptiness here means the identity of yes and no. In this system of thought the gentle art of undoing with one hand what one has done with the other is considered as the very quintessence of fruitful living. The Buddhist sage is depicted as a kind of faithful Penelope, patiently waiting for the coming of the Ulysses of enlightenment. He should really never commit himself to either 'yes' or 'no' on anything. But, if he once says 'yes', he must also say 'no'. And when he says 'no', he must also say 'yes', to the same.

Emptiness is that which stands right in the middle between affirmation and negation, existence and non-existence, eternity and annihilation. The germ of this idea is found in an early saying, which the scriptures of all schools have transmitted. The Buddha says to Kātyāyana that the world usually bases its views on two things, existence and non-existence. 'It is' is one extreme; 'it is not' is another. Between those two limits the world is imprisoned. The holy men transcend this limitation. Avoiding both extremes, the Tathāgata teaches a Dharma in the middle between them, where alone the truth can be found. This Dharma is now called emptiness. The Absolute is emptiness and all things also are empty. In their emptiness Nirvāṇa and this world coincide, they are no longer different but the same.

The anattā doctrine openly disagrees with common sense. The doctors of the Old Wisdom School had admitted the conflict as irreducible by distinguishing two kinds of truth: ultimate truth consists of statements about dharmas, conventional truth speaks of persons and things. The ultimate events of this school have very much the same function as atoms, cells, and similar entities, also normally ignored in daily life, to which the propositions of modern science properly refer. The New Wisdom School takes the concept of ultimate truth a step further. It is now found exclusively in relation to the one ultimate reality, which is the Absolute in its emptiness. Ultimate truth means no longer scientific but mystical truth. It is obvious that in this sense anything we may say is ultimately untrue. Emptiness cannot be the object of a definite belief. We cannot get at it, and even if we could, we would not recognize it, since it has no distinctive marks. All doctrines, even the Four Holy Truths, are ultimately false, evidence of ignorance. Theories cover up the Ineffable Light of the One, and they are only conventionally true, in the sense that they conform to peoples' varying capacities for understanding spiritual experiences. In accordance with the inclinations and gifts of beings, the teaching can, and must, be varied indefinitely.

The doctrine of emptiness is frequently expressed by way of simile. The Old Wisdom School had already compared this world around us to a mass of foam, a bubble, a mirage, a dream, a magical show. The similes had the purpose of bringing home the insight that the world is relatively unimportant, worthless, deceptive, and unsubstantial. Poets in the West have often used the same similes with a similar intention:

> But what are men who grasp at praise sublime
> But bubbles on the rapid stream of time,
> That rise and fall and swell and are no more
> Born and forgot, ten thousand in an hour.[*]

---

[*] Edward Young, 'Night Thoughts'.

Or, the more famous

> This world is all a fleeting show,
> For man's illusion given;
> The smiles of joy, the tears of woe,
> Deceitful shine, deceitful flow –
> There's nothing true but Heaven.[*]

When the New Wisdom School, in its turn, compares all dharmas to a dream, an echo, a reflected image, a mirage, or a magical show, it does so in a more technical sense. The Absolute alone is not dependent on anything else; it is ultimately real. Any relative thing is functionally dependent on other things, and can exist, and be conceived, only in and through its relations with other things. By itself it is nothing, it has no separate inward reality. 'A borrowed sun is not one's own capital,'[†] as Candrakīrti puts it. But if each and every thing is 'devoid of an own-being', and does not really exist, like 'the daughter of a barren virgin carved in stone',[‡] how is it that we can see, hear, and feel the things around us which are really just emptiness? The similes of a dream, etc., are intended to answer that question. One sees a magical show, or a mirage, one hears an echo, one dreams a dream, and yet we all know that the magical appearance is merely deceptive (see p.145), that there is no real water in the mirage, that the echo does not come from a man's voice and that an echo is not someone speaking, and that the objects one loved, hated, and feared in one's dream did not really exist.

Many misunderstandings of the Mādhyamika conception of emptiness would have been avoided if full weight had been given to the terms that are used as synonymous with it. One of the most frequent synonyms is 'non-duality'. In the perfect gnosis, all dualities are abolished, the object does not differ from the subject, Nirvāṇa is not distinguished from the world, existence is no longer something apart from non-existence. Discrimination and multiplicity are the hallmarks of ignorance. From another point of view emptiness is called 'suchness', because one takes reality such as it is, without superimposing any ideas upon it.

---

[*] Thomas Moore, 'This world is all a fleeting show'.

[†] *Prasannapadā* 263

[‡] cf. *Laṅkāvatāra Sūtra* 105, 188, 266

The statements the Mahāyāna philosophers make about true knowledge cease to be paradoxical and absurd when one realizes that they attempt to describe the universe as it appears on the level of complete self-extinction, or from the point of view of the Absolute. If it is a meaningful and rational undertaking to describe this world as it appears to God, then the sūtras of the Mahāyāna are full of meaning and rationality. Meister Eckhart and Hegel attempted a similar task. Their writings also suggest that God's meaning is not always easily understood.

SALVATION

Salvation, as the New Wisdom School understands it, can be summed up in three negations – non-attainment, non-assertion, non-relying – and one positive attribute – omniscience. A profusion of argument is expended on showing that Nirvāṇa cannot be attained, that salvation cannot really take place, and that the long and laborious struggle of the Bodhisattva really leads nowhere at all – 'In emptiness there are neither attainment nor non-attainment.'* The Unconditioned is by definition devoid of any relation to anything else, or, as the sūtras put it, it is absolutely isolated and solitary. It is therefore impossible for a person to enter into any kind of relation with it, much less to possess or gain it. Further, one could never know that one had attained Nirvāṇa. Emptiness has no properties, no marks, it has nothing by which it could be recognized, and so we can never know whether we have it or not.

Non-attainment amounts really to self-extinction, or forgetting oneself in complete self-surrender. It is characteristic of the highest virtues of all that one cannot be aware of them without losing them. It is so with simplicity and humility. One cannot deliberately acquire an unstudied simplicity, nor can one reflect on one's humility without pandering to pride. One cannot say that one has gained Nirvāṇa without making a distinction between oneself and Nirvāṇa, between one's former state and one's present state, between Nirvāṇa and its opposite. And all these distinctions are signs of that very ignorance which excludes one from the other shore.

---

* *Prajñāpāramitāhṛdaya*

It is really a danger inherent in the very use of language that any statement one makes looks like the assertion of something. In a system in which non-assertion is one of the marks of salvation, one must always remember that it is not put forward as a positive theory or as a metaphysical system. 'This sublime doctrine is not a cockpit for logicians.'* The doctrine of emptiness is not taught to support one theory against others, but to get rid of theories altogether. It would therefore be quite unjust to the intentions of the New Wisdom School if one were to regard emptiness as a kind of Absolute behind the conditioned world, as a kind of basis for it, as a kind of anchor for us. This is certainly not so – 'Nirvāṇa is not in the least distinct from birth-and-death.'† It is not a separate reality at all. It would be equally fallacious to describe it as a metaphysical monism directed against the pluralism of the Sarvāstivādins. It is true that the Mādhyamika doctrine is often so represented in textbooks of philosophy. It would, however, be against the spirit of a doctrine which avoids falling into dualism, to posit a One as against a Many. The mind of Nāgārjuna was more subtle than such philosophizings. Emptiness is the non-difference between yes and no, and the truth escapes us when we say 'it is', and when we say 'it is not'; but it lies somewhere between these two. The man who dwells in emptiness has neither a positive nor a negative attitude to anything. Nāgārjuna's doctrine is not a metaphysical one at all, but it describes a practical attitude of non-assertion which alone can assure lasting peace. Nothing is more alien to the mentality of the sage than to fight or contend for or against anything. This peacefulness of the true sage is the germ of the Mādhyamika dialectics. It is clearly expressed already in scriptures much older than Nāgārjuna. It is found clearly and unmistakably in the very ancient *Sutta Nipāta* (verses 796–803). And in the Saṁyutta Nikāya the Buddha states:

I do not fight with the world, but the world fights with me, for one who knows about Dharma never fights with the world. And what the learned in the world regard as non-existent, that also I teach as non-existent. And what the learned in the world regard as existent, that also I regard as existent.‡

* *Sūtrālaṁkāra* i.7
† *Prasannapadā* 535
‡ *Saṁyutta Nikāya* iii.138

The purpose of Nāgārjuna's dialectics was not to come to any definite conclusion at all, but to destroy all opinions and to reduce all positive beliefs to absurdity.

The New Testament tells us concisely in one short sentence that 'the son of man has not where he can rest his head.' Through an almost infinite variety of expressions, the New Wisdom School preaches the gospel of non-relying. The clue to the doctrine lies in the importance of anxiety in our lives (see p.11). This anxiety forces us to hold perpetually on to something which is different from us. We cling to one person after another, and nothing terrifies us so much as to be quite solitary, by ourselves, without even the thought of something to flee into. In order to be saved, we must reject all these supports one by one, and learn to view without trembling the emptiness of our soul, as it is naked by itself. When we are thus without any stable support, without any hope of one, then we are said to 'rely on nothing but perfect wisdom', or on emptiness, which is the same thing.

From a positive point of view, salvation is described as omniscience. This ambition to become omniscient appears rather curious to us and requires some words of explanation. It is a result of a double development, which, on the one side, makes the final Nirvāṇa of Buddhahood into the goal after which the believer should strive, and which, on the other side, stressed omniscience as the essential attribute of a Buddha. The first is, as we saw, implied in the Bodhisattva ideal. In what sense, then, is the Buddha held to be omniscient? The Mahāyānists claim that the Buddha was omniscient in the strictest sense of the term. With unimpeded cognition, he knew correctly all the aspects of existence, in all its details. Finite minds could, of course, not hope to understand the workings of an infinite intellect. The Buddha's thoughts would really be quite different from ours qualitatively. They would be 'absolute' thoughts, thoughts of an Absolute by an Absolute. When properly considered, the thought of the Buddha would really not be a thought at all, because an unconditioned thought cannot be included in the skandha of consciousness, and because it is not separated from its object, but identical with it. In any case, omniscience could not be attributed to the Buddha in so far as he was a human being, or even in so far as he was in his 'glorified body', but it would be essentially bound up with the Buddha as a pure spiritual principle, with the Dharma body of the Buddha. Not all Buddhists seem to have believed that strict omniscience on the part of the Buddha would be necessary to invest his religion with the required authority. If he knew everything that was essential to salvation, that would be sufficient to make him into a trustworthy guide. In some passages of the Pāli scriptures, as a matter of fact, the Buddha expressly disclaims any other kind of omniscience. The Mahāyāna, on the other hand, explains that while primarily the omniscience of the Buddha consists in his acquaintance with the means of attaining heaven and liberation, he also comprehends all things without exception, including such unnecessary pieces of information as the number of insects in the world. If the Buddha were deficient in this respect, he would be hampered by things outside the range of his knowledge and he would fall short of identity with the Absolute.

Leaving aside the philosophical implications of this problem, the search after omniscience is, from a practical point of view, identical with the search after self-extinction, and therefore it is salutary to hold it up as a goal of the spiritual life. If we take ourselves in our natural condition, we probably have to agree that we have no particular desire to become totally omniscient. To the average seeker after Dharma, all-knowledge is certainly not one of the fruits, it is not the reward he really seeks. The state of being which one often expects from the pursuit of the Dharma would be marked, I think, by three chief properties: (1) protection from physical pain, (2) deliverance from fear, anxiety, and apprehension by the removal of all attachment to self, and of its consequences, such as death, and finally, (3) there would be some hope of becoming the centre or abode of a calm, pure strength that would overcome and dispel the world. Our historical documents suggest that in the ancient Buddhist order in India these were the motives which inspired the efforts of a considerable section of the community of monks. Before their mind was an ideal state of Unconcernedness, almost like the Stoic ideal of *apatheia*. It is against them that the Mahāyāna's stress on omniscience is directed. If you are all the time dominated by a desire to escape from the evils of the world, your idea of self-extinction may very well come to resemble a perpetual dreamless sleep. The Buddha, however, is one who is awake all the time, and in Sanskrit the root *budh* denotes both 'to wake up' and 'to know'. That is one of the reasons the Mahāyāna stressed omniscience as a goal for all.

In addition, the virtue of omniscience lies precisely in that I have not the slightest desire for it. Not one of our instincts impels us to seek all knowledge. As a goal it is quite alien to our natural constitution. We are obviously faced with a contradiction: My goal, as a follower of the Path, must be attractive to me, because otherwise I would not try to reach it. It must, however, also be unattractive to me, because otherwise I would try to reach it. But the goal is where my present I, and all that it values and understands, has ceased to be, and cannot enter at all. It is clearly ridiculous for me, or for anyone else, seriously to pretend that they want to know every detail of the entire universe. Compared with the vast universe, the whole of mankind is less than a small spot of fungus on a pebble in the Atlantic Ocean as compared with the Atlantic Ocean itself. How much less am I. Omniscience and I can never be brought together. But when I am no longer I, anything may happen.

It is not easy, it is against our nature, to accept this contradiction, and to remain contented with it. To persons constituted as we are, it is tempting to conceive of our goal as something to be got hold of – like a butterfly caught in a net, or like an interest-bearing bank account. We like an emancipation which, in the words of Eckhart, we can 'wrap into a blanket, and put underneath a bench'. To correct the error of trying to approach the goal as a thing out there, one may say that the goal is nothing at all, i.e. emptiness, or the identity of yes and no. Or, alternatively, one may say that it is all things – not the sum of all things, but a totality of all things which both includes and excludes each individual thing. Clearly unthinkable, but in all-knowledge an object identical with its subject. To do all things, not conscious of doing anything. To think all things, and not be conscious of any thing. To strive for all things, and be content never to get to them. That is the miracle we must perform to be rid of ourselves. 'One who does not train himself to get hold of all-knowledge, he trains himself in all-knowledge, he will go forth into all-knowledge.'[*]

PARALLELS

The ideas of the Prajñāpāramitā and of the Mādhyamikas are apt to appear strange to Europeans, as standing completely outside the

* *Aṣṭasāhasrikā* ii.43

stream of our own philosophical tradition. It may therefore be useful to remind the reader that we have here not a peculiarly Indian phenomenon, but that the Mediterranean world knows, or knew, a number of similar developments.

The a-theoretical attitude of the Mādhyamikas had, for instance, a striking parallel in the so-called Greek Sceptics. The founder of this school is Pyrrho of Elis (c. 330BC). Except for the stress on omniscience, his view of life corresponds in all its details closely to that of the Mādhyamikas. Pyrrho had no positive doctrines. To be his disciple meant to lead a kind of life similar to that of Pyrrho.

> He wanted to reveal to men the secret of happiness, by showing
> them that 'salvation' can be found only in the peace of a thought
> which is indifferent, a sensibility which is extinct, a will which is
> obedient; and further, that this quest requires an effort which is, on
> the part of the individual, an effort to die to himself.[*]

Freedom from passion is the great aim of life, and even-mindedness is the attitude one must strive to cultivate. All external things are the same, there is no difference between them, and the sage does not distinguish between them. To gain this state of indifference one must sacrifice all natural instincts. All theoretical views are equally unfounded and one must completely abstain from forming propositions and from passing judgments. There is, in Pyrrho's philosophy, the same distinction between conventional truth, the appearances (*phainomena*) on the one side, and the ultimate truth (*adēla*) on the other. The ultimate truth is completely hidden. 'I do not know that honey is sweet, but I agree that it appears to me so.'

Pyrrho's inhibition of all theoretical judgement is technically called *epokhe*. Its meaning is very clearly explained by Aristocles of Messene, under three headings: (1) What is the inner nature (= own-being, *svabhāva* in Sanskrit) of things? It can be characterized only by negations, because all things are equally in-different, im-ponderable, un-decided. They are all equal and none weighs more than another. One cannot say of any thing that it is more *this* than it is *not this*. One might equally well affirm that it *is* and *is not*, or deny that it *is* or *is not*; (2) What is our situation with regard to them? We should not trust more in one than in another. We should not incline towards

---

[*] L. Robin, *Pyrrhon et le scepticisme grec*, 1944, p.24

them. We should not be agitated by them; (3) How should we conduct ourselves towards them? The wisest attitude is a speechless silence, imperturbability, and indifference. Non-action is the only action possible.

From this parallel, one can incidentally draw a conclusion as regards the date of the appearance of the Mādhyamika views in India itself. This conclusion sounds rather extravagant, but I think it has sufficient plausibility to be mentioned here. It is a fact that Pyrrho founded his school immediately on his return from Asia, which, together with his teacher, Anaxarchos, he had visited in the train of Alexander's army. It has further been asserted by Robin, and other authorities, that the Sceptic philosophy was something quite new to Greece, and that none of the preceding indigenous Greek developments led up to it. One can therefore infer with some probability that Pyrrho acquired his views in India or Iran. If he did not acquire them in Iran, the tenets of the Mādhyamikas would already have been present in India by about 350BC. They were, of course, not necessarily transmitted to Pyrrho by Buddhist monks. It is perhaps more probable that he was in contact with the Digambara Jains, who, in the Greek accounts, occur under the name 'gymnosophists', the naked ascetics. The Jains and Buddhists lived in close contact with each other, and the doctrine of each shows the influence of the other. It is, for instance, curious that the Jains have a list of twenty-four successive *tīrthaṅkaras* (saviours), and that ancient Hīnayāna Buddhism knows a list of twenty-four predecessors of Śākyamuni. I believe that the Mahāyāna doctrine of omniscience has also been profoundly influenced by the Jain views on that subject. As a matter of fact, a typical Jain doctrine is recorded among the sayings of Pyrrho. He gave as his reason for writing no books that he was resolved to exert no pressure on anybody's mind. The Jains, before him, had drawn, from their injunction of 'inoffensiveness', the logical conclusion that one must not do violence to anyone by imposing one's views upon him. However that may be, if it is granted that Pyrrho owed his basic ideas to his conversion by Indians, and if his philosophy is very similar to that of the Mādhyamikas, then the Mādhyamika doctrines, which are known to us only from writings certainly not older than about 100BC, must go back in their essentials to c. 350BC, i.e. to within 150 years after the Buddha's Nirvāṇa.

Whatever the merits of this argument, the extraordinary fact remains that during the same period, i.e. from c. 200BC onward – two
distinct civilizations, one in the Mediterranean, the other in India,
constructed out of their own cultural antecedents, a closely analogous set of ideas concerning Wisdom, each one independently, as it
seems. In the eastern Mediterranean we have the Wisdom books of
the Old Testament, nearly contemporaneous with the Prajñāpāramitā in its first form. Later on, under the influence of Alexandria,
the Gnostics and Neoplatonists developed a literature which as-
signed a central position to Wisdom (*sophia*) and which, from Philon
to Proclus, reveals a profusion of verbal coincidences with the
Prajñāpāramitā texts. Among the Christians, this tradition was continued by Origenes and Dionysius Areopagita; among others, the
magnificent church of Hagia Sophia is an eloquent witness to the
importance of wisdom in the Eastern branch of the Christian church.
Numerous are the parallels, or coincidences, between the treatment
of Chochma and Sophia, on the one hand, and the Buddhist texts
dealing with perfect wisdom on the other. To explain these coincidences by 'borrowing' does not get us very far. We do not 'explain'
Lloyd George's social legislation by saying that he 'borrowed' it from
Germany. A real explanation would have to go into the *motive* of the
borrower. Mere borrowing also would not explain the fact that both
in Buddhism and Judaism the conception of wisdom, as it evolved
after 200BC, grew quite naturally out of the preceding tradition, and
is in no conflict with any of their basic concepts. To note only one
difference: Sophia plays a definite role at the creation of the world,
while the Prajñāpāramitā has no cosmic functions, and remains
unburdened by the genesis of this universe. The iconographies of
Sophia and Prajñāpāramitā also seem to have evolved independently. I was, however, interested to come across a Byzantine
miniature of the tenth century (Vat. Palat. gr.381 fol.2) which is said
to go back to an Alexandrian model. There, the right hand of Sophia
makes the gesture of teaching, while the left arm holds a book. This
is not unlike some Indian statues of the Prajñāpāramitā. In all this
we may have parallel developments, under the influence of local
conditions, from a general widely diffused pattern of human culture.
Or, of course, there may be some hidden rhythm in history which
activates certain archetypes – as Jung would call them – at certain
periods in widely distant places.

6

THE BUDDHISM OF FAITH AND DEVOTION

THE RECEPTION OF BHAKTI

The New Wisdom School was the movement of an élite which from compassion regarded the interests of the common people as their own. It could therefore not content itself with formulating the highly abstract metaphysics described in the previous chapter. In order to fulfil its mission, it had to supplement its metaphysical doctrines with a mythological system.

The Bodhisattva was committed to skill: he could not possibly confine his activities on behalf of the salvation of others to the advice to meditate on emptiness, otherwise the majority of the people would be left out, by their lack of metaphysical inclinations, their preoccupation with earning a living, and their deep-rooted attachment to property, family, and home. Since, however, the layman also is involved in suffering, and, as originally divine, endowed with spiritual longings and potentialities, the word of the Buddha is addressed to him as well.

Incapable of wisdom, he must use Faith. The way of transcendental wisdom is supplemented by that of faith, or *bhakti*. Nāgārjuna distinguishes the easy way of Faith from the hard and difficult way of Wisdom. Both lead to the same goal, just as one can travel to the same town either by water or on land. Some prefer the method of zealous vigour, of austerities, and of meditation. Others can, by the easy practice of the helpful means of Faith, simply by thinking of the Buddha while invoking his names, rapidly attain to a state from which there is no falling back, i.e. from which they go on to full enlightenment, in the certainty of reaching it.

Faith, a rather subordinate virtue in the Hīnayāna, now comes to rank equal with wisdom itself. Its power to save is much greater than the old schools assumed. The increasing degeneration of mankind had to be recognized. The hard way of self-trained, vigorous wisdom was no longer feasible for many, if not for the majority, even among the monks. Under these circumstances, the easy way of Faith was the only one of which people were still capable.

From c. 400BC onward a movement of bhakti had gathered momentum in India, and about the beginning of our era it had gained great strength. *Bhakti* means the loving personal devotion to adored deities conceived in human form. About the time of the Christian era the bhaktic tendencies of the Indian masses, which had influenced Buddhism for a long time, invaded it in full force. The metaphysics of the New Wisdom School was sufficiently elastic to absorb the trend towards bhakti, and to provide it with a philosophical foundation. The result of the organic fusion between the 'new wisdom' Buddhism and the bhaktic movement is what we shall call the Buddhism of Faith.

The Mahāyāna had insisted on the universality of salvation as against a Hīnayāna that seemed incomplete not least because it had concentrated on the élite, and had few effective means of helping the less endowed to salvation. The Mahāyānist takes his duty towards his less developed fellow beings most seriously. He must make the Dharma, if not intelligible, then at least accessible to them. The inner logic of perfect wisdom leads to its negation in faith. If Nirvāṇa and the world are identical, if everything is the same as everything else, then there is no real difference between the enlightened and the unenlightened, between the wise and the fools, between purity and impurity, and everyone must have the same opportunity for salvation. If the Buddha's compassion is unlimited, he must save also the fools. If the Buddha nature is equally present in all, then all are equally near Buddhahood. The Mahāyāna Buddhism of Faith draws the practical conclusions. It evolves methods which remove the difference between poor and rich, between ignorant and learned, between sinners and saints, between the pure and the impure. Since all have the same claim to salvation, it must be made equally accessible to all.

LITERARY HISTORY

The literature of this school combines the terms, phrases, and ideas of the New Wisdom School with devotion to personal saviours. It began in India about the beginning of our era. 400 or 500 years later it was more and more submerged by Tantric ideas. To an increasing extent, it became preoccupied with the provision of 'spells'[16] by which one could approach deities, and induce them to do one's will (see p.155 *et seq.*).

One of the first Buddhas to become an object of bhakti was Akṣobhya (the Imperturbable), who rules in the east, in the Buddha-land of Abhirati. He is mentioned in quite a number of early Mahā-yāna sūtras. This worship must have been fairly widespread, but only fragments of his legend have survived. The cult of Amitābha shows strong Iranian influence, and began about the same time. Amitābha is the Buddha of Infinite (*amita*) Light (*ābhā*) and his kingdom is in the west. He is also known as Amitāyus, because his life-span (*āyuḥ*) is infinite (*amita*). A great number of texts are devoted to Amitābha. The best known among them is the *Sukhāvatīvyūha*, the 'Array of the Happy Land', which describes his Paradise, its origin and structure. In addition, Bhaiṣajyaguru, the Buddha of healing, enjoyed a great popularity. In China and Japan, Amitābha has been much more popular than any other Buddha. In India he seems never to have occupied such an overtowering position, although Huei-je, a Chinese pilgrim who visited India between 702 and 719, reports that everyone spoke to him about Amitābha and his Paradise.

Other texts, again, dealt with the Bodhisattvas. Like the Buddhas, they are very numerous, and we can mention only a few. Among the creations of the mythological imagination of the Buddhism of Faith, Avalokiteśvara is easily the most outstanding. By the power of his magic, and by his infinite care and skill, he affords safety to those who are anxious. The word Avalokiteśvara is a compound of the word *iśvara* ('lord, sovereign'), and of *avalokita*, which means 'he who looks down with compassion', i.e. on beings suffering in this world. Avalokiteśvara personifies compassion. The texts and the images suggest that in India one may distinguish three stages in his development. At first, he is a member of a trinity, consisting of Amitāyus, Avalokiteśvara, and Mahāsthāmaprāpta (i.e. 'the one who has at-tained great strength'). This trinity has many counterparts in Iranean religion, i.e. in the Mithras cult and in Zervanism, a Persian religion which recognised Infinite Time (*Zervan Akarana* = *Amita-āyus*) as the fundamental principle. Assimilated by Buddhism, Avalokiteśvara becomes a great Bodhisattva, so great that he is nearly as perfect as a Buddha. He possesses a great miraculous power to help in all kinds of dangers and difficulties. In the second stage, Avalokiteśvara acquires a number of cosmic functions and features. He 'holds the world in his hand', he is immensely big – '800,000 myriads of miles.... Each of the pores of his skin conceals a world system.'* He is the Lord and Sovereign of the world. From his eyes come the sun and the moon, from his mouth the winds, from his feet the earth. In all these respects Avalokiteśvara resembles the Hindu god, Brahmā. Finally, in the third stage, at a time when the magical elements of Buddhism come to the fore, he becomes a great magician who owes his power to his mantras, and he adopts many of the charactenstics of Shiva. This is the Tantric Avalokiteśvara. In some ways Mañjuśrī was Avalokiteśvara's equal in popularity. He personifies wisdom. A number of sūtras were composed in his honour, some before 250AD. Many other Bodhisattvas, like Kṣitigarbha and Samantabhadra, could be enumerated, but for the details we must refer the reader to Ch. Eliot's book on Japanese Buddhism.

THE AGENT OF SALVATION

To judge from the scriptures of the Old Wisdom School, self-reliance seems to have been one of the outstanding traits of its adherents. It was taken for granted that one could only save oneself by one's own personal effort and that 'none could be saved by another'. Three new ideas helped to undermine, in the Buddhism of Faith, such an attitude of exclusive self-reliance. They were the doctrine of the Transfer of Merit, the notion that the Buddha nature is present in all of us, and the invention of a large number of saviours.

The belief that merit can be transferred from one person to another runs counter to the law of karma as it had been understood in the old order. The original belief seems to have been that each one of us has his own series of karma, that the punishment for his misdeeds must be suffered by him, and that the rewards for his good deeds

* *Lokeśvara Śataka* 71; Kāraṇḍavyūhasūtra, in de Mallmann, Avalokiteśvara, I, 1948, pp.43, 105

are enjoyed only by him. This excessive individualism was not essential to the karma doctrine, and just as historically the notion of collective responsibility preceded that of individual responsibility, so, in the Vedas, it had been assumed that the members of a family or clan all share one common karma. The individualistic interpretation of the law of karma throws each individual on his own resources, and seems to deny any solidarity between the different persons as regards the more essential things of life, i.e. as regards merit and demerit. We hear of a Brahmin who objected to the Buddha's teaching on the count that, when carried into practice, it created merit only in one single person. The Buddha replied that the actions of the saints affected usually a multitude of people whom they inspired with their example, but there is no sign that any Buddhist scripture before 200BC definitely teaches the transfer of merit from one person to another.

Merit is that quality in us which ensures future benefits to us, be they material or spiritual. It is not difficult to perceive that to desire merit, to hoard, store, and accumulate merit, does, however meritorious it may be, imply a considerable degree of self-seeking. It has always been the tactics of the Buddhists to weaken the possessive instincts of the spiritually less-endowed members of the community by withdrawing them from such objects as wealth and family, and directing them instead towards one aim and object, i.e. the acquisition of merit. But that, of course, is good enough only on a fairly low spiritual level. At higher stages one will have to turn also against this form of possessiveness, one will have to be willing to give up one's store of merit for the sake of the happiness of others. The Mahāyāna drew this conclusion and expected its followers to endow other beings with their own merit, or, as the scriptures put it, 'to turn over, or dedicate, their merit to the enlightenment of all beings'.

> Through the merit derived from all my good deeds I wish to appease the suffering of all creatures, to be the medicine, the physician, and the nurse of the sick as long as there is sickness. Through rains of food and drink I wish to extinguish the fire of hunger and thirst. I wish to be an inexhaustible treasure to the poor, a servant who furnishes them with all they lack. My life, and all my rebirths, all my possessions, all the merit that I have acquired or will acquire, all that I

abandon without hope of any gain for myself in order that the
salvation of all beings might be promoted.[*]

This is the intention. It is carried out by the great Bodhisattvas in the
last stages of their spiritual progress, and it is embodied in their
vows. A portion of their immeasurable merit is transferred to the
believer, if asked for in faith.

Secondly, the emphasis on the identity of the Buddha with this
world had accustomed the Mahāyānists to the idea that the Buddha
nature dwells in every part of the universe, and therefore in the heart
of each one of us.

> The Lord Buddha on his lion-throne
> Dwells in each particle of sand and stone.

If one assumes that by our own efforts we ourselves strive for
salvation, which part of ourselves is it then that seeks Nirvāṇa? Is it
our individual self, or perhaps our 'higher self', our 'Buddha-self',
which does the seeking? The Mahāyāna came to the conclusion that
it is really the Buddha in us who does the seeking and that it is the
Buddha nature in us that seeks Buddhahood.

Thirdly, the Buddha had been a teacher and not a saviour. In the
Buddhism of Faith the higher Bodhisattvas developed into the saviours of the faithful. Once a Bodhisattva had saturated himself with
the perfection of wisdom, and annihilated himself by a thorough
understanding of emptiness, his being underwent a complete transformation. All self-interest and attachment are then abolished. A
Bodhisattva could, on principle, extinguish himself at this point, but
compassion prevented him. He would continue to act, but his activity would be perfectly pure. A true king, he enjoys sovereignty over
the world. A Bodhisattva at this stage acquired all kinds of unearthly
and supernatural qualities. He could be miraculously reborn at will
wherever, and in whatever shape, he desired; he possessed an unlimited power of transformation, etc. The New Wisdom School had
conceived of the possibility of such supernatural beings. The Buddhism of Faith conceived of them as concrete individuals, and fur-
nished them with names, legends, and a definite and tangible
individuality.

---

[*] Śāntideva, *Bodhicaryāvatāra* iii.6–10

Akṣobhya and Amitābha, Avalokiteśvara and Mañjuśrī, all the celestial Buddhas and Bodhisattvas of this school, are, however, obviously productions of the mind, and without historical or factual basis. It is not easy to understand that the Mahāyānists could admit this, as they did, and yet deny that these new saviours were mere creatures, nay figments, of the imagination, subjective and arbitrary inventions. It is impossible to explain their attitude by the absence of a historical sense generally found among Hindus, since we know that the Indian Buddhists of the Hīnayāna used to argue that they could not believe in the celestial Buddhas and Bodhisattvas of the Mahāyāna because there was no evidence of their actual existence.

It seems to me that we have here a philosophical difference which corresponds to the age-old cleavage between 'Nominalism' and 'Realism'. To the Nominalist only the individual has real existence, to the Realist the universal. Similarly, in religion, one type of mind requires an actual historical fact to base its belief on, while another regards the productions of the creative mythological imagination as in no way inferior to the products of human history. Many Christians set much store by the assertion that Jesus Christ was a historical person. To the mythological school, the question of historical existence seems to be quite irrelevant. Such a mentality considers only Christ as religiously and spiritually significant, and not the man Jesus. In early Christian history, the Mahāyānist attitude was represented by some Gnostic sects, who claimed that the Christ descended on the man Jesus at baptism and left him again on the Cross, at the point where Jesus said, 'My God, my God, why hast thou forsaken me?'

Philosophers distinguish between what a person is and the fact that he is. In the traditional conception of the Christ there is not one single element which is not pre-Christian, which is not shared by other religious systems, which does not recur in the legends about the Messiah, about Osiris, about Hercules, and many others. The mythological school regards the mythological concept as the essential thing. Whether it is embodied, or not, in a person in history appears as a quite incidental and trivial detail. The names of Amitābha, etc., may be invented, but the reality behind them, the Absolute, is there all the time.

In China, this attitude of the Mahāyāna came up against the keen and accurate historical sense of the Chinese literary tradition, and ·

we find an inclination to seek a historical nucleus of the celestial Bodhisattvas. One said, for instance, of Mañjuśrī, that he was originally a Chinese prince, who lived in the first century, at Wu-t'ai-shan, the Mountain of the Five Peaks (Pañcaśīrṣa), at the time of the Emperor Ming-ti. Thus located in time and space he was satisfactorily accounted for. Similarly, Green Tārā was traced back to a Chinese princess. The Tibetan king, Songtsen Gampo (d.650) had two wives, one Chinese and one Nepalese. They were identified with two goddesses, White Tārā and Green Tārā. To the Indian mind this was an ordinary case of incarnation of a pre-existing spiritual force. Some Chinese reversed the process. To their instinctive Euhemerism it appeared that the princesses were deified as the two Tārās, that the goddess Tārā was an apotheosis of the historical persons, who, far from being the embodiment of an idea, were its real starting point. In the large cosmic perspective of the early Mahāyāna this insistence on the puny data of human history would have appeared quite incomprehensible.

THE AIMS OF THE FAITHFUL

What, then, did the faithful expect of the Buddhas and Bodhisattvas? In the Buddhism of Faith the saviours have, in the main, four functions:

(1) They promote the virtues of the faithful, help to remove greed, hate, and delusion, and protect from ghosts and men who may maliciously try to interfere with spiritual practices.

(2) In addition, they bestow material benefits. Since the Buddhas and Bodhisattvas are all-merciful, it was natural, and, in some ways, logical to assume that they should concern themselves with the actual wishes of their adherents, protect their earthly fortunes, and ward off disasters. Avalokiteśvara, for instance, protects caravans from robbers, sailors from ship wreck, criminals from execution. By his help women obtain the children they desire. If one but thinks of Avalokiteśvara, fire ceases to burn, swords fall to pieces, enemies become kind-hearted, bonds are loosened, spells revert to whence they came, beasts flee, and snakes lose their poison. This aspect of the Buddhism of Faith stands in logical contradiction to the emphasis on the need for renunciation which pervades the Buddhist doctrine. As a magical doctrine, Buddhism promises to remove evils

physically, as a spiritual doctrine it aims at purging the mind of a wrong attitude to them. We have stated before (p.6) that what is contradictory in thought may well co-exist in life.

(3) The Buddhas and Bodhisattvas become an object of the desire to love. Now the word 'love' is extremely ambiguous, and harbours a great multiplicity of meanings. In this context, love in the sense of bhakti means a personal relationship with a person whom one not only cherishes and adores, but whom one wishes to see, wishes to be with, whom one does not want to let go, whom one wants to persist. The orthodox view which the 'Wise' had formed of the Buddha had made him quite unsuitable as an object of such love. He was said to be extinct, and, after his Nirvāṇa, to have gone to nowhere at all. He was really lost to the world, quite isolated from it. Only his Dharma, an impersonal entity, remained. This theory had, from the very start, proved emotionally quite unsatisfactory to those whose religion meant love. Ānanda, among the immediate disciples of the Buddha the chief representative of bhaktic mentality, a man who loved the Lord as a person, could not resign himself to his loss. He formed the quite heretical opinion that, when he entered Nirvāṇa, the Buddha had gone up to the Heavens of Brahmā, Just as at birth he had come down from the Tushita Heavens.

As time went on, the bhaktic trend grew in India. Buddhism was not exempt from it. Increasingly the faithful wished to 'dwell in the sight of the Buddha', or to 'see the Tathāgatas'. In spite of official discouragement, they wished to believe that the Lord Buddha was not really extinct, but that somewhere he was present and in existence. Wisdom and devotion were in open conflict. Wisdom consisted in giving up all supports whatsoever. Devotion was unhappy without some persisting person as its support. The Mahāsaṅghikas came to the rescue of the devotional needs of the laity by fostering the belief that the Buddha, as a supramundane being (see p.99) had not quite passed away, but persisted after his Nirvāṇa in some form or other. The Mahāyāna greatly developed this idea, and filled the entire universe to the utmost limits of space with Buddhas and Bodhisattvas who were alive and thus could be loved and treasured.

(4) Finally, the Buddhas and Bodhisattvas provided favourable conditions for the attainment of enlightenment in a future life. In this respect the Mahāyāna merely continued the line of its predecessors. The majority of the faithful had obviously never expected to

obtain the highest goal of Nirvāṇa in this very life. Instead, they could only hope to gain access to a plane of the universe which offered fewer obstacles to the attainment of full enlightenment than the world of men. Rebirth in the heavens was to them the immediate reward of a holy life, and of the act of taking refuge in the Three Treasures. There, among the gods, the virtuous might 'finally pass away' (parinibbāyati), 'not to return from that world'. All the Mahā-yāna did was replace the heavens of the old Hindu gods with the heavens of the Buddhas and Bodhisattvas, and to increase the op-portunities of the average man by multiplying the paradises in which he could be reborn. Even within the Hīnayāna, the Paradise of Maitreya (see p.95) had become increasingly popular as a place of future rebirth. Maitreya, the next Buddha, at present reigns and preaches in the Tushita Heavens, which, inhabited by the Satisfied Gods, are the regular abode of a future Buddha of this world system in his last existence but one. The pious aspired, after death, to go to Maitreya's kingdom and to stay there until they would be with him in his final life on Earth.

Looking out on the starry sky in its immensity, the Mahāyāna perceived such paradises everywhere. Just as the Buddha Śākya-muni appeared in this world system, so other world systems have their Buddhas also. In assigning different Buddhas to different world systems, the Mahāyāna was not original. The Mahāsaṅghikas and Sautrāntikas had already done so. The originality of the Mahāyāna consisted in the development of the notion of a Buddhafield (buddha-kṣetra), or Buddhaland, and in the distinction they made between pure and impure Buddhafields.

Each Buddha has a certain limited field of influence, in which, with a 'deep, sublime, and wonderful voice', he teaches the Dharma to creatures, and thereby helps them to win enlightenment. A Buddhafield is a kind of kingdom of God, a mystical universe, inhabited by the Buddha and by the beings whom he rules and matures. According to Buddhaghosa, a Buddha has a twofold rela-tion to his universe: (1) In his omniscience he knows the entire universe, which is a field of his knowledge; (2) by his sovereignty he exercises authority and influence over a certain range of world systems. The first relation is clearly developed in earlier Hīnayāna literature. The second idea – that of a spatially limited magical influence of the Buddha, of his sovereignty over a particular area (as distinct from his supreme eminence in it) – is almost completely absent from earlier Hīnayāna literature, and was adopted by Buddhaghosa from the Mahāyāna.

But this is not all. Many Buddhafields are identical with the natural and impure world systems that are inhabited by creatures in all the six states of existence (see p.36 *et seq.*). Other Buddhafields again, like that of the Buddha Amitābha, for instance, are 'Pure Lands'. Some Buddhas create realms which are not natural, but ideal, or transcendent in the sense that they stand outside the 'triple world' of sense-desire, form, and formlessness; devoid of women, animals, ghosts, and the damned; inhabited only by Bodhisattvas of great spiritual perfection, either gods or men, 'pure in body, voice, and mind', come into being by apparitional birth. There one sees the radiant body of the Buddha, listens to his preaching, and undergoes further and further purification until Buddhahood is reached by all. This 'paradise' is often described with much sensory imagery. It is bright, made of lapis lazuli, free from stones and gravel, holes and steep precipices, gutters and sewers. It is even, lovely, calming, and beautiful to behold, adorned with jewel trees that are fastened in a chequerboard marked off with gold threads, covered with flowers, etc.

> Beings who are born in that land will never suffer untimely death, will be abundantly rich, doers of good, truthful and sincere, tender in talk. Their families and relatives will never be scattered. They will be skilful in reconciling quarrels, ever benefiting others when speaking. They will never be envious or angry, but ever maintain right principles.[*]

All this is straightforward popular religion. It is, however, characteristic of Buddhism that great efforts are made to integrate these popular conceptions with the basic ideas of the New Wisdom School. It would go against the spirit of the doctrine of universal emptiness if one would have those paradises as a kind of crude actuality out there in space. As a matter of fact, they are really produced by the minds of the Bodhisattvas. To quote the *Avataṁsaka*:

> The Buddhalands as innumerable as particles of dust are raised from one thought cherished in the mind of the Bodhisattva of mercy,

[*] *Vimalakīrtinirdeśa, The Eastern Buddhist,* vi.394

Who, practising meritorious deeds in numberless kalpas has led all
beings to the truth.
All the Buddhalands rise from one's own mind and have infinite forms,
Sometimes pure, sometimes defiled, they are in various cycles of
enjoyment or suffering.[*]

The Buddhafield is the result of a Bodhisattva's altruism, which does
not aim at isolation from the evil-doers but at their conversion. The
Ratnamegha is instructive on this point:

> If the Bodhisattva learns of peoples' grasping greed and violence, he
> must not say, 'Away with these people so grasping and violent,' and
> on that account be depressed and turn back on them. He makes a
> vow to have a very pure field in which the very name of such
> persons shall not be heard. But if the Bodhisattva turns his face away
> from the welfare of all creatures, his field is not pure and his work
> not accomplished.[†]

Few of us would at present believe that one can create a world by
merely wishing to. The creative power of ethically relevant actions
is as axiomatic to the Buddhists as it is strange to us. The environment in which beings have to live is to a great extent, especially in
regard to its pleasantness or unpleasantness, determined by their
deeds (karma). The various hells, for instance, are produced by the
deeds of the creatures who are reborn there. We have waterless
deserts in our world because of our small merit. The world of things
(*bhajanaloka*) is really nothing more than a kind of reflex of people's
deeds. An environment can exist only as long as there are persons
whose karma compels them to perceive it. In the same spirit one now
claims that the merit of a Bodhisattva may be great enough to create
a Pure Land not only for himself, but also for others to whom he
transfers it.

As a popular religion, the Buddhism of Faith teaches a multiplicity
of Buddhafields. As an offshoot of Wisdom-Buddhism, it knows that
this multiplicity is only provisionally true. Ultimately all fields are
one field, and one field is all fields. Ultimately, the natural and the
ideal Buddhafields are one and the same. The Buddha is omnipresent,

---

[*] *Avataṁsaka Sūtra, The Eastern Buddhist,* i.153
[†] *Ratnamegha, Śikṣāsamuccaya* 283

and this world is essentially the ideal world, if one will only recognize it as such. 'Here in this very chamber,' says Vimalakīrti, 'all the magnificent heavenly palaces and all the Pure Lands of all the Buddhas are manifested.'* This world of ours seems quite impure, replete with all kinds of woes and sorrows, wretched and full of terrors. To those, however, who have a true faith, this same world appears with all the features of a Pure Land, 'made of lapis lazuli, forming a level plain, forming a chequerboard of eight compartments with gold threads, set with jewel trees'.† It is again Vimalakīrti who brings out the paradoxical character of this teaching, when he says

> Beings, because of their sins, cannot see the pureness of this
> Buddhaland of ours. Really this land of ours is ever pure. The
> impurities are in your own mind. I tell you, Śāriputra, the
> Bodhisattva, pure in his firm mind, looks upon all things impartially
> with the wisdom of a Buddha, and therefore this Buddhaland is to
> him pure without blemish. This world of ours is ever pure as this,
> and yet, to save beings of inferior capacities is this wicked and
> impure world shown.‡

METHODS

The goal having been thus defined, we can proceed to enumerate the five methods by which one hopes to gain rebirth in one of the 'Lands of the Blessed':

(1) One should lead a pure life, and cultivate the desire to become like the Buddhas.

(2) As the Mahāyāna developed, more and more stress was laid upon worship of the Buddhas as a means of accumulating merit. Worship comprises such acts as praising the Buddha's virtues, doing homage to his beauty, delighting in the thought of him, requesting to be reborn one day as a perfect Buddha (pranidhana), and the giving of gifts to the Buddha. The matter is a particular source of merit. The merit to be obtained from a gift is the greater the more exalted its recipient. Some individuals and groups, especially the saints and the

---

* Vimalakīrtinirdeśa, The Eastern Buddhist, iii.347

† Saddharmapuṇḍarīka xvi p.286

‡ Vimalakīrtinirdeśa, The Eastern Buddhist, vii.145

Sangha, were from early on regarded as the world's 'peerless field of merit'.* In the Mahāyāna, the Buddha became increasingly the supreme 'field of merit'.

(3) One should think of the Buddha while repeatedly pronouncing his name. Since the name contains the power of the Buddhas and Bodhisattvas, its invocation is an act of the highest virtue. Innumerable formulas of invocation were elaborated. The most famous of all is 'Homage to the Buddha Amitābha!' '*oṁ namo amitābhāya buddhāya*' in Sanskrit, '*oṁ o-mi-to-fo*' in Chinese, '*namo amida butsu*' in Japanese. While on the one hand the professionals surpassed themselves in the number of their repetitions of the holy name, it was conceded to the laymen that 'one single act of devotion', 'one single thought of the Buddha', 'for one single moment' will effect his salvation.

(4) One should believe firmly that one's chosen Buddha or Bodhisattva has made a 'vow' to save all, and that therefore he is both willing and able to save you, and to take you to his paradise. A firm belief is recognized by three features: It must be sincere; one must be deeply convinced of one's own wretchedness and the power of the Buddha's vow; one must 'transfer', or deflect, one's merits to the Paradise and form a vow to be reborn therein. The collaboration of compassion on the part of the Buddha, and of faith on ours, brings about the desired rebirth.

(5) One should concentrate in one's meditations on the perfection of a Buddhaland, and one should train the visual imagination to see the Buddhas and Bodhisattvas, and the senses of sound, sight, and smell to perceive the sensory beauty of the Buddhalands.

These are the five methods. Some authorities assume that it is the faith which saves, others that it is the repetition of the holy name. There was much controversy on the first and the fifth of the above methods since, according to some, they savoured too much of self-reliance. In general, the Buddhism of Faith in India was disinclined to disregard the moral worth of the worshipper. Gross sinners, and 'those who calumniate the holy Dharma', cannot be saved by faith alone. How can they claim to love the Buddha with all their heart if they offend against his moral teachings, if they refuse to do his will? It was left to the later developments of Amidism in Japan to proclaim

---

* *Aṅguttara Nikāya* i.208

a kind of totalitarianism of Faith, in which faith becomes all-powerful, regardless of moral conduct (see Chapter 9).

SELF-EXTINCTION AND FAITH

The specific features of the Buddhist schools which developed after the first 500 years are due partly to social pressure, and partly to the latent implications of the problem of self-extinction. The Mahāyāna, by adopting the ideal of a Bodhisattva, tries, as we saw (p.103 *et seq.*), to drive out the last residue of self-seeking. The bhaktic trend eliminates, in faith, all reliance on *self-power*, all reliance on one's own ability to plan and control one's own life and salvation. As soon as we judge it by the standard of self-extinction, the 'Buddhism of Faith' is in the direct line of Buddhist orthodoxy. Surrender in faith involves a high degree of extinction of separate selfhood, partly because one does not rely on oneself, or one's own power, partly because one sees the futility of all conscious and personal efforts and allows oneself to be carried to salvation, and partly because one does not claim any special privileges, as due to superior merit or wisdom. Elementary modesty lets us perceive that any merit we may claim compares as nothing with that of the Buddhas and Bodhisattvas, and with the power of their help. Pride had always been a sin to which the more advanced Buddhists were particularly prone. Now they were taught humbly to accept gifts from another, whom they could only perceive in faith. All pride in our intellect, all pride in the purity of our heart, sets up a self against others. If the intellect is seen as futile, the heart as corrupt, that self is deflated. The grace of the Absolute alone can carry us across, and our own personal schemes and endeavours are quite trivial, for it must never be forgotten that that which is represented to the relatively ignorant in the form of a personal saviour and of a paradise is exactly the same thing as that which is taught to the relatively learned as the Absolute itself. Following out the logic of the Buddhist dialectics, Buddhist perfection is found only in its extinction, and it is manifested only where it becomes quite indiscernible. The distinctive Buddhist life must go so that Buddhism may be fulfilled. A sincere heart and belief, unaware of the merit of its sincerity, is all that is needed. The Buddha's demand that, in order to be saved, one should learn to do nothing in particular, is fulfilled in this way as perfectly as in any other.

7

THE YOGĀCĀRA

WISDOM AND TRANCE

During the first centuries of our era a new school, known as the *Yogācāra*, began to grow up. After 500AD it came to dominate the thought of the Mahāyāna more and more. The theories of this school are very complex, and do not easily lend themselves to popular exposition. They presuppose a greater familiarity with the methods and effects of trance (*samādhi*) than most of us possess nowadays.

The initial impulse of Buddhism contained all the later systems of thought in its system of practices (pp.76, 80). The various practices were grouped under the three headings of Morality, Trance, and Wisdom (pp.77 *et seq.*). The theoretical developments discussed in Chapters 1–4 were inaugurated by specialists in Wisdom, and the methods of the Abhidharma were the real driving force behind the theoretical work. But what about morality and trance? Morality does not enter into the controversies at all until quite late, when the Left-handed Tantra repudiates it (pp.166 *et seq.*). As for the special approach and the experiences of those who concentrated on the practice of ecstatic meditation, the theoretical formulations of the doctrine had not taken them sufficiently into account. It was the function and purpose of the Yogācāra to give due emphasis to the outlook on the world revealed by withdrawal into trance. Trance would suit better the temperament of some monks, Wisdom that of others. In the Samyutta Nikāya (ii.115), the difference between the two roads is exemplified by the persons of Musīla and Nārada. The *Bhagavad Gītā* devotes a great deal of its space to contrasting the two under the names of Sāṁkhya and Yoga. The 'men of wisdom' are chiefly intellectual, the 'men of trance' chiefly meditative and ascetic. The former are 'devoted to Dharma', the latter just 'muse' (jhāyin).[17] The Wise are led to insight, while trance leads to calm. The Wise pay little attention to magic, the others a great deal. According to the orthodox doctrine, only both wings together could carry one to enlightenment. The Sarvāstivādins always emphasized the primacy of wisdom, understood as the contemplation of dharmas. In the case of some of them, like for instance Harivarman, the ecstatic practices of trance have quite faded into the background. Again, among the Mādhyamikas all the attention is given to Wisdom, here understood as a refined dialectics which kills all thought. The Yogācāra represented a reaction against such overemphasis on thought-processes with its consequent neglect of the practice of Trance.

What then was the distinctive doctrine of the Yogācāra? They taught that the Absolute is Thought. Not that this theory, as such, is really new. It had been clearly stated in the scriptures of all schools, and we must try to understand why it had been neglected for so long, and for what reasons the Yogācārins developed it now.

In the Pāli scriptures the Buddha states expressly that the well-directed mind is like the pellucid water of a clear pool, free from any scum on the surface. 'Self-luminous through and through (pabhassara) is that thought, but usually it is defiled by adventitious taints which come from without.'* In other words, when the mind is face to face with the Truth, a self-luminous spark of thought is revealed at the inner core of ourselves and, by analogy, of all reality. The teachers of the Old Wisdom School, without expressly denying the statement, had made little of it. The Abhidharma wholly dominated their theorizings, and the Abhidharma considered reality as composed of a succession of dharmas, or momentary events. We see the world as it truly is when we see that 'there are dharmas only' (dhamma-matta), to quote Buddhaghosa's short formula. The formula of the Yogācāra, 'thought-only' (cittamātra) derives a great deal of its meaning from its contrast to the traditional Abhidharma.

In the Prajñāpāramitā, again, emptiness is the ultimate fact of life. To describe that emptiness as Thought, as the Yogācāra did, seemed to the Mādhyamikas to fulfil no useful purpose whatever. Not that

---

* Aṅguttara Nikāya i.8–10

the Prajñāpāramitā sūtras ignore the tradition about a self-luminous thought at the centre of everything. The fact that it is 'Thought' does not interest them at all, however. All that concerns them is the dialectical nature of the thought of the absolute, or of an absolute thought (see p.91 *et seq.*), which is self-contradictory, and identical with its own negation. Of course, thought 'in its essential original nature', when free from all greed, hate, and delusion, is 'a state of transparent luminosity', and on that level it constitutes 'the essential being of all dharmas.' But, as the sūtra continues, that thought 'is really no thought', and it neither exists, nor does it not exist. The preoccupation with wisdom, understood as the dialectical dissolution of everything, determines in this case clearly the approach to the problem.

Nor did the career of an absolute 'self-luminous thought' end here. Chinese Buddhists, with their insistence on passivity and non-action, took up the saying of the Prajñāpāramitā, and claimed that salvation consisted in attaining to a state of 'no-thought'. They rejected all mental activity, and argued that only stupid people practise virtues and meditate. Their thesis that 'one should not think of anything' found little favour with their Indian brethren of the Madhyamaka School.

The Yogācāra, in their turn, gave quite a different meaning to the old saying. What seemed important to them was the statement that the Absolute is 'Thought', in the sense that it is to be sought not in any object at all, but in the pure subject which is free from all objects. Before we go on with the explanation of this somewhat cryptic doctrine, we must, first of all, give a sketch of the history of the school.

LITERARY HISTORY

A trend in the direction of the Yogācāra School started about 150AD with the *Saṁdhinirmocana Sūtra*. Between 150 and 400 we have several other literary documents which teach 'thought-only'. The *Laṅkāvatāra Sūtra*, the *Avataṁsaka*, and the *Abhisamayālaṁkāra* occupy a position midway between Madhyamaka and Yogācāra. The *Abhisamayālaṁkāra* is an influential commentary on the Prajñā-pāramitā which has guided its exegesis from c. 350AD onward, and which is still the basis of the explanation of the Prajñāpāramitā in the monasteries of Tibet and Mongolia. The *Avataṁsaka* takes up the teaching of the *sameness* of everything (see p.111), and interprets it as the interpenetration of every element in the world with everything else. The one eternal principle of the universe, which is the serenity of Mind, is reflected in the cosmos, its presence charges everything with spiritual significance, its mysteries can be beheld everywhere, and by means of any object one may generate all virtues and fathom the secrets of the entire universe. The *Avataṁsaka Sūtra* was the basic text of a school which became powerful in China as the Hua-yen-tsung, in Japan as the Kegon-shū. Fa-tsang (643–712) was its greatest theoretician. The school did a great deal to refine the attitude to nature in the Far East, and it has inspired many artists in China and Japan. In India it represents an important link between the Yogācāra and the Tantra. The Yogācāra School was founded about 400AD by two brothers, Asaṅga and Vasubandhu, natives of north-west India. Some scholars place Asaṅga as early as 320AD. Asaṅga and Vasubandhu systematized the theory of 'mind-only', and in addition elaborated three further doctrines, concerning the *store-consciousness*, the three kinds of *own-being*, and the three *bodies* of the Buddha. The school evolved an extremely complicated scholastic system, and was not entirely free from speculative exuberance.

From the ranks of the Yogācāra School came the men who developed a Buddhist version of the science of Logic. Buddhist Logic was founded by Dignāga, c. 440AD, and a great deal was written in India on the subject up to about 1100AD. Interest in logic was stimulated by its great value for propaganda. During the Indian Middle Ages, rulers were in the habit of arranging tournaments in which ascetics of different schools, before huge audiences, were pitted against each other in debate. Victory in debate carried with it enhanced prestige and increased patronage. A training in logic gave the Buddhists an advantage over their rivals, and the Hindu sects were soon compelled to elaborate logical systems of their own. Dignāga's logic had an important indirect consequence. Wherever the Yogācārins were influential, interest was deflected from the traditional Abhidharma to the new logic, and so, without being expressly repudiated, the Abhidharma was increasingly neglected. The tradition of Yogācāra logic is still active in Tibet. In China we have a fairly extensive, and in Japan, up to the fifteenth century, a vast literature connected with Indian logical texts.

Together with Buddhism, the Yogācāra School disappeared from India about 1100AD. It was brought to China by several teachers. Among them were two first-class intellects, Paramārtha (500–69) who came from Ujjayini (Ogein) in East India in 546AD, and Hsüan Tsang, the great pilgrim (c. 650). Hsüan Tsang's school is known as Wei-shih.

Hsüan Tsang summed up his teachings in the *Ch'eng Wei-Shih Lun*, the 'treatise on the achievement of (the insight that everything is) nothing-but-idea', which is still the classical textbook of the school in the Far East. The work is an abstract of ten Indian commentaries to Vasubandhu's *Thirty Stanzas*. Hsüan Tsang relied chiefly on Dharmapāla, abbot of Nālandā, rather neglecting the other nine. A great and influential exponent of the Wei-shih School was Hsüan Tsang's disciple K'uei-chi (632–85). He wrote a great number of commentaries, and also an *Encyclopedia of the Doctrines of the Great Vehicle*. The Wei-shih School soon fell apart into a Northern and a Southern branch. In addition to Paramārtha's school and the Wei-shih some other versions of the Yogācāra tradition were current in China, where long scholastic disputes on the intricacies of the doctrine marked its history. In 653, and again in 712, the school was brought to Japan, as the Hossō (= Chinese: *fa tsiang tsong*, 'mark of dharma') sect. In the Tempyo period it flourished greatly through the exertions of the Sojo Gien (d.728). It survives even now as one of the smaller Japanese sects, with forty-four temples and monasteries and seven hundred priests.

'MIND-ONLY'

Mind, Thought, and Consciousness are used as interchangeable terms in Buddhist philosophy. In describing Nirvāṇa in positive terms – calling it mind-only, *or* thought-only, *or* consciousness-only – the Yogācārins seem to deviate from the Buddhist tradition which has always preferred negative names for the Absolute. The word *Nirvāṇa* itself means 'to be blown out', and where other traditions speak of eternal life, Buddhism speaks of the Deathless. It wishes jealously to guard the transcendence of the Absolute, and to avoid the danger of misconceptions which arise if the same name which applies to something found in this world is also given to what is absolutely different from the world – as when Christians call God a 'person'. Why then should the Yogācārins choose 'Consciousness' among all the constituents of the world, and designate the Absolute by it?

They intended to point to a spot in the world, to a dimension of self-awareness, where we are most likely to find it. In all our experience, an object stands out against a subject. The subject is identified by the Abhidharma with the skandha of consciousness, defined by *awareness* as its essential mark. Just as the blade of a knife cannot cut itself, so we cannot experience consciousness directly, as an object in front of us, for as soon as we turn to the subject, it becomes an object and ceases to be the subject. Introspection can thus never hope to meet the subject face to face. The final subject – which might be at the end of the infinite regress – is completely beyond our experience, it is not really of this world, it is transcendental. To try to get to it would be to attempt the impossible. This is exactly what the Yogācārins set themselves out to do.

By ruthless withdrawal from each and every object, in the introversion of trance, one could hope to move towards such a result. In any condition in which my personality might normally find itself, the subject is always associated with some object. If, on the other hand, there is, in the absence of an object standing up against the subject, no such admixture of any relation to an object, then I could be said to have realized my inmost self in its purity. Salvation could then be said to consist in a revulsion from all objective and external accretions to that inmost self itself, which is realized when it can stand alone, without an object or the thought of one. 'There is no grasping where there is nothing to be grasped.'*

We can now see more clearly the link between this line of reasoning, and the experience of ecstatic trance. The wisdom schools had annihilated the objects around us by a ruthless *analysis* which found but countless momentary dharmas, too impersonal or fragile to bear much attachment, and by a ruthless *dissociation*, which cuts off identification with all objects in turn by the thought, 'I am not this, this is not mine, this is not myself.' The ruthless *introversion* of ecstatic meditation also removes the object, but by withdrawing from it. The experience of it gave their special tone to the Yogācāra theories. We remember (pp.81 *et seq.*) that the stages of *dhyāna* proceed by the successive withdrawal from all external stimuli or

* Vasubandhu, *Triṁśika* v.29

objects, which impinge less and less on the mind, until the six organs of sense are in repose; in the highest trance there is no external object left at all. The yogi seeks happiness and fulfilment not in outer things, but in the quiet calm of the pure inwardness of his own thought. The wisdom schools had always maintained that we are troubled because we falsely identify with our true self something we find in our empirical self. The Yogācārins now define the true self as the ultimate subject. Then, as a natural consequence, the root of all evil must lie in our proclivity to see anything as separated from, or as external to, that inmost self, in the way of an object. In reality all things and thoughts are but mind-only. The basis of all our illusions consists in that we regard the objectifications of our own mind as a world independent of that mind which is really its source and substance. As a philosophical doctrine, this is very similar to the Idealism of Berkeley. Bishop Berkeley said that

> some truths are so near and obvious to the mind that a man need
> only open his eyes to see them. Such I take this important one to be,
> viz. that all the choir of heaven and furniture of the earth – in a word,
> all those bodies which compose the mighty frame of the world – have
> not any subsistence without a mind.[*]

The external world is really Mind itself. The multiplicity of external objects is 'mere representation', 'nothing but ideas'. 'Just as in a mirage there is no real water, and yet the notion of real water is produced, so there is no object, but the notion of an object is engendered.'[†] The highest insight is reached when everything appears as sheer hallucination. The Yogācārins based this conviction not merely on a number of logical arguments which proved the impossibility of an external object, but on the living experience of ecstatic meditation. In the higher stages of trance the yogi was accustomed to meet with vivid visual images without a corresponding external stimulus. In the course of his exercises he saw directly before him such objects as a blue circle, or a skeleton, which were mere hallucinatory ideas, or, as interpreted by Asaṅga, mere thought. The world is like a dream. A dream is merely an awareness of ideas; the corresponding objects are not really there. Just as one perceives the lack of objectivity in the

---

[*] G. Berkeley, *A Treatise Concerning the Principles of Human Knowledge*, part 1, section 6
[†] *Mahāyānasaṁgraha* ii.27, 2

dream pictures after one has woken up, so the lack of objectivity in the perceptions of waking life is perceived by those who have been awakened by the knowledge of true reality.

'STORE-CONSCIOUSNESS'

The Yogācāra concept of a 'store-consciousness' (ālaya-vijñāna) is of interest less for its actual value than for the motive behind it. Asaṅga postulated an overpersonal consciousness which is the foundation of all acts of thought. The impressions of the whole of past experience are stored up in it, all deeds and their fruits. It is not an individual soul, bound to a psychophysical organism, but it is the objective fact which in our ignorance and self-love we mistake for an individual soul, or self. As worked out by the Yogācārins, the concept of a store-consciousness is far from intelligible, and it has led to little more than ardent discussions.

That such a concept, unsatisfactory as it is, should have been worked out at all, indicates an important difficulty in the Buddhist system of thought. The anattā doctrine had claimed that there was in fact no individual self, or permanent ego, which could account for the self-contained unity of an individual. What appears as an individual is really a series of momentary dharmas which continuously succeed each other. But there remained the relative unity of each series, and its distinction from the others. There remained the observation of common sense that I remember my own inner experiences so much better than those of others, which, in fact, I do not remember at all. There remained the teaching of karma, according to which I experience the fruit of my deeds, and am not punished or rewarded for the deeds of another. There remained the observation that some of my own past experiences are, as it were, stored up for a time in a kind of unconscious, and influence my actions at a later date. The illusion of individuality may indeed be due to craving, but it is strongly fortified by ordinary observation. One could, of course, brush all this aside, and refer the enquirer to the state of Nirvāṇa in which all these observations would appear in quite a different light.

To all those who have not gone so far, the belief in individuality must, however, seem so plausible that they would expect it to have some kind of objective foundation somewhere. Here was the weak spot in the Buddhist armour, and the problem has harassed the

Buddhist theoreticians throughout their history. The heresy of a belief in a self invaded even the ranks of the Order. The followers of one of the eighteen traditional sects – the Sammitīyas – were known as Pudgalavādins, 'upholders of the belief in a person'. They attempted to retain some form of belief in a self, or a soul, without quite doing so. They spoke of an indefinable principle called the *pudgala*, the person, who is neither different nor not different from the five skandhas. It persists through the several lives of a being until he reaches Nirvāṇa. It has a sort of middle position between our true and our empirical self. On the one hand it accounts for our sense of personal identity (like the 'empirical self'), and on the other it lasts into Nirvāṇa (like the 'true self'). Among all controversial issues, this one was considered as the most critical of all. Throughout the centuries the orthodox never wearied of piling argument upon argument to defeat this admission of a Self by the Pudgalavādins. But the more tenaciously and persistently one tries to keep something out of one's mind, or out of a system of thought, the more surely it will come in. The orthodox, in the end, were forced to admit the notion of a permanent ego, not openly, but in various disguises, hidden in particularly obscure and abstruse concepts, like the 'subconscious life-continuum' (*bhavanga*) of the Theravādins, the 'continued existence of a very subtle consciousness' of the Sautrāntikas, the 'root-consciousness' of the Mahāsaṅghikas, etc. The store-consciousness of the Yogācārins is conceived in the same spirit. As soon as the advice to disregard the individual self had hardened into the proposition that 'there is no self', such concessions to common sense became quite inevitable.

Once the Yogācārins had given way to the desire to probe into the origins of our illusions, they found themselves carried into an ocean of boundless speculation. Beginning with the store-consciousness, they set themselves the task of deducing the actual world from it, and to trace the exact process of evolution by which the ultimate subject became estranged from itself and unfolded itself into an objective world. In doing so, they built up an extremely involved and complicated system of speculative metaphysics which has no direct bearing on the practice of emancipation. They departed from the theoretical simplicity of the past, which was more concerned with undoing illusions than with explaining them. The bulk of Yogācāra philosophy, though occasioned by the difficulties inherent in the anattā doctrine, represents really an invasion of Buddhism by the Sāṃkhya system of Hindu philosophy which, at about the time of Asaṅga, was used by Patañjali (c. 450AD) for his theoretical exposition of the yoga methods still current in India. A complete change had taken place in the mental climate of India between the time of the Abhidharma and the centuries which saw the growth of the Yogācārins. In the old times the monks were very little concerned with the universe in general. Mental states and psychological methods were all that mattered if one wanted to know oneself. Now, however, when no longer individual but universal salvation is sought after, mental states are considered in their relation to the evolution of the cosmos to which more and more attention is directed. This shift in emphasis began with the Yogācārins, and became more and more marked in the Tantric developments to which we will soon turn.

FURTHER DOCTRINES

Apart from their identification of Nirvāṇa with Thought, and their speculations about the store-consciousness, the Yogācārins are remembered for the final systematic form they gave to two old ideas, the one ontological, the other Buddhological.

As to the first, they distinguished three kinds of 'own-being'. It is sufficient to mention this doctrine in passing. It means that anything can be viewed from three angles: First, as common sense sees it, in its imagined appearance as an object, where a thing is simply itself, and distinct from others. Secondly, in its dependent aspect, one views, more scientifically, events in so far as they are conditioned by one another. Finally, there is a side to everything where it is fully and perfectly real. It then no longer stands out as an object, and it is intuited by yoga. All things are then one Suchness, mind-only, undifferentiated, both transcendent and immanent in everything.

The doctrine of the three bodies of the Buddha must be mentioned because it is the final result of many centuries of thought about the three aspects of the Buddha we have described above (pp.21 *et seq.*). The three bodies are the Dharma body, the enjoyment body, and the apparitional body. The Dharma body is the Buddha as Absolute. In his Dharma body alone is the Buddha truly himself. It is one and single, the other two bodies emanate from it and are supported by it. The enjoyment body of the Buddha is his manifestation to the Bodhisattvas in different pure Buddhafields. In different assemblies a different enjoyment body is seen and heard. This body bears the thirty-two marks, and many miraculous manifestations issue from it. It is mind-made, and comes into being without the ordinary processes of procreation and birth. The apparitional body, finally, is a person who is a fictitious magical creation which goes through the motions of descending from heaven, leaving home, practising austerities, winning enlightenment, gathering and teaching disciples, and dying on Earth, in order to aid and mature beings of little insight. The Buddha's humanity, always more or less unimportant, has now become a mere figment or phantom. In the Hīnayāna, already, the Buddha was credited with the miraculous power of conjuring up an appearance of himself, a 'nimitta-Buddha', which preached elsewhere while he went begging. The Hindu gods also had such powers. So we read in the Dīgha Nikāya that Brahmā Sahampati, when he appears in the assembly of the 'Gods of the Thirty-three', manifests himself in a material body. 'For his shape, as it naturally is, is unbearable to the sight of those Gods.'* This idea is now used in the Mahāyāna to define the relation of the historical Buddha to the One Eternal Buddha. The One Buddha, the Dharma body, has existed at all times, but on various occasions it has projected into this world phantom bodies of Buddhas to do its work.

The magical connotations of such ideas have been of great historical importance. The world itself, in which the 'Buddha-frames' appear, is no more than a magical show (māyā). When teaching the world as a magical illusion, the Buddhists do not mean to say that it is just non-existent. It is tangibly and visually real, but it is deceptive, because one mistakes it for what it is not. It is not genuine, and as a magical trick it should not be treated too seriously. In this practical sense, the things of the world had been called māyā from the beginning of Buddhist history. Now the application of the term is extended. As the Buddha had said to the juggler Bhadra in the Ratnakūṭa: 'The enjoyments of all beings conjured up by the māyā of their deeds; this Order of monks by the māyā of the Dharma; I myself by the māyā complexity of conditions.'† The world, in other words,

---

* Dīgha Nikāya ii.209
† Bhadramāyākāravyākaraṇa n.18, trans. K. Regamey, 1938, p.70

is a kind of phantasmagoria, in which magically created beings are saved from a magically created suffering by a magically created saviour, who shows them the unsubstantiality of all that comes into being. It is no wonder that the conviction began to spread that magical methods alone could deal effectively with such a universe. This conviction found shape in the Tantra, to which we must now turn.

8

THE TANTRA, OR MAGICAL BUDDHISM

THE PROBLEM OF THE TANTRA

As distinct from modern Europeans, Asiatics were quite familiar with the magical feats of conjurers, jugglers, etc., who formed a regular part of their daily lives. At this point, I think, a concrete example will be helpful to show how the average Hindu, Arab, or Chinese viewed these things. In the fourteenth century, Ibn Batuta, an Arab traveller, visited the Viceroy of Hang-chau fu. A juggler

took a wooden ball, with several holes in it, through which long ropes were passed, and, laying hold of one of these, slung it into the air. It went so high that we lost sight of it altogether. There now remained only a little of the end of a thong in the conjurer's hand, and he desired one of the boys who assisted him to lay hold of it and to mount. He did so, climbing by the rope, and we lost sight of him also! The conjurer then called to him three times, but getting no answer, he snatched up a knife as if in a great rage, laid hold of the thong, and disappeared also! Bye and bye he threw down one of the boy's hands, then a foot, then the other hand, and the other foot, then the trunk and last of all the head! Then he came down himself, all puffing and panting, and with his clothes all bloody, kissed the ground before the Amir, and said something to him in Chinese. The Amir gave some order in reply, and our friend then took the lad's limbs, laid them together in their places, and gave a kick, when, presto! there was the boy, who got up and stood before us! All this astonished me beyond measure. The Kazi Afkharuddin was next to

me, and quoth he, 'Wallah! 'tis my opinion there has been neither
going up nor coming down, neither marring nor mending; 'tis all
hocus pocus.'*

According to the Prajñāpāramitā, the whole process of salvation is
of the same nature as this conjuring trick. Witness this dialogue
between the Lord Buddha and Subhūti.

> *Lord:* 'Just as if, Subhūti, a clever magician, or magician's apprentice,
> would conjure up at the crossroads a great crowd of people, and,
> after he had conjured them up, he would make that great crowd of
> people vanish again. What do you think, Subhūti, has there anyone
> been killed by anyone, or murdered, or destroyed, or made to
> vanish?'
> *Subhūti:* 'No, indeed, Lord!'
> *Lord:* 'Even so, a Bodhisattva, a great being, leads innumerable and
> incalculable beings to Nirvāṇa, and yet there is not any being that has
> been led to Nirvāṇa, nor anyone who has led one. If a Bodhisattva
> hears this, and does not tremble, is not frightened, nor terrified, then
> he is to be known as "armed with the great armour."'†

The Buddhist Tantra draws the practical consequences. It is the
logical outcome of the developments which preceded it, and the
difficulties which it has presented to many scholars are of their own
making. Of course, if one makes up one's mind that 'original' Buddhism was a perfectly rational religion, after the heart of the 'Ethical
Society', without any touch of the supernatural or mysterious, then
the Tantra will become an almost incomprehensible 'degeneration'
of that presumed original Buddhism. In actual fact, Buddhism has
always been closely associated with what to rationalists would appear as superstitions (see pp.63 *et seq.*). The reality of extraordinary
psychic, nay of wonderworking, powers, was never questioned
(pp.84 *et seq.*). The cultivation of such powers was, for those suited
to it, part of the program of salvation, although for others a dubious
blessing. The existence of many kinds of disembodied spirits and the
reality of magical forces were taken for granted, and the belief in
them formed part of the current cosmology.

---

* Quoted in H. Yule, *The Book of Ser Marco Polo*, I, 1903, 316–7
† *Aṣṭasāhasrikā* i.21

Europeans who write about the Tantra are often beside themselves with emotion. Their revulsion is partly intellectual, because they believe they have outgrown the magical beliefs of our forefathers. In addition, the Tantra is apt to provoke their moral indignation. It seems to them that in the history of Buddhism an abstract metaphysics of great sublimity has slowly given way to a preoccupation with personal deities and with witchcraft, with the mumbo jumbo of magical ritual and all manner of superstitions. Deliberate immorality seems to replace the lofty austerity of the past. The former disinterested non-attachment to the world seems supplanted by a desire to coerce it to fit in with the basest desires, and resignation to circumstances by a wish to gain power over them. Where poverty had been a prime condition of spiritual growth, one now thinks of propitiating Kuvera and Jambhala, gods of wealth. And so on.

This hostile attitude does little justice to the Tantra. It is true the Tantra proclaims that it has two aims – success (*siddhi*) in winning full enlightenment in this life, and success in gaining health, wealth, and power. But this illogical combination of worldly and other worldly aims is as old as Buddhism itself, and it has been one of the main pillars of its strength (see pp.67 *et seq.*). The immorality is, as we shall see, not an immorality of men of the world, but of saints. The claim that charms and magical ritual are the surest way to full enlightenment is, indeed, new in its emphasis, but a long historical development has led steadily up to it. Far from being a nightmare of a few deluded perverts of doubtful respectability, the Tantra was, and is, an inevitable phase of Buddhist history.

THE HISTORY OF THE TANTRA

It is impossible at present to indicate the exact time when Tantric practices were first thought of. The Tantrists are habitually inclined to secrecy. Occult and esoteric views must have circulated in small circles of initiates for a long time before they came out into the open. As a more or less public system of thought, the Tantra gathered momentum after 500 or 600AD. Its beginnings do, however, go back to the dawn of human history, when an agricultural society was pervaded by magic and witchcraft, human sacrifice and the cult of the mother goddess, fertility rites and chthonic deities. The Tantra is not really a new creation, but the result of an absorption of primitive beliefs by the literary tradition, and their blending with Buddhist philosophy.

The Tantric literature of Buddhism is very bulky, and largely unexplored. Very little has been translated, and the language of the texts is difficult and obscure, often intentionally so. Like the Hindus, the Buddhists distinguish a 'right-handed' and a 'left-handed' Tantra. In Hinduism the two groups are distinguished by the fact that the 'right-hand' observers (*dakṣiṇācārins*) attach greater importance to the masculine, the 'left-hand' observers (*vāmācārins*) to the feminine, principle in the universe. In Buddhism, the difference between the two lies chiefly in their attitude to sex (see pp.166 *et seq.*). It is convenient to reserve the term Śaktism for the left-handed form. Hindu Śaktism is associated with Shivaism. Shaiva doctrines had a great influence on Buddhist Śaktism. A Śakti is the creative energy, or 'potency', of a deity, personified as his wife or consort. In Shivaism, Śakti-worship is directed towards Shiva's wife – Pārvatī or Umā – also known as the Great Goddess, and the Great Mother. It is a peculiarity of Śaktism that many deities exist both in a benign and a terrible form. The terrible form of Pārvatī is Durgā, the Unapproachable, or Kālī, the Black. The terrible forms are associated with death and destruction, with necromancy, with animal and human sacrifices. At the same time, Shivaism possesses a profusion of feminine deities, of sorceresses, witches, and ogresses, many of whom were incorporated into Buddhist Śaktism. The followers of the more extreme Shivaite practices did not always command the respect of their contemporaries. The Shiva magician Bhairavananda sings, in an Indian drama of 900AD, the following song:

> As for black book and spell – they may all go to hell!
> My teacher excused me from practice for trance.
> With drink and with women we fare mighty well,
> As on – to salvation – we merrily dance!
> A fiery young wench to the altar I've led.
> Good meat I consume, and I guzzle strong drink;
> And it all comes as alms – with a pelt for my bed.
> What better religion could anyone think?
> Gods Vishnu and Brahm and the others may preach
> Of salvation by trance, holy rites, and the Vedies.

'Twas Umā's fond lover alone that could teach
Us salvation plus brandy plus fun with the ladies.[*]

The scholarly investigation of the Tantric documents is still in its beginnings. As far as we can judge at present, among the multitude of Tantric sects, two great schools were historically the most important, the left-handed form of the Vajrayāna, and the right-handed form of the Mi-tsung (School of Secrets). The Vajrayāna is the 'Adamantine Vehicle'. The *vajra* is literally the thunderbolt which Indra, like Zeus and Thor, used with great effect as a weapon. Itself unbreakable, it breaks everything else. In later Buddhist philosophy the word is used to denote a kind of supernatural substance which is as hard as a diamond, as clear as empty space, as irresistible as a thunderbolt. The vajra is now identified with ultimate reality, with the Dharma and enlightenment. The Vajrayāna mythologizes the doctrine of emptiness, and teaches that the adept, through a combination of rites, is reinstated into his true diamond nature, takes possession of a diamond body, is transformed into a diamond being (*vajrasattva*). The beginnings of the Vajrayāna may go back to c. 300AD. As it is known to us, the system developed from c. 600AD onward. The *Guhyasamāja-tantra* is one of its earliest scriptures. The Vajrayāna was founded by a succession of teachers, among whom a second Nāgārjuna (c. 650) was one of the first. Their names are recorded up to about 1100AD. The Vajrayāna originated apparently in the extreme north of India, both in the east, in Bengal and in the hills of Assam, and in the west, in a district called Uḍḍiyāna, which may perhaps be the region around Pesawar. Non-Indian influences had something to do with the shaping of Tantric ideas. The erotic mysticism and the stress on the female principle owed much to the Dravidian stratum of Indian culture which, in the cult of the Village Goddess had kept alive the matriarchal traditions about the Mother Goddess to a greater extent than the Vedic religion had done. In Bengal, the patronage of the Pāla dynasty (750–1150) enabled the Tantric doctrines to develop and organize themselves. The official Buddhism of that period was a mixture of Prajñāpāramitā and Tantra. The monks who lived in Nālandā, and in the settlements founded by the Pāla kings – such as Odantapurī, Vikramaśīla,

[*] Rājaśekhara, *Karpūra-mañjarī*, i.22–4, trans. C.R. Lanman, 1901

Jaggadala, Somarupa – combined metaphysics and magic, almost like the Gerbert of Rheims and Albert the Great of medieval folklore. Their range of interest is well typified by Vagīśvarakīrti, c. 1000AD, about whom Tāranātha says:

> By constantly looking on the face of the holy Tārā, he resolved all his doubts. He erected eight religious schools for the Prajñāpāramitā, four for the exposition of the *Guhyasamāja*, one for each of three other kinds of Tantra. He also established many religious schools with provisions for teaching the Mādhyamika logic. He conjured up quantities of the elixir of life, and distributed it to others, so that old people, 150 years old and more, became young again.[*]

This combination of Prajñāpāramitā and Tantra has shown an astounding vitality. It was destroyed in Bengal by the Muslims, but it spread to Java and Nepal, and in Tibet it still continues as a living tradition.

The right-handed Tantra is chiefly known to us through the system of Amoghavajra (705–74) which is preserved in China. This doctrine also claims to descend from Nāgārjuna. The Chinese Mi-tsung School combined two Tantric systems, each embodied in a magical circle (*maṇḍala*). The circle of the womb (*garbha-dhātu-maṇḍala*) and the circle of the thunderbolt (*vajra-dhātu-maṇḍala*) are said to be, in a higher sense, identical and to represent different aspects of the supreme reality. The Buddha Mahāvairocana is here the universe. His body is divided into two complementary constituents, the passive, mental womb-element, and the active, material diamond-element. The whole world is the Buddha's revelation to himself, and it is represented in those two maṇḍalas. This doctrine came to Japan with Kōbō Daishi about 800AD, and as the Shingon ('True Word') School it is still one of the largest Japanese sects, with 8,000,000 members and 11,000 priests in 1931. Other esoteric doctrines were adopted by the Tendai School, founded by Dengyō Daishi, who supplemented them with a more 'open' doctrine, founded on the *Lotus of the Good Law*. Śaktism never spread very much in China or Japan. Erotic tendencies developed in the Tachikawa sect of the Shingon in the eleventh century, but the sect was soon suppressed.

---

[*] Tāranātha, *Geschichte des Buddhismus in Indien*, trans. A. Scheifner, 1869, p.236

In 1132 a reformed Shingon School, the Shingi-shingon-shū, was established.

Tantric literature consists of treatises, spells, hymns, and descriptions of mythological beings. Tantric deities often bear the same names as those of the bhaktic tradition. The identity of the names hides a profound difference in the function of the pantheon. Bhaktic deities are creatures of the mythological imagination who are loved and implored for help. Tantric deities are personifications of spiritual and magical forces which are conjured up and utilized as steps on the road to salvation.

TANTRIC PRACTICES

Like all other schools of Buddhism, the Tantra developed a number of practices which are peculiar to it. Essential to the Tantra is the difference between the initiated and the uninitiated, and, corresponding to it, a sharp division between an exoteric and an esoteric doctrine. The Buddha, as he is depicted in the scriptures of Pāli Buddhism, took pride in the fact that he kept nothing hidden 'in his closed fist', as far as any item of knowledge conducive to salvation was concerned. The Tantra now, on the contrary, assumes that the really efficacious methods of salvation and their proper use cannot be learned from books, but that they can be taught only by personal contact with a spiritual instructor, called a guru. Only a guru, to whom we submit in complete obedience, and who for us stands in the place of the Buddha, can translate the true secrets and mysteries of the doctrine. Small circles of initiates gather around a guru, and what is taught outside these small circles of initiates is really very far from the truth.

Without initiation one cannot even begin a spiritual training. Initiation in this system of Buddhism has the same decisive importance as it had in the Mystery cults of Greece and Rome. In addition, we may note that initiation has always been important in primitive societies, and that in this as in many other ways, Tantric Buddhism is a reversal to primitive ways of thinking and acting. The Sanskrit word for the initiation ceremony is *abhiṣeka*, which literally means besprinkling. The initiated is sprinkled with holy water, and there is in this respect some similarity with Christian baptism. The ceremony derives from the ancient Indian ritual of the inauguration of a crown prince. In theory, a crown prince was, through that ceremony, transformed into a world ruler. Similarly in this case, the water of knowledge is supposed to enable the devotee to become a spiritual world ruler, i.e. a Buddha. It would lead us here too far to describe all the varieties of worship and ritual which were practised by the initiates. There are three methods, however, with which we must deal in some detail. They are: (1) the recitation of spells, (2) the performance of ritual gestures and dances, (3) the identification with deities by means of a special kind of meditation.

(1) With regard to the use of spells, we have to distinguish three periods. At first the Buddhists, like all the other inhabitants of India at the time, expected from magical formulas protection from danger, and furtherance of their worldly interests. The use of spells for such purposes was widespread among all nations in the pre-industrial period of human history. It implied at least two assumptions, i.e. that diseases and many other misfortunes are due to the influence of some demonic power, and that words have the power to deal effectively with the demon, by either driving him out, or driving him away, or by mobilizing some greater benevolent magical power against him. The belief in the efficacy of magical words was greatly encouraged by the priests and doctors, who had a kind of vested interest in them. There were, of course, always some sceptics, who pointed out, as the famous Buddhist Vasubandhu did, that very often the herbs or the medicine are the curative agent, but that the doctors, who fear that 'one will do without us, and we will get no more money,' claim that the drug is successful only through the *mantra* (Sanskrit for 'spell'), which is their professional secret. A mantra is an incantation which effects wonders when uttered. The Buddhists employed for protection not only the traditional mantras of Brahmanism, but used also some of the shorter Buddhist sūtras as charms. Hsüan Tsang, the Chinese pilgrim, told Hwui-Li, his biographer, how the *Sūtra of the Heart of Perfect Wisdom* helped him to cross the Gobi Desert, by calling forth the aid of Kuan-Yin, who had taught this sūtra. In the Gobi Desert Hsüan Tsang

> encountered all sorts of demon shapes and strange goblins, which
> seemed to surround him behind and before. Although he invoked
> the name of Kuan-yin, he could not drive them all away; but when he
> recited this sūtra, at the sound of the words they all disappeared in a

moment. Whenever he was in danger, it was to this alone that he trusted for his safety and deliverance.[*]

From the third century AD onward, the Buddhists made an ever-increasing use of mantras for the purpose of guarding their spiritual life from interference by malignant deities. Special chapters on spells are added to some of the best known sūtras, like the *Lotus of the Good Law* (chapter 21), the *Laṅkāvatāra Sūtra* (pp.260–2), etc.

Thirdly, from the seventh century onward, the mantras become, among a section of the community, the chief vehicle of salvation. The permissible, but so far subsidiary, practice of murmuring spells becomes, in the Mantrayāna, the 'vehicle of the mantras', the very key to emancipation from the fetters of existence. If applied according to the rules, there is nothing the mantras cannot achieve. Their power 'can confer even Buddhahood – how much more anything else one may want!'[†] About 200BC Nāgasena in *The Questions of King Milinda*,[‡] had still taught that charms can protect only where they are unopposed by hostile karma – evidence being the case of Maudgalyāyana, the disciple of the Buddha, who was most proficient in magic, and who yet could not protect himself from being punished for a wrong action in his remote past by being beaten to death by robbers.[§] In the Tantra, on the other hand, the mantras and dharanis act infallibly if only the rules, which are numerous and minute, are strictly observed. Innumerable mantras were thought out by the Tantric Buddhists, and the whole subject was treated as a most elaborate science, with numerous laws of its own. For instance, a mantra addressed to a male deity must end with *hūṁ* or *phaṭ*; if the deity, however, is feminine, the last word should be *svāhā*; and if neuter, it should be *namaḥ*. Leaving these details to look after themselves, we must say a few words about the reasoning that induced the Tantra to assume that the mumbling of usually quite meaningless syllables could produce such great effects in the world. It is, of course, the power of mind which makes the mantras efficacious. The mantra is a means of getting into touch with the unseen forces around us through addressing their personifications. Benevolent higher beings

[*] Hwui-Li, *The Life of Hiuen-tsiang*, trans. S. Beal, pp.21–2

[†] *Sādhanamālā*, p.270

[‡] ed. Trenckner, p.150

[§] *ibid.*, p.188

have given us those mantras. The famous '*oṁ maṇi padme hūṁ*', for instance, which in Tibet is everywhere – on the rocks, on the houses, in the praying wheels, and on the lips of the people – is one of Avalokiteśvara's most precious gifts to this suffering world. The *Mahāvairocana Sūtra*, in its fourth chapter, explains the power of mantras as follows: 'Thanks to the original vow of the Buddhas and Bodhisattvas, a miraculous force resides in the mantras, so that by pronouncing them one acquires merit without limits.'[*] The same text says that 'success in our plans through mantras is due to their consecration by the Buddha which exerts upon them a deep and inconceivable influence'.[†] To pronounce a mantra is a way of wooing a deity and, etymologically, the word mantra is connected with Greek words like *meimao*, which express eager desire, yearning, and intensity of purpose, and with the Old High German word *minn-ia*, which means 'making love to.'

In order to appreciate the place of mantras in the ritual of Tantric Buddhism, we may in conclusion describe briefly the four operations which the *Mahāvairocana Sūtra* distinguishes in the process of the recitation, or *jāpa*, of mantras: (a) the contemplative recitation, which has four aspects: (i) one recites the mantra while contemplating in one's heart the shape of the letters – this is called the 'heart enlightenment'; (ii) one distinguishes well the sound of the different letters, and (iii) understands well the significance of the phrases; finally, there is (iv) 'the practice of breathing', in which one regulates one's breath in order to contemplate the mutual interpenetration of the faithful and the Buddha. On that follows (b) the recitation, accompanied by (c) offerings to the deity, such as flowers, perfume, etc. Finally, there is (d) the 'recitation of realization', when one attains success (*siddhi*), through the power of the mantras.

(2) In addition to the sounds of the mantras, ritual gestures are of great importance in the Tantra, which worked out a complicated classification of the magically efficacious positions of the hands. A few of the more common ritual gestures are known from the statues of Buddhas and Bodhisattvas, and they are an important guide to the identification of these statues. This is not the place to go into the details. Dancing is to the Hindus a form of 'singing with the body';

[*] *Mahāvairocanasūtra* iv, in R. Tajima, Etude sur le M., 1936, p.116
[†] *Mahāvairocanasūtra* vi, *ibid.*, p.118

it gained considerable importance in the north of India and in the countries under Tibetan influence. In any case, according to the Tantric theory, a valid ritual action must involve all three sides of our being, i.e. body, speech, and mind. The body acts through the gestures, the speech through the mantras, and the mind through trance (*samādhi*).

(3) The Tantra combines the devotional needs of the masses with the meditational practices of the Yogācāra School, and with the metaphysics of the Mādhyamikas. In other words, the Tantra took over the vast pantheon of popular mythology, with its bewildering variety of deities, fairies, witches, etc. The Tantrists agreed, however, with the metaphysical assumptions of the Prajñāpāramitā, according to which only the one reality of emptiness is fully real, whereas any kind of multiplicity would be ultimately unreal, and the fictitious product of our diseased imagination. The multiplicity of gods would be really nothing but a fiction of the imagination, and not one of those deities would be really there. Our free-thinking modern mind would wholeheartedly agree with that postulate. There is, however, the important difference that, according to our modern assumptions, the multiplicity of things around us is real and the deities a less real fabrication due to the disappointments of our instinctual life when confronted with the hard facts of everyday 'reality'. According to the Tantra, things and gods alike are equally unreal compared with the one vast emptiness, but on the whole the data of mythology represent a kind of fiction far more worthwhile than the data of our everyday practical experience, and when properly handled, can greatly assist us in winning emancipation from the fetters of existence.

The Tantra worked out a system of meditation on deities which is marked by a sequence of four steps. First of all, there is the understanding of emptiness and the sinking of one's separate individuality into that emptiness. Secondly, one must repeat and visualize germ syllables (*bīja*). Thirdly, one forms a conception of the external representation of a deity, as shown in statues, paintings, etc. Fourthly, through identification, one becomes the deity.

(1) We remember that, according to the New Wisdom School, emptiness is the one ultimate reality; the Yogācārins identified this emptiness with Thought, and taught that outside Thought there is nothing in the external world. From its very beginning Buddhism in all its forms regarded the illusion of individuality as the root of sin,

suffering, and failure. The Tantra now advises the yogi to 'develop emptiness' by cultivating the thought 'I am, in my essential being, of diamond nature.' A successful cultivation of this thought would finally abolish the individual personality. As the *Sādhanamālā* puts it: 'Through the fire of the concept of emptiness, all the five skandhas are destroyed without return.' Once we have identified ourselves, or our self, with emptiness, our state of mind is called the 'thought of enlightenment' (*bodhicitta*).[*]

(2) From the Vedas onward, sound has been treated far more seriously in India than it has been in the West. Western philosophy is almost throughout dominated by the visual appearance of things, and sound is relegated to a comparatively subordinate position, almost on a level with smell and taste. We have somehow got the conviction that the visual and tactile appearance of things corresponds more closely to what is really there than their sound. In the magical tradition of all ages, however, sound comes much nearer to the essence of a force than anything else. Each word can be analysed into its syllables, and according to the Tantra, different syllables not only correspond to different spiritual forces or deities, but a syllable, or letter, can be used to conjure up a deity, and therefore it can, in a sense, be called the 'germ' of that deity, just as a grain of wheat contains the plant in itself. It seems logical to assume that if one can, as the first step, dissolve oneself into emptiness through concentrated thought, then it must also be possible to conjure up from emptiness the entire world of phenomena. With the help of certain sounds – such as *oṁ, hūṁ, svāhā* – one does actually create the deities out of the void. In the belief that these deities did not exist objectively before they were created by the yogi with the help of sounds, the Tantra seems to be fairly unique, and only the Egyptian priests have credited themselves with a similar power. Most mythological systems would be afraid to rob their deities of objective and independent existence. Normally, it is regarded as derogatory to a deity to say that it is 'not there'. Here, however, the deities are a mere reflex. The creative imagination is supreme, though restrained by tradition.

(3) The indefiniteness and prolixity of individual fantasy is brought into some kind of order by a tradition concerning the visual appearance

---

[*] *Sādhanamālā*, fol.100, quoted in A. Foucher, Etude, 1905, p.9

of the deities. That is described with meticulous care in the so-called *sādhanas*, some of which go back to about 500AD. It was the task of artists to carry out those prescriptions. The overwhelming majority of the Tantric images which have come down to us agree closely with the prescriptions of the sādhanas. It is only on rare occasions that artists have introduced alterations of their own for artistic reasons, e.g. in order to increase the symmetry of many-armed images. The artistic image is regarded as a basis for visualizing the deity. It is a kind of prop which should be dispensed with in due course, when what we would call the 'hallucination' of the deity takes its place.

(4) It is a commonplace of magic that identification with a deity allows us to participate in his or her magical powers. The deity, to be sure, is illusory, and so are the benefits we derive from them. It is again the emptiness of everything which allows this identification to take place – the emptiness which is in us coming together with the emptiness which is the deity. Step three brought about the vision of the deity. By step four we actually do become the deity. The subject is actually identified with the object, the faithful with the object of faith. 'The worship, the worshipper, and the worshipped, those three are not separate.'[*] This is the mental state which is known as yoga, concentration (*samādhi*), or trance (*dhyāna*).

An important aid to Tantric meditation are the 'magical circles' or *maṇḍalas*, which are known to all lovers of Buddhist art. A maṇḍala is a diagram which shows deities in their spiritual or cosmic connections, and it is used as a basis for winning insight into the spiritual law which is thus represented. A maṇḍala is either painted on cloth or paper, or drawn on the ground with coloured rice or pebbles, or it may be engraved on stone or metal. Each system of the Tantra had its own maṇḍalas. The deities are shown either pictorially, in their visible form, or by the Sanskrit letters, which form their germ syllables, or by various symbols. Some maṇḍalas give a detailed, though condensed, representation of the entire universe, and they include not only the Buddhas and Bodhisattvas, but also the gods and spirits, mountains and seas, the zodiac and the great heretical teachers. The maṇḍalas are in the direct line of the ancient tradition of magic. The first step of a magician who wishes to conjure up a magical power has always been to mark off from its profane surroundings a

[*] *Journal Asiatique* 225, 1934, p.9

charmed circle, in which the power can manifest itself. In recent years, C.G. Jung found that some of his patients spontaneously drew pictures similar to the Buddhist maṇḍalas. The circle and the square are, according to him, the essential elements of a maṇḍala, and, although Jung has never really understood the Buddhist methods of meditation, his attempt to bring together the Tantric tradition and the psychology of the unconscious is a fruitful starting point for further work in this field.

TANTRIC PHILOSOPHY

If the Tantra expects salvation from sacred actions, it must have a conception of the universe according to which such actions can be the lever of emancipation. The cosmos consists of a great number of forces, which are modes of the activity of the world force; through sacred actions we adapt ourselves to those forces and render them serviceable to our purposes, which in themselves are also the purposes of the cosmos. The Buddha is no longer just a transcendent spiritual reality. The omnipresence of the Buddha nature results from the fact that the Buddha is conceived as a 'cosmic body'. The six elements, which are the material of everything: earth, water, fire, air, space, and consciousness, are the substance of that cosmic body, and the actions of body, speech, and mind are its functions. The world is nothing but a reflection of the Buddha's light, more concentrated in one place, and more diffused in another, as the case may be. The Buddha is the secret reality in all things, their heart, the living and central truth in them. We ourselves are not strange elements external to it, and all we have to do is to realize that we ourselves are the Buddha and the cosmos. Logical reasonings and discussions are quite unavailing. Only actions of mystical value can help us to realize our intimate and universal community, or identity with the Buddha.

It is easy to see that this theory is a logical development rendered inevitable by the trends in Buddhism which preceded it. To the Old Wisdom School, Nirvāṇa had been the absolute opposite of this world. The early Mahāyāna had identified Nirvāṇa and this world in the one Absolute Reality of emptiness. Now, in the Tantra, the world becomes a manifestation of the Dharma body of the Buddha. And again, the old Buddhist urge for total self-extinction is expressed through the new metaphysical formulation.

When we consider ourselves, as well as all other beings, as a
manifestation of the eternal principle of life, we act in a feeling of our
own personal nullity, free from personal and egoistical interests.
Then, and only then, can we devote ourselves to earthly work
without doing damage to our spiritual progress. For through our
changed mental attitude to this world of phenomena, we have
practically overcome this world.[*]

TANTRIC MYTHOLOGY

From the very beginning the personality of man was interpreted as
a complex of the skandhas. The Tantra now transfers this conception
to the Buddha himself, and claims that he is composed of five
skandhas. The skandhas themselves are Buddhas. In European literature, they are often called Dhyāni Buddhas, but this term, introduced by Hodgson about a century ago, is not only faulty Sanskrit:
it has never been found in any Tantric text. It is time to discard it. The
texts themselves always speak of the 'five Tathāgatas', or the 'five
Jinas'. Jina means 'victor' or 'conqueror', and is an old epithet of the
Buddha, referring originally to his conquest over passion. The Tibetans always speak of the five Jinas, and I shall follow their example.
The five Jinas are Vairocana, the Illuminator, or the Brilliant; Akṣobhya,
the Imperturbable; Ratnasambhava, the Jewel-born; Amitābha, the
Infinite Light; and Amoghasiddhi, the Unfailing Success. These five
Buddhas were introduced about 750AD, and they differ completely
from all the other Buddhas known to Buddhism up to then. All the
Buddhas one had heard about in the pre-Tantra period had com-
menced their career as ordinary human beings, or even as animals,
and then, through progressive purification, in many millions of lives,
had worked their way slowly and gradually up to Buddhahood. The
five Jinas, on the other hand, always were Buddhas from the very
beginning, and had never been anything else.

The five Jinas constitute the body of the universe. In addition, the
Tantra worked out a system according to which these five Jinas
'corresponded' mystically to the various constituents of the universe, who severally 'participated' in them. Five elements correspond to the five Jinas, five senses and sense-objects, and five

[*] H. von Glasenapp, *Zeitschrift der Deutschen Morgenländischen Gesellschaft* 90, 1935,
p.563

cardinal points (the centre being the fifth). At the same time there are further correspondences with letters of the alphabet, with parts of the body, with the various kinds of 'vital breath', with colours, sounds, etc. This is not all. Each celestial Buddha is reflected in a celestial Bodhisattva, and in a human Buddha, and is united with a feminine force, *śakti*. Further, by introducing the idea that each Jina presides over a mystical 'family', this system can, on principle, group all the other deities under the five Jinas as accessory divinities.

The system of the five Jinas was the most influential, but by no means the only, mythological system of the Tantra. Just as Buddhism could consider the human personality as constituted of five skand-has, without postulating a unifying principle over and above them, just so a reduction of the universe to the five Tathāgatas as its ultimate constituents would satisfy the logical requirements of the majority of Buddhists. It appears, however, that after 800AD a doctrine was propounded, in various places and in varying forms, which tried to derive the five Tathāgatas as emanations from one original, first, or primeval Buddha, who is sometimes called the Ādi-Buddha, and who is the one eternal living principle of the entire universe.

The traditions about the Ādi-Buddha were considered as a particularly secret part of the teaching, and we are at present not in a position to distinguish clearly between the different schools of thought. Many schools seem to have singled out one of the five Jinas, usually Vairocana, as the chief. Others introduced a sixth person to preside over them. This person bears the name sometimes of Mahāvairocana, sometimes of Vajradhara, and sometimes he is simply called the Ādi-Buddha.

It is at this point that Buddhism at last deviates completely from its original teachings, and prepares the way for its own extinction. It is quite clear that this kind of teaching must tend in the direction of henotheism. As we saw before, it has always been a basic conviction of the Buddhist tradition that the object of thinking about the world was escape from it, and not explanation of its origin. As far as the origin of the appearance of this universe around us was concerned, one was content to put it down to ignorance and not to God. The Yogācārins were the first to build up an extremely complicated and involved system which was designed to deduce the appearance of a world of external objects from ignorance as the cause, and from the 'store-consciousness' as the basis of the universe. 500 years later, about 950, some Tantric scholars, who lived near the Jaxartes, came to regard a near-monotheistic cosmogeny as the very centre of the Buddhist doctrine. Up to then the Tathāgata had been the one who delivers the true teaching about the cause of the universe. Now the Tathāgata himself becomes the cause. In the Kalacakra Tantra, and in some Chinese systems, the Buddha acts as a kind of creator. As Lords of the yogis, the Buddhas were transformed into magicians, who created this world by means of their meditation. All things are their magical creations. Everything that exists, they see in their creative meditation. And what they see in their meditation must be real because, except for this meditation, nothing at all exists, and every-thing, as it is, is really Thought. It had been usual for many centuries, in Yogācāra circles, to describe ultimate reality as the 'womb of the Tathāgatas'. It is now from this womb of the Tathāgatas that the world is said to issue. The elaboration of this cosmogeny was the last creative act of Buddhist thought. Once it had reached this stage of development it could do no more than merge into the monotheistic religions around it.

LEFT-HANDED TANTRA

In our historical survey, we have drawn attention to the difference between the Left-handed and the Right-handed Tantra (see pp.150 *et seq*.). The chief features of the Left-handed Tantra are: (1) the worship of śaktis, female deities, with whom the male deities are united in the embrace of loving union, and from whom they derive their energy; (2) the presence of vast numbers of demons and terri-fying deities, the worship of the God Bhairava (the Terrible), and an elaborate ritual connected with the burial ground; (3) the inclusion of sexual intercourse, and other forms of 'immoral conduct', among the practices which conduce to salvation.

The Left-handed Tantra has met with much disapproval, and moral indignation has prevented most observers from attempting to understand it. Its vitality has, nevertheless, been surprising; for centuries it has been a historical force of the first magnitude in the East, and we must try to arrive at some appreciation of its three salient features.

(1) The Old Buddhism had been a severely masculine system, and only a few quite subordinate feminine deities were admitted. The

higher gods are sexless, so are the inhabitants of the Buddhafields. Femininity was on the whole a bar to the highest spiritual attainment, and on approaching Buddhahood the Bodhisattva ceased to be reborn as a woman. A woman cannot possibly become a Buddha.

The Prajñāpāramitā and Tārā were the first autonomous Buddhist deities. The cult of Tārā seems to have entered Buddhism about 150AD. Tārā, from Sanskrit *tārayati*, is the saviouress who helps us to cross to the other shore, who removes fear and dread and who grants the fulfilment of all our wishes. Tārā was a creation of the popular mind. The Prajñāpāramitā, on the other hand, originated among small groups of ascetic metaphysicians. In the Mahāyāna, the Prajñā-pāramitā was not only a virtue, a book, and a mantra, but also a deity. The personification of transcendental wisdom seems to have started about the beginning of our era. In the Prajñāpāramitā sūtras, she is described as the 'mother of all the Buddhas'. What is the meaning of this phrase? Just as a child is born of the mother, so the full enlightenment of a Buddha comes forth from the Perfection of Wisdom. It is she who shows them their way about in the world. In this way a feminine principle was placed side by side with the Buddha, and to some extent even above him. It is interesting to note that the Prajñāpāramitā texts, with their emphasis on the feminine principle in the world, originated in the south of India, where the Dravidian environment had kept alive many matriarchal ideas, which the more exclusively masculine Brahmanism had suppressed in the north of India. Almost everywhere in ancient thought we find the notion of a principle which represents both wisdom and femininity, and which combined motherhood with virginity. In the Mediterranean world we meet, at the same period, with a Sophia, who is modelled on Ishtar, Isis, and Athene; she represents a fusion between the idea of wisdom and the idea of the Magna Mater, and is placed by the side of the supreme being. Like Ishtar and the Virgin Mary, the Prajñā-pāramitā was in essence both mother and virgin. She is the 'mother of all the Buddhas', i.e. she is not barren but fertile, fruitful of many good deeds, and her images lay great stress on her full breasts. Like a virgin, on the other hand, she remains 'unaffected, untouched', and the scriptures emphasize her elusiveness more than anything else.

While thus Buddhism acknowledged the importance of feminine attitudes to the world, and personified them into a multitude of feminine deities, a sexual attitude to femininity was generally discouraged, and the sexual implications, both of femininity and of the relation between the masculine and the feminine principle, were glossed over. In the Left-handed Tantra, concepts derived from sexual life were openly introduced into the explanation of spiritual phenomena. It is, of course, well known to psychologists that sexuality, almost undisguised, has often intruded into mystical experiences. Even abstract metaphysical thought is not entirely without its libidinous side. This has been felt even by a philosopher whom one usually regards as almost inhuman in his withdrawal from all normal human affections. Somebody asked Immanuel Kant why he had never married. Kant replied that all his life he had had one 'mistress'; that had been metaphysics, and he had wished to remain faithful to her. Similarly, the authors of the Prajñāpāramitā sūtras were aware that the pursuit of perfect wisdom could easily assume the character of a love affair with the Absolute. The persistent elusiveness of perfect wisdom on its own would maintain interest to the end. We are, as a matter of fact, told explicitly that a Bodhisattva should think of perfect wisdom with the same intensity and exclusiveness with which a man thinks of a 'handsome, attractive, and beautiful woman' with whom he has made a date, but who is prevented from seeing him.

What, however, is only implied in most treatises on wisdom, is brought out in the open in Śaktism. The highest reality is conceived as a union of a masculine (active) and a feminine (passive) principle. The active principle is called 'skill in means', the passive principle being 'wisdom'. Only the union of the two can lead to salvation. The one Absolute is a union of the two, and that act of union fills it with the 'highest bliss.' The art of this school, as is well known, represents the Buddhas and Bodhisattvas in the act of sexual intercourse – called by the Tibetans the *yab-yum* (father-mother) attitude.

(2) The emphasis on the terrifying aspect of the universe is connected with the purpose of yogic practices in the Left-handed Tantra. The Left-hand path aims at stripping man of his ego, so that he may become completely identified with the divine principle. The object is to bring about a complete and total destruction and obliteration of all the elements which build up the ego, i.e. of our desires and passions. The concentration on self-destruction would, to some extent, account for the appearance of the many terrifying deities,

which represent the yogi's own destructive efforts. As Dr P.H. Pott puts it,

> the idea of destruction awakens naturally the association with the burial ground where the material body is destroyed. The place where the acts of consecration of the 'left-path' should be performed is by preference the burial ground. The ritual is inspired by its atmosphere.[*]

Esoterically, the burial ground stands for the place where the last remaining link between man and his world is severed.

(3) Finally, we must consider the arguments that are put forward in justification of all kinds of immoral conduct. One does not really expect the followers of any religion to advocate, for instance, 'daily intercourse in out of the way places with twelve-year-old girls of the Candala caste',[†] as a kind of sacred duty. The *Guhyasamāja-tantra*, one of the earliest – and also one of the most sacred – scriptures of the Left-handed Tantra, seems to teach the very opposite of what Buddhist asceticism stood for. It tells us that we will certainly easily attain Buddhahood if we 'cultivate all sensual pleasures, just as we may desire'.[‡] Hardships and austerities fail, where the 'satisfaction of all desires' succeeds. Just the most immoral, the most tabooed, actions seem to have a particular fascination for the followers of this doctrine. One is enjoined to defy the prohibitions which restrict the food permitted to ascetics. One must feed on the flesh of elephants, horses, and dogs, and all food and drink should be mixed with ordure, urine, or meat. No wonder that the doctrine has so often been called an aberration of the human mind.

The purpose of these doctrines should be perfectly familiar to anyone who has studied the mentality of mysticism. What is wanted here is to bring the senses purposely into contact with the objects that stimulate them, either by way of strong attraction, or repugnance. On the one hand, one can come to a full realization and understanding of the vanity and relativity of the pleasures of the senses only by exposing oneself to them. On the other hand, we know also of Christian saints who strove to overcome their sensuous

---

[*] P.H. Pott, *Yoga en Tantra*, 1946. p.159

[†] *Guhyasamāja Tantra* xv.2, p.94

[‡] *Guhyasamāja Tantra* vii.3, p.27

repugnance of disgusting things by putting them into their mouths. Such conduct would be really in keeping with the spirit of asceticism. It is further easy to see that the metaphysics of the Mahāyāna could very well lead to such conclusions. Nirvāṇa and this world were taught to be one. Then the passions are also not outside Nirvāṇa, 'the passions are the same as Nirvāṇa'.* Both branches of the Tantra agreed on that. The Right-handed form maintained that the passions had to be sublimated before they could become wings to enlightenment. Sensual love, the love of self, of women, of worldly possessions, are justified in so far as they are the starting point of a universal and all-embracing love. The passions, therefore, should not be suppressed, but ennobled and transformed. The Left-handed Tantra, on the other hand, believed that the passions in their direct and unsublimated form could be made into vehicles of salvation. One must further, I think, admit that the objection to immoral practices carried out in the name of religion is not so much a religious as a social one. It is possible that the Left-hand yogis lacked in spirituality, but it is certain that they were sadly deficient in respectability. It is equally certain that they did not wish to be respectable. In order to understand this better, we must realize that religion can exist either in an institutionalized or in a highly individualistic form. In an institutionalized religion, religious doctrine and practice is rarely in conflict with ordinary social morality. The more individualistic mystics, on the other hand, see no real reason why religion and morality should be necessarily tied together. The ordinary morality of the common people is based on little more than social taboos, i.e., essentially on the fear of social isolation which the mystic regards as the ideal breeding ground for spiritual emancipation. While they are still under the influence of the fear of the taboos of society, the yogis have not gained the 'freedom of the spirit' that they aim at. During that stage of their spiritual progress, in which they still feel bound to the moral rules of their social environment, they may find that it is salutary to break their attachment to them, and to bear living apart in isolation from the cosy warmth of tribal approval. Such revolt against social restraints is called antinomianism. It has made its appearance at different times in all religions, and in Buddhism it is not confined to the Tantras, but it is also observed among the

---

* e.g. *Ratnacūḍa Sūtra, Śikṣāsamuccaya* 236

Amidists, and in the Ch'an. Immoral conduct is therefore a perhaps necessary stage of transition for the attainment of a-moral conduct. We find an almost exact counterpart to Buddhist a-moralism in Ruysbroek's description of the views of certain 'followers of the free spirit'.

> Hence they go so far as to say that so long as man has a tendency to virtues, and desires to do God's very precious will, he is still imperfect, being preoccupied with the acquiring of things. Therefore they think they can never either believe in virtues, or have additional merit, or commit sins. Consequently, they are able to consent to every desire of the lower nature, for they have reversed to the state of innocence, and laws no longer apply to them. They claim indeed to be free, outside of commandments and virtues. Free in their flesh they give the body what it desires. To them the highest sanctity for man consists in following without compulsion and in all things his natural instinct, so that he may abandon himself to every impulse in satisfying the demands of the body.[*]

THE CONTROL OF THE BODY

It would be misleading, however, to make too much of the disagreement which separates the doctrinal formulations of the Tantra from those of the older Buddhism. In one decisive particular, the Tantra, in all its branches, has remained faithful to the spirit of Buddhist tradition. The physical body is here, as always, regarded as the chief object of all endeavour. We have pointed out before (p.77) that a mindful discipline of the body is the very cornerstone of Buddhist training. This applies to all schools, in spite of their divergences.

It had been the dignified physical bearing of a monk which had converted Śāriputra. The privations of a homeless life demanded a considerable mastery over the body. The monk, as the Buddha said to Śāriputra, must be able to endure cold, excessive heat, the pangs of hunger; he must not fear gadflies, snakes, or attacks from men or beasts; he must not brood discontentedly on where he will eat or sleep. The work on the body belonged to the essential routine of the Buddhist life which went on quietly, unaffected by doctrinal disputes. The comfort of the skin is consistently disregarded and

---

[*] Untraced at time of publication

opposed. Muscular movements are subjected to perpetual mindfulness, i.e. one tries to be consciously aware of what one does, when walking, standing, sitting, etc. Rhythmical and mindful yogic breathing controls the lungs and respiratory system. One combats the demands of the alimentary canal by fasting, by the rule that no food must be eaten after midday, and by a set meditation on the onerous and disgusting aspects of feeding. The sense organs, as we saw above (p.79), are rigidly guarded. The control and mortification of the body is of the essence of the spiritual life. At the same time, the body, though a burden, should not be despised. The highest trance is, as we saw (p.81), achieved through the body. It gives great beatitude and complete calm, and since all thought is extinct, the realization of this state depends on the body. One is said to 'touch the deathless element with one's body'.*

Anyone who has ever tried to meditate must have observed that the weaknesses and disturbances of the body are apt to interfere with continuous meditation. Accordingly, the *Sukhāvatīvyūha* had taught that in Amitābha's paradise the physical bodies of beings will be 'as strong as the diamond of Nārāyaṇa.'† The Tantra took up this idea, and adopted many yogic practices which would transform this body into a 'diamond body', make it into a fit vehicle for the spiritual journey, and render it ripe, strong enough to bear the strain imposed upon it by spiritual work. In this connection the physiology of hatha yoga was accepted as authoritative. The body is believed to contain an immense number of nerves, or arteries (*nāḍi*), channels of occult force, and four vital centres which are called nerve-plexuses (*cakra*) or lotuses (*padma*). The lowest centre is in the region of the navel, another in the heart, another just below the neck, and another in the head. Among the innumerable nerves, three are the most important: Two by the two sides of the spinal cord, and one in the middle. The left nerve represents Wisdom, the right Skill in Means, and the centre Absolute Unity. With the help of esoteric practices, which are quite unintelligible without the guidance of a guru, the yogi causes a union of Wisdom and Skill in Means to take place in the lowest nerve centre, thus producing there the thought of enlightenment (*bodhi-citta*). This must then be moved upwards along the middle nerve

---

* *Aṅguttara Nikāya* iii.355
† *Sukhāvatīvyūha* viii.25

until it becomes a state of motionless bliss in the highest nerve centre. Systematic breathing exercises play a big part in this technique, because they are said to regulate the 'vital winds' which in their turn determine the flow of the occult force in the nerves. All this, as put down here in general terms, sounds quite fantastic, and it would take many pages to make it even vaguely plausible. I must refer the reader to the ample treatises on hatha yoga that are available.

In this context we are concerned only to show the seriousness with which the Tantra regarded the body. The truth is within the body, and arises out of it. In the *Hevajra-tantra* the Lord explains that, although everything is empty, there is need for the existence of a physical body, because the highest bliss could not be gained without it. The ultimate truth resides within the body.

> He is within the house, but you are enquiring about him outside. You are seeing your husband within, yet you are asking the neighbours as to his whereabouts. [*]

So Saraha, a Tantric poet of Bengal.

> The scholars explain all the scriptures, but do not know the Buddha residing within the body. [†]

It was the arduous struggle with his own physical constitution which filled the life of the Tantric yogi, and any theories he might have were no more than minor by-products of his exertions.

---

[*] Quoted in S. Dasgupta, *Obscure religious cults*, 1946, p.104

[†] Quoted *ibid.*, p.105

9

NON-INDIAN DEVELOPMENTS

SURVEY
The schools we have considered so far had their origin in India, and, although they were accepted outside India, their fundamental tenets were not seriously modified there. Three schools outside India have, however, profoundly modified the Indian impulse. They are, in the Far East, the Ch'an (Zen) and Amidism, in Tibet the Nyingma.

Buddhism had spread to China from Central Asia. It was first introduced about 50AD. Always suspect to the Confucians, Chinese Buddhism took a great deal of its colour from the native Taoism. It had a great success under the Liang dynasty in the sixth century and during the greater part of the T'ang dynasty (618–907). From c. 1000AD onward, two schools have drawn to themselves the majority of the Chinese monks. The meditational Ch'an sect is a development of Mahāyāna metaphysics, of the Prajñāpāramitā, and of the Yogācāra, reshaped by Chinese and Japanese conditions. Amidism is the form which, in the course of time, the 'Buddhism of Faith' took in China and Japan.

Monks from Bengal carried, about 700AD, the Buddhist religion to Tibet. The native, Bön, religion of Tibet had been a form of magical Shamanism. Buddhism did not by any means succeed in superseding it. Until this day, after nearly 1,200 years of Buddhist rule, the Bön religion still remains a vital force. The monks of Tibet have always been sharply divided in their attitude to the indigenous Shamanism. Some absorbed a great deal of it, others much less. After 1400AD the less magical school, known as the Yellow Church, has, through the reforms of Tsongkhapa, gained the upper hand. Many of the more magical Red sects continue to exist, and the Nyingmapas represent that branch of the Tibetan Tantra which has yielded more than any other to the influence of Bönism.

CH'AN

The word *ch'an* is the Chinese equivalent of the Sanskrit word *dhyāna*, and means 'meditation'. Four stages can be distinguished in the development of the Ch'an School:

(1) A formative period, which began about 440 with a group of students of Gunabhadra's Chinese translation of the *Laṅkāvatāra Sūtra*. About 520 we have the legendary figure of Bodhidharma. After that, a few groups of monks round men like Seng-t'san (606), whose poem, called *Hsin Hsin Ming* ('On believing in mind') is one of the finest expositions of Buddhism I know of, and Hui-neng (637–713), of southern China, who is held up to posterity as an illiterate, practically-minded person, who approached truth abruptly and without circumlocution. Much of the traditions about the early history of Ch'an are the inventions of a later age. Many of the sayings and songs of the patriarchs which are transmitted to us are, however, very valuable historical and spiritual documents.

(2) After c. 700AD, Ch'an establishes itself as a separate school. In 734 Shen-hui, a disciple of Hui-neng, founded a school in the south of China. While the northern branch of Ch'an died out in the middle of the T'ang period (c. 750), all the later developments of Ch'an issue from Shen-hui's school. Whereas so far the Ch'an monks had lived in the monasteries of the Lu-tsung (Vinaya) sect, about 750 Pai-chang provided them with a special rule of their own, and an independent organization. The most revolutionary feature of Pai-chang's Vinaya was the introduction of manual work. 'A day without work, a day without food.' Under the T'ang dynasty (618–907), the Ch'an sect slowly gained its ascendancy over the other schools. One of the reasons was the fact that it survived the bitter persecution of 845 better than any other sect. The five great masters among Hui-neng's disciples initiated a long series of great T'ang masters of Ch'an, and this was the heroic and creative period of Ch'an.

(3) By about 1000, Ch'an had overshadowed all Chinese Buddhist sects, except Amidism. Within the Ch'an School, the Lin-chi sect had

gained the leadership. Its approach was now systematized, and to some extent mechanized. In the form of collections of riddles and cryptic sayings, usually connected with the T'ang masters, special textbooks were composed in the twelfth and thirteenth centuries. The riddles are technically known as *kungan* (Japanese *kōan*, literally 'official document'). An example is this one: 'Once a monk asked Tung-shan: "What is the Buddha?" Tung-shan replied: "Three pounds of flax."'

(4) The final period is one of permeation into the general culture of the Far East, its art and the general habits of life. The art of the Sung period is an expression of Ch'an philosophy. It was particularly in Japan that the cultural influence of Zen made itself felt. Ch'an had been brought to Japan about 1200 by Eisai and Dōgen. Its simplicity and straightforward heroism appealed to the men of the military class. Zen discipline helped them to overcome the fear of death. Many poems were composed testifying to the soldier's victory over death:

> Neither heaven nor earth give me shelter.
> I rejoice to know that all things are void – myself and the world.
> Honour to the sword wielded by the great Yuan swordsmen.
> Strike, and it cuts through a spring breeze, like a lightning flash.[*]

A detailed description of the far-reaching influence of Zen on Japanese painting, and calligraphy, gardening, tea-ceremony, fencing, dancing, and poetry would lead us too far here, and I must refer the reader to D.T. Suzuki's excellent works on the subject.

The specific features of Ch'an Buddhism can also be grouped under four headings:

(1) The traditional aspects of Buddhism are viewed with hostility. Images and scriptures are held up to contempt, conventions are derided by deliberate eccentricities. Ch'an evinces a spirit of radical empiricism, very similar to that shown by the Royal Society in England in the seventeenth century. There also the motto was, 'Don't think, try!' and 'With books they meddle not farther than to see what experiments have been try'd before,' (Sprat). Ch'an aimed at a direct transmission of Buddhahood outside the written tradition. The study of the scriptures was therefore neglected. In the monasteries they are placed for occasional reference in close proximity to the

[*] Quoted in E. Steinilber-Oberlin, *Les sectes bouddhiques japonaises*, 1930, p.143

lavatory. To discuss commentaries, ransack the scriptures, brood over words, is regarded like investigating the sand at the bottom of the sea. 'What use is it to count the treasures of other people?' 'To see one's own nature is Ch'an.' By comparison with that, nothing else matters. Historians have often attributed these attitudes to the practical turn in the Chinese national character. This cannot be the whole truth because anti-traditionalism pervaded the whole Buddhist world between 500 and 1000, and the Indian Tantra in this respect offers many parallels to Ch'an.

(2) Ch'an is hostile to metaphysical speculation, averse to theory, and intent on abolishing reasoning. Direct insight is prized more highly than the elaborate webs of a subtle thought. The truth is not stated in abstract and general terms, but as concretely as possible. The T'ang masters were renowned for their oracular and cryptic sentences, and for their curious and original actions. Salvation is found in the ordinary things of everyday life. Hsüan-chien was enlightened when his teacher blew out a candle, another when a brick dropped down, another when his leg got broken. This was not an altogether new phenomenon. The Pāli *Psalms of the Brethren* and *Psalms of the Sisters* show that also in the Old Wisdom School trivial incidents could easily start off the final awakening. The Ch'an masters flaunt their disapproval of mere tradition in startling actions. They burn wooden statues of the Buddha, kill cats, catch shrimps and fishes. The master assists the pupil not so much by the wise words which issue from his mouth, but by the 'direct action' of pulling at his nose, hitting him with the staff (*pang*), or shouting at him (*pang-ho*). The kōans, which are the basis and support of meditation, consist of riddles and puzzling stories which one should think about until intellectual exhaustion leads to a sudden realization of their meaning. Again, the kōan is not, as is so often asserted, a peculiar creation of the Chinese genius. It is nothing but the Chinese form of a general Buddhist trend which, at the same time, is clearly visible in Bengal, where the Tantric Sahajiyas taught by riddles and enigmatic expressions, partly to guard the secrets of their thoughts, partly to avoid abstractions by concrete imagery.

(3) 'Sudden enlightenment' was the distinctive slogan of the southern branch of Ch'an. Enlightenment according to Hui-neng and his successors is not a gradual but an instantaneous process. The purport of this teaching has often been misunderstood. The Ch'an masters

did not intend to say that no preparation was necessary, and that enlightenment was won in a very short time. They just laid stress on the common mystical truth that enlightenment takes place in a timeless moment, i.e. outside time, in eternity, and that it is an act of the Absolute itself, not our own doing. One cannot do anything at all to become enlightened (p.91). To expect austerities or meditation to bring forth salvation is like 'rubbing a brick to make it into a mirror.' Enlightenment just happens, without the mediacy of any finite condition or influence, and it is, as we might put it, a totally 'free' event. It is not the gradual accumulation of merit which causes enlightenment, but a sudden act of recognition. All this teaching is, in its essence, impeccably orthodox. The Ch'an sect deviated from orthodoxy only when it drew the inference that one need not adhere to the minor prescriptions of discipline, and thus cultivated a moral indifference which enabled it to fall in with the demands of Japanese militarism.

(4) Like Amidism, the Mādhyamikas, and to some extent the Tantra, Ch'an believes that the fulfilment of the Buddhist life can be found only in its negation. The Buddha dwells hidden in the inconspicuous things of daily life. To take them just as they come, that is all that enlightenment amounts to. 'As regards the Ch'an followers, when they see a staff they simply call it a staff. if they want to walk, they just walk; if they want to sit, they just sit. They should not in any circumstances be ruffled and distracted.' Or: 'How wondrously supernatural! And how miraculous this! I draw water, I carry fuel!' Or, once more:

> In spring, the flowers, and in autumn the moon,
> In summer a refreshing breeze, and in winter the snow.
> What else do I have need of?
> Each hour to me is an hour of joy.

AMIDISM

The cult of Amitābha had originated in the north-west of India, in the borderland between India and Iran. Missionaries from the same area had carried it to China about 150AD. About 350 Hui-yuan founded the Pure Land School, which taught an easy way to salvation, based on the *Sukhāvatī Sūtra* (p.122). For a long time the Buddhism of Faith in China centred round the figures of Śākyamuni

(Shih-chia) and Maitreya (Mi-lo), and a number of Bodhisattvas like Avalokiteśvara (Kuan-yin) and Kṣitigarbha (Ti-t'sang) were widely revered. Although Maitreya has always remained popular, and the cult of Mañjuśrī (Wên-shu) and Vairocana (Pi-lu-che-na) spread widely in the eighth century, the inscriptions and images suggest that Amitābha (A-mi-t'o) came to the fore about 650AD, and Kuan-yin became then firmly associated with his cult. While in India so far scarcely any portrayals of Amitābha and none of his paradise have been found, China offers an abundance of such images. We do not know the reasons why just Amitābha's paradise should have stirred the imagination of the Chinese to such an extent. The Egyptian 'Fields of Reeds', or the Paradise of Osiris, the Iranian 'Var', and the Greek 'Islands of the Blessed and the 'Gardens of the Hesperidae' also lie in the west, and Chinese folklore already possessed the notion of a fairy palace on the Kun-lun mountains, inhabited by Hsi-wang-um, 'Royal Mother of the West.' After 650 Amidism was provided with an elaborate theology. Tzu-min (680–748) was one of the earliest to concentrate on the mere repetition of the name of Amitābha. The school has retained its popularity until today.

In Japan, the ideas of Amidism began to spread after 950AD. In the Kamakura period the movement was organized into a number of schools of which two are the most important: Hōnen founded the Pure Land School (*Jōdo*) in 1175, and one of his disciples, Shinran Shonin (1173–1262) the True Sect of the Pure Land (*Jōdo Shin Shū*). In 1931 the Pure Land schools had in Japan 16,000,000 adherents, with 23,000 priests. Slightly less than half of all Japanese Buddhists belonged to them.

It is customary to reckon the sect of Nichiren (1222–82) as one of the schools of Amidism. It would be more appropriate to count it among the offshoots of nationalistic Shintoism. Nichiren suffered from self-assertiveness and bad temper, and he manifested a degree of personal and tribal egotism which disqualify him as a Buddhist teacher. He did not only convince himself that he, personally, was mentioned in the *Lotus of the Good Law*, but also that the Japanese were the chosen race which would regenerate the world. The followers of the Nichiren sect, as Suzuki puts it: 'even now are more or less militaristic and do not mix well with other Buddhists'.[*]

---

[*] D.T. Suzuki, *Essays in Zen Buddhism* iii, 1934, p.328

From the point of view of Buddhist thought, the chief interest of the Far Eastern development of Amidism lies in its increasing radicalism which reaches its culmination in the Shin sect. The Shin Shū, intent on magnifying the power of faith and of Amida's vows, to cheapen salvation and to simplify the doctrine, rejects all ritualism, philosophy, and even the mild asceticism of a monastic life. All men, whether honest or criminal, are, without distinction, admitted to Amida's paradise. Faith in Amida's grace is the one and only condition of admission. We are all equally sinful, and Amida is a god of compassionate love. Unlike the Christian God, he is not a judge. The idea that morality counts as nothing compared with faith goes back a long time. It is attested already a millennium before Shinran. About 150AD we find in the *Divyāvadāna* (pp.258–9) a story which illustrates how lightly even at that time moral rules might be regarded. Dharmaruci, who lived three aeons ago, had killed his parents, killed an Arhant, and burnt down a monastery. Nevertheless, the future Śākyamuni ordained him with the words: 'Of what use are the rules? Only repeat constantly the formula, "Homage to the Buddha, Homage to the Dharma!"' The priests of the Shin Shū may marry, and eat fish and meat. They carry to its logical conclusion the old idea that one should accommodate oneself to the world. By doing as the world does, by living like other ordinary people, the priests avoid setting up barriers, and they can meet the laity on easier terms. The Shin sect tends in the direction of the abolition of all specific religious observances. The motive for the abrogation of celibacy is, of course, quite different from that prevalent in the Tantra. There, the idea was to utilize the whole body for salvation, and there was no reason why the sexual parts should be left out. Sex was a form of physical drill, and a temptation bravely borne. In the Shin Shū, marriage is a means of sharing the burdens of the low and humble, of observing the customs and duties of the society in which one lives and which it would be presumptuous to reject. The main task is to live like any one else, and to serve both the world and the Buddha. The democratic spirit of the Shin Shū and its sanction of social duties have made for success in the world of today. Alone among all Buddhist schools, the Shin sect has during the last fifty years shown that Buddhism can adapt itself to industrial conditions, although such 'adaptation' of Buddhism could easily be mistaken for its abolition.

THE NYINGMA

In Tibet the ancient Red sect, whose adherents wear red instead of yellow gowns, preach and practise an esoteric doctrine which was originally introduced by the Indian prince Padmasambhava about 750AD. Padmasambhava was a wonder-worker who paid no more than two brief visits to Tibet. During the short eighteen months of his stay he exerted, however, an influence which is still felt in Tibet today, in spite of the fact that the official Yellow Church has combated his doctrine now for five centuries. The chief reason for Padmasambhava's lasting influence seems to lie in the fact that his interpretation of Buddhism – a form of the Tantra – is very much akin to Bönism, the indigenous religion of Tibet. The followers of Padmasambhava are usually called the Nyingmapa, literally 'ancient ones'. The reason for this epithet is to be found in the fact that their doctrines were introduced between roughly 750 and 850, i.e. in the period before the great persecution of Buddhism by King Langdarma (836–41).

It is quite obvious that secret magical doctrines, since they do not claim to be justified by reasoning alone, require some form of inspiration to lend them authority. The Nyingma tradition claims to be based on two sources of authority. The initial foundations of the doctrine were transmitted direct from the Indian masters. In addition, however, the Nyingma chose to believe, like the Hermetic tradition of the Mediterranean world, that the tradition has an additional basis in the discovery of buried texts (*termas*). Padmasambhava, and other masters, buried certain texts in out-of-the-way places, which would be found at the appointed time by predestined persons whenever the need for a supplementary revelation should arise. Similarly, the Hermetic texts dealing with astrology, alchemy, magic, and so on, do in many cases claim to represent books written by ancient sages, to be 'found' and edited when the time was ripe. This seems again to confirm our view that a great deal of the Tantra is a fusion between the Egyptian magic in its gnostic form on the one side, and the metaphysics of the Mahāyāna on the other. The buried texts in Tibet were dug up from c. 1125 onward. Among them are some extremely valuable works.

In its essentials the Nyingma doctrine is a branch of the Left-handed Tantra. The worship of tutelary deities plays an important part, and this system knows of a hundred such deities, of whom fifty-eight are serene and forty-two angry. In addition, of course, there is the cult of the terrible deities, who are in their essence conceived as the destroyers of the three traditional arch-enemies of our peace of mind, i.e. of greed, hate, and delusion. The physiological practices of hatha yoga play an important part. The manipulation of the 'arteries' (see p.169) and of the semen virile is held to result in the production of happiness, light, and thoughtlessness. The different classes of practices are normally performed in the following order: first, there should be the mental creation of the images of the tutelaries, brought about by reciting formulas and meditating on the visions thus raised. Secondly comes the physical-mental control of the arteries and of the semen virile; and thirdly, a realisation of the true nature of one's own mind which is emptiness itself. The distinctive idea of this school is that it tries to utilise what the Buddhists generally discard, i.e. the emotions of anger and lust, etc., and secondly that it tries to employ the material body, a dreaded shackle of the spirit to other Buddhists, as a profitable means to help the spirit. The magical nature of the Nyingma is seen in their doctrine of Thod-gyal, 'surpassing of the uppermost', according to which there is a way of salvation or emancipation in which the material body may vanish in the rainbow, or in the manner of the colours of the rainbow.

The doctrines of this school are very involved in their details, and it would be quite impossible to give a short explanation of them. Readers who are interested in this side of Buddhism are referred to some of the texts which Evans-Wentz has made available in English. A particularly fascinating doctrine which the Nyingmapas have preserved is the doctrine of the *bardo*. Bardo is the name of the experience a person undergoes in the interval between death and a new rebirth. Many Buddhists assume that a new birth follows instantaneously on death. Others, however, postulate an interval, and the Nyingma School give us a most detailed description of the experiences of the 'soul' on the bardo plane, which has been rendered accessible to us by Evans-Wentz's admirable translation of the *Tibetan Book of the Dead*.[18] Some of the traditions which it contains obviously go back to the Stone Age. The book gives advice to the soul of the dying man by preparing him for the typical experiences to which he will be exposed. In this work a great deal of Egyptian wisdom lives on until today.

EUROPEAN BUDDHISM

The Jesuit missionaries had, in the seventeenth and eighteenth centuries, acquired a fairly accurate knowledge of Chinese and Japanese Buddhism, but it was a German philosopher, Arthur Schopenhauer, who first made Europe acquainted with Buddhism as a living faith. Without any knowledge of the Buddhist scriptures, guided only by the philosophy of Kant, a Latin translation of a Persian translation of the *Upanishads*, and his own disillusionment with life, Schopenhauer had, by 1819, evolved a philosophical system which in its insistence on the 'negation of the will to live', and on compassion as the one redeeming virtue, breathed a spirit very akin to that of Buddhism. The ideas of Schopenhauer, expressed in a lively and readable style, have had a great influence in Europe. Richard Wagner was deeply impressed by the teachings of the Buddha, and in recent years Albert Schweitzer lived the life which Schopenhauer only recommended.

In the course of the nineteenth century, the invasion of Asia by European merchants, soldiers, and missionaries was accompanied by a slow infiltration of Asiatic ideas into Europe. The infiltration took the two forms of scientific research and popular propaganda. The scholarly investigation of writings and art has continued now for 120 years without interruption. The history of Buddhism has, in each generation, attracted a considerable number of scholars of great ability. Many of them, especially at first, studied Buddhism as one watches an enemy, intent on proving the superiority of Christianity. A few were convinced that they had to deal with a faith of supreme purity from which Europe could learn a great deal. The majority investigated the documents with the detachment with which one solves crossword puzzles. As the result of the labours of four generations, the exploration of Buddhism has made great progress, though much remains to be done. Sociologically, orientalism in Europe was bound up with imperialism. With the decline of European imperialism, orientalism is at present in the throes of a deep crisis, and one wonders how it will fare in the future. In the USSR Buddhist studies seem to have petered out, although Russians had contributed much to Buddhist scholarship in the past. It may be that the mysticism of the Buddhists is not to the taste of the dialectical materialists.

The year 1875 marks an event of great importance. Madame Blavatsky and Colonel Olcott founded the Theosophical Society. Its activities accelerated the influx of knowledge about Asiatic religions, and restored self-confidence in the wavering minds of the Asiatics themselves. At that period, European civilization, a blend of science and commerce, of Christianity and militarism, seemed immensely strong. The latent dynamite of national war and class war was perceived by only a few. A growing number of educated men in India and Ceylon felt, as the Japanese did about the same time, that they had no alternative but to adopt the Western system with all that it entails. The Christian missionaries looked forward to speedy mass conversions. But then the tide turned, rather suddenly and unexpectedly. A few members of the dominant race, white men and women from Russia, America, and England, Theosophists, appeared among the Hindus and Ceylonese to proclaim their admiration for the ancient wisdom of the East. Mme Blavatsky spoke about Buddhism in terms of the highest praise, Colonel Olcott wrote a 'Buddhist Catechism', and A.P. Sinnett published a very successful book in which all kinds of mysterious, but fascinating, ideas were presented as 'Esoteric Buddhism'. The myth of the Mahatmas located those invisible, wise and semi-divine leaders of mankind in the Himalayas, in Tibet, a Buddhist country, which became surrounded by an aura of superhuman wisdom. By its timely intervention, the Theosophical Society has done a great service to the Buddhist cause. Although later on it became, as an organization, corrupted by wealth and charlatanism, it has continued to be an impetus to Buddhist studies and has inspired many to seek further. To the ranks of the Theosophists belonged also Edwin Arnold, whose poem, *The Light of Asia*, has led many hearts to love and admire the Buddha for the purity of his life, and his devotion to the welfare of mankind.

After 1900, a few missionaries were sent from Asia, who laboured, in London and elsewhere, without much success. In the European capitals, in Paris, London, and Berlin, small propaganda organizations were established. In England, the Buddhist Society has, under the able leadership of Christmas Humphreys, shown a great deal of initiative in 'beating the drum of the Dharma'. So far, however, European Buddhism has been unable to find its feet. The organization of the Sangha has been, as we saw (p.38) the one permanent and stable element in Buddhist history. Monks and monasteries are the indispensable foundation of a Buddhist movement, which aims at being a concrete, living social reality. A number of European

Buddhists who felt drawn to the monastic life have gone to Ceylon, China, and Japan. The obstacles to the establishment of Buddhist monasteries in Europe are great, but probably not greater than they were originally in China. As the bankruptcy of our civilization becomes ever more patent, many more people will be drawn to the wisdom of the past, and some of them to its Buddhist form. It remains to be seen when and where Europeans garbed in the saffron robe will make their first appearance.

NOTES

1   This is how Conze translates the terms *samādhi* (see e.g. p.157) and *dhyāna* (see e.g. p.159). 'Meditation' is now a more common translation of both terms.

2   'Delusion' is the usual term. See, for example, page 179.

3   Nowadays, Buddhists generally refer to 'rebirth' rather then 'reincarnation', the latter suggesting as it does a pre-existing unchanging ego-entity that is reborn. See for example Sangharakshita, *A Guide to the Buddhist Path*, second edition, Windhorse, Birmingham 1996, p.83.

4   But see, for example, H. von Glasenapp, *Buddhism: a Non-Theistic Religion*, George Allen and Unwin, London 1970, chapter 2.

5   This term was invented by Humboldt in the nineteenth century to mean a distinct stellar system, such as our solar system, but it was never taken up by astronomers.

6   'Supress' would be a better word here, as this does not mean 'repress' in the modern psychological sense.

7   Annam = Vietnam.

8   Now called Sri Lanka, Myanmar, and Thailand.

9   i.e., Indo-China.

10   But see Paul Williams, *Buddhist Thought*, Routledge, London 2000, p.257, for details of recent research.

11   'Commandment' is a misleading term, and Conze employs the more usual 'precept' elsewhere. A precept is a principle of training, rather than a command that must be obeyed. See, for example, Sangharakshita, *A Guide to the Buddhist Path*, second edition, p.127, where these terms are contrasted.

12   But see for example Paul Williams, *Buddhist Thought*, Routledge, London 2000, chapter 3, for details of recent research.

13 i.e., the parinirvāṇa or passing away of the Buddha, rather than his Enlightenment.

14 i.e., the Christian or common era.

15 i.e., Maitreya.

16 'Spell' is Conze's translation of 'mantra'. See p.154.

17 The Pali Text Society's *Pali-English Dictionary* defines *jhāyin* as 'meditative, self- concentrated, engaged in jhāna-practice'.

18 Evans-Wentz was the *compiler and editor* of Lama Kazi Dawa-Samdup's translation of the *Bardo Thödol*, a title published in English as *The Tibetan Book of the Dead*, but which more literally translates as 'the liberation through hearing in the in-between state'.

THE MAIN DATES OF BUDDHIST HISTORY

Am = Amidism, B = Buddhism, Ch = China, Chinese, Hī = Hīnayāna,
MY = Madhyamaka-Yogācāra, NW = New Wisdom, S = Sarvāstivāda, T = Tantra,
Th = Theravāda, Y = Yogācāra, YL = Yogācāra Logic, Z = Zen (Ch'an)

After Buddha	BC	History	Hīnayāna	Mahāyāna	Art
80	480	480 Death of Buddha			
		325 Alexander in India			
		315 Candragupta			
260	300	274 Aśoka begins to rule	246 Mahinda brings B. to Ceylon		
			240 Sthaviravādins and Mahāsaṅghikas split		
		236 Aśoka d.			
360	200	160 Menandros		Original Prajñāpāramitā (NW)	120 Gates at Sāñci
460	100		80 Pāli Scriptures written down	80 Mahāyāna sūtras: Saddharma Puṇḍarīka etc.	to 500AD Gandhāra to 200AD Mathurā
560	AD	25–60 Kadphises I B. spreads to China			Amarāvatī
		61 Dream of Mingti			
		78–103 Kaniṣka		Large Prajñāpāramitā (NW)	Reliquary of Peshawar
660	100		100 Aśvaghoṣa		
			140 Vibhāṣa (S) in Kashmir	160 Saṁdhinirmocana Sūtra (Y), Nāgārjuna (NW), Āryadeva (NW)	150–350 Bulk of Amarāvatī
760	200	220 B spreads to Annam			Buddhist painters in South China
					265 First pagoda in China
					to 600 Gupta art Ellora, Ajanta
860	300	355 Ch edict permits monkhood		333 Hui-Yüan (Am) b. Laṅkāvatāra sūtra (Y) Maitreyanātha (MY)	Ku k'ai chih

After Buddha	AD	History	Hīnayāna	Mahāyāna	Art
		357–385 Fu kien protects B			
		372 B spreads to Korea			
		385–414 Candragupta II		385 Kumārajīva to China	
		399–414 Fa hien in India			
960	400		Vasubandhu (S)		
		414–455 Kumaragupta I founds Nālandā	420 Buddhaghosa (Th)	Vasubandhu (Y) Asaṅga (Y) Kumārajīva (NW)	to 500 B sculpture in N. Ch
		438–452 To-pa Tao persecutes B. B spreads to Burma, Java, Sumatra	440 Mahāvaṁsa (Th)	416 Hui-yuan d. Dignāga (YL)	414–520 Grottos of Yun-kang
		452 seq. To-pas protects B	460 Dhammapala	498–561 Bodhidharma (Z) Paramārtha (Y)	Wei sculpture
1060	500	518 Oldest catalogue of Ch Tripiṭaka			
		552 B spreads to Japan		560 Sthiramati d.	
		572 Shotoku Taishi b.			
		573 Second persecution in China		580 Tien tai founded San-lun founded	Renaissance of art in China
1160	600	B spreads to Sumatra		Hua-yen founded	
		606–647 Harshavardhana		606 Sang ts'an (Z) d.	
		621 Shōtoku Taishi d.		635 Dharmapāla (Y)	Grotto I in Ajanta
		629–645 Hsüan Tsang in India		637 Hui-Neng (Z) b. Lu-tsung founded	
		642 seq. Songtsen Gampo (Tibet)		645–664 Hsüan Tsang (Y) works in China	Li-szu-hsun
		642 B spreads to Tibet		643 Fa-tsang (Hua-yen) Dharmakīrti (L)	
		651 First B temple in Tibet		650 Candrakīrti (NW)	
		671–695 I'tsing's travels		691 Śāntideva (NW) b.	Nara temples
1260	700	B spreads to Annam Mahāyāna official religion of Srivijaya			

After Buddha	AD	History	Hīnayāna	Mahāyāna	Art
		710–784 Nara period		713 Hui-Neng (Z) d.	Wu tao tze Java
		711 Sindh lost to Islam		716 Shingon founded	to 1000 Tun-hu-ang
		720 B (Hī) spreads to Siam		Śubhakarasimha (T) Vajrabodhi (T) Amoghavajra (T)	
		749 First monastery (Samye) in Tibet	740 Anuruddha, Abhidhammattha-saṅgaha	747 Padmasambhava to Tibet (T) Śantarakṣita (T)	747 Gigantic Buddha at Nara
		760 Arabs take central Asia Odantapurī founded Pāla Dynasty		774 Amoghavajra d.	Borobudur Todaiji
		770–815 Dharmapāla			
1360	800	Shivaism supersedes B in Kashmir		Haribhadra (NW)	802 Angkor founded
		Mahāyāna develops in Cambodia		805 Dengyo Daishi founds Tendai on Mt Hiei	
		845 Persecution by Wu-tsang		840 Kōbō Daishi (T) d.	
		850–1350 Korye Dynasty in Korea			
1460	900	Langdharma Islam supersedes B in Central Asia		Kōan system	to 1300 Korean art
			920 King Aba Salamevan Kasup V (Ceylon)	949 Yun-men (Z) d. Kuya (Am)	
				942–1017 Genshin (Tendai)	
				965 Kalacakra (T)	
				980 Atīśa b.	
1560	1000	1000–1200 B enjoys royal support in Annam			
				1020 Pi-yen-chi (Z)	1017 Yeishin Sozu d.
		1077 King Anuruddha of Burma d.	1040 Theravādins win Burma	1038–1122 Milarepa	
		1086–1112 King Kyanzittha of Burma		1039 Atīśa goes to Tibet	
				1052 Atīśa d.	

After Buddha	AD	History	Hīnayāna	Mahāyāna	Art
1660	1100			1100 Ryonin (Tendai, Am)	
			1140 Theravādins win Siam	1133 Hōnen Shonin (Am) b.	
		1180–1205 Dvayavarman VII (Cambodia)		1173 Shinran (Am) b.	Art flourishes in Tibet
		1197 Nālandā destroyed by Islam		1191 Eisai brings Zen to Japan	Art of Bayon in Cambodia
1760	1200	1202 Śākyapanditya arrives in Tibet		1200 Dōgen (Z) b. Jōdō Shū founded (Am)	
				1211 Hōnen Shonin d. (Am)	
				1215 Eisai (Z) d. Dōgen (1200–53) founds Sōtō (Z)	
		1227–63 Tokiyori favours Zen		1222 Nichiren b.	
				1225 Jōdō Shin Shū founded	
				1228 Mumon Kwan (Z)	1252 Kamakura Dai Butsu Engakuji temple
		1251–84 Hojo Tokimune favours Zen	1240 Dhammakitti	1239 Ippen Shonin (Z) b.	
				1253 Dōgen (Z) d.	
		1260–94 Kublai Khan favours B. Tea ceremony comes to Japan		1267 Dai-o Kokushi (1235–1308) founds Rinzai (Z), Eison (1202–90) revives Ritsu (Vinaya) school	
			1280 Jinacarita	1282 Nichiren d.	
				1289 Ippen Shonin (Am)	
				1288 Bu-ston (T) b.	
1860	1300	1320 Mahāyāna declines in Cambodia			
		1340 Laos converted		1357 Tsongkhapa b.	

After Buddha	AD	History	Hīnayāna	Mahāyāna	Art
		1360 B (Hī) official religion of Siam		1365 Nagarakirtagama (T) in Java	
		1392 B declines in Korea		1385 Royogo Shogei's Jugi (Am)	
				1392 Gelug (T) founded	
1960	1400	to 1500 Persecution in Annam		1419 Tsongkhapa d.	1420–1506 Sesshiu (Z)
		1480 Java: Hinduism supersedes B. Sumatra: Islam supersedes B			
2060	1500	1576 Kumbum founded		Shi yen ki of Wu Ch'eng-en (Am)	
		1577 Final conversion of Mongols		1573 Tārānātha b.	1582–1645 Miyamoto
				1573–1645 Takuan (Z)	
				1599–1655 Chih-hsu	
2160	1600	1603 Tokugawa in Japan Decline of B	1620 Yogāvacara's Manual		
		1642 Fifth Dalai Lama becomes priest-king of Tibet			
		1643 Potala built		1685–1768 Hakuin (Z)	1643–94 Basho
2260	1700	1718 Mongol armies assist Gelugpa			
		1769 Nepal turns to Hinduism			
		1785 First Burjat monastery			
2360	1800	1819 Schopenhauer's Welt als Wille und Vorstellung			
		1840 Burnouf			
		1850–65 Tai-ping rebellion destroys many monasteries			
		1875 Theosophical Society founded			

After Buddha	AD	History	Hīnayāna	Mahāyāna	Art
2460	1900	1879 E. Arnold's *Light of Asia* 1890 Revival of B in Japan 1891 Mahabodhi Society founded 1904 British expedition to Lhasa 1909 Tai Hsu revives Ch B 1926 English Buddhist Society founded 1928 Amis du Bouddhisme founded		1924–29 Taisho Issaikyo	

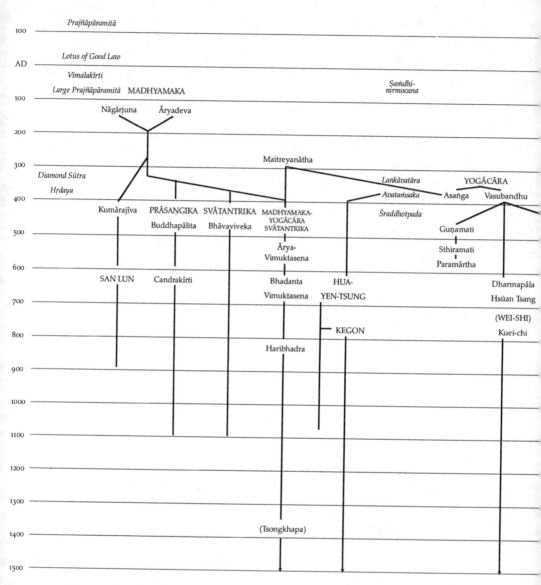

BC

100 Prajñāpāramitā

AD Lotus of Good Law

Vimalakīrti

Large Prajñāpāramitā MADHYAMAKA Saṁdhi-nirmocana

100

Nāgārjuna Āryadeva

200

300 Maitreyanātha

Diamond Sūtra Laṅkāvatāra YOGĀCĀRA

Hṛdaya Avataṁsaka Asaṅga Vasubandhu

400 Kumārajīva PRĀSAṄGIKA SVĀTANTRIKA MADHYAMAKA-YOGĀCĀRA SVĀTANTRIKA Śraddhotpada

Buddhapālita Bhāvaviveka Guṇamati

500 Ārya-Vimuktasena Sthiramati

Paramārtha

600 SAN LUN Candrakīrti Bhadanta Vimuktasena HUA-YEN-TSUNG Dharmapāla

Hsüan Tsang

700 (WEI-SHI)

KEGON Kuei-chi

800 Haribhadra

900

1000

1100

1200

1300

1400 (Tsongkhapa)

1500

Authors are shown in ordinary print
Works are shown in *italics*
Schools are shown in CAPITALS

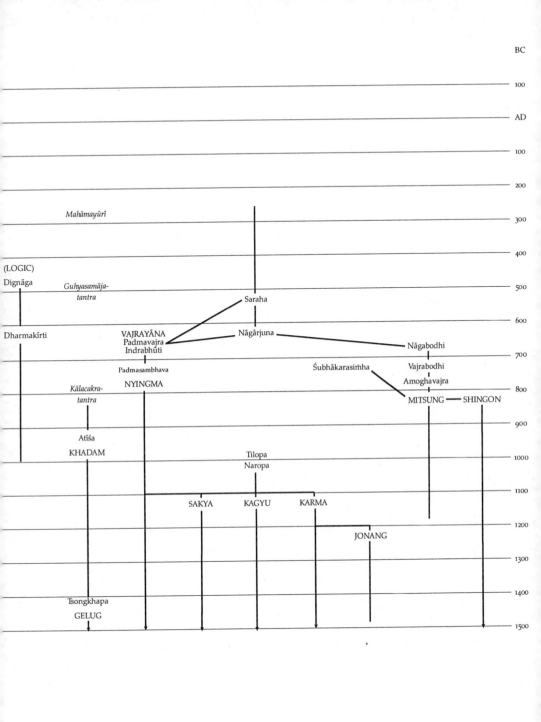

FURTHER READING

SURVEYS AND INTRODUCTIONS

Heinz Bechert and Richard Gombrich (eds.), *The World of Buddhism: Buddhist Monks and Nuns in Society and Culture*, Thames and Hudson, London 1984

C. Bell, *The Religion of Tibet*, Motilal Banarsidass, Delhi 2000

Har Dayal, *The Bodhisattva Doctrine in Buddhist Sanskrit Literature*, Motilal Banarsidass, Delhi 1996

Rupert Gethin, *The Foundations of Buddhism*, Oxford University Press, Oxford 1998

C. Eliot, *Hinduism and Buddhism*, Curzon Press, London 1998

Peter Harvey, *An Introduction to Buddhism: Teachings, History and Practices*, Cambridge University Press, Cambridge 1990

Damien Keown, *Buddhism: A Very Short Introduction*, Oxford University Press, Oxford 1996

H. Kern, *Manual of Indian Buddhism*, Motilal Banarsidass, Delhi, 1989

Richard H. Robinson, Willard L. Johnson, *The Buddhist Religion, A Historical Introduction*, Wadsworth Publishing Company, Belmont USA 1997

Sangharakshita, *A Survey of Buddhism*, Windhorse, Birmingham, 2001

Sangharakshita, *The Three Jewels*, Windhorse, Birmingham, 1998

Andrew Skilton, *A Concise History of Buddhism*, Windhorse, Birmingham, 1997

E. Steinilber-Oberlin, *The Buddhist Sects of Japan*, Greenwood, London 1971

D.T. Suzuki, *Essays in Zen Buddhism*, Munshiram Manoharlal, New Delhi 2000

E.J. Thomas, *The Life of Buddha as Legend and History*, Dover Publications, New York 2000

L.A. Waddell, *The Buddhism of Tibet*, Asian Educational Services, 1998

Paul Williams with Anthony Tribe, *Buddhist Thought, A Complete Introduction to the Indian Tradition*, Routledge, London 2000

TEXTS

Theravāda

Buddhaghosa, *The Path of Purity*, P.M. Tin (trans.), Pali Text Society, Oxford 1975

A.K. Coomaraswamy and I.B. Horner, *The Living Thoughts of Gotama the Buddha*, Dover Publications, New York 2000

Bhikkhu Ñāṇamoli and Bhikkhu Bodhi (trans.), *The Middle Length Discourses of the Buddha*, Wisdom Publications, Boston 1995

H. Saddhatissa (trans.), *Sutta-Nipāta*, Curzon Press, London 1985

Maurice Walshe (trans.), *The Long Discourses of the Buddha*, Wisdom Publications, Boston 1995

Mahāyāna

S. Anacker (trans.), *Seven Works of Vasubandhu, the Buddhist Psychological Doctor*, Motilal Banarsidass, Delhi 1984

E. Conze, *Buddhist Texts Through the Ages*, Shambhala, Boston 1990

E. Conze, *Buddhist Wisdom Books: The Diamond Sūtra and Heart Sūtra*, Vintage, 2001

E. Conze (trans.), *The Perfection of Wisdom in 8,000 Lines and Its Verse Summary (Aṣṭasāhasrikā Prajñāpāramitā)*, Four Seasons Foundation, Bolinas 1973

Garma C.C. Chang (ed.), *A Treasury of Mahāyāna Sūtras: Selections from the Mahāratnakūṭa Sūtra*, The Pennsylvania State University Press, Pennsylvania and London 1983

W.Y. Evans-Wentz (ed.), *The Tibetan Book of the Dead*, Oxford University Press, London 1960

W.Y. Evans-Wentz (ed.), *Tibet's Great Yogi Milarepa*, Oxford University Press, New York 2000

Jay L. Garfield (trans.), *The Fundamental Wisdom of the Middle Way: Nāgārjuna's Mūlamadhyamakākarikā*, Oxford University Press, Oxford 1995

Bunno Kato et al. (trans.), *The Threefold Lotus Sūtra*, Kosei, Tokyo 1995

M. Mueller (trans.), *Buddhist Mahāyāna Texts*, Motilal Banarsidass, Delhi 1985

A.F. Price and Wong Mow-lam (trans.), *The Diamond Sūtra and the Sūtra of Hui-Neng*, Shambhala, Boston 1990

Śāntideva, *The Bodhicaryāvatāra*, Kate Crosby and Andrew Skilton (trans.), Oxford University Press, Oxford 1995

Śāntideva, *Siksha Samuccaya*, C. Bendall and W.H.D. Rouse (trans.), Motilal Banarsidass, Delhi 1990

W. Soothill (trans.), *The Lotus of the Wonderful Law*, Curzon Press, London 1992

D.T. Suzuki (trans.), *The Laṅkāvatāra Sūtra*, Kegan Paul International, London 2000

D.T. Suzuki (ed.), *Manual of Zen Buddhism*, Rider, London 1983

Paul Williams, *Mahāyāna Buddhism*, Routledge, London 1989

Sarvāstivāda (and Sautrāntika)

L.M. Pruden, *Abhidharmakośa and Abhidharmakośabhāṣya*, (four volumes), Asian Humanities Press, Berkeley, California 1988–90

ART

A. Foucher, *The Beginnings of Buddhist Art*, Asian Educational Services, 1996

A. Getty, *The Gods of Northern Buddhism*, Dover Publications, New York 2000

R. Beer, *The Encyclopedia of Tibetan Symbols and Motifs*, Serindia, London n.d.

INDEX

The Windhorse symbolizes the energy of the enlightened mind carrying the Three Jewels – the Buddha, the Dharma, and the Sangha – to all sentient beings.

Buddhism is one of the fastest-growing spiritual traditions in the Western world. Throughout its 2,500-year history, it has always succeeded in adapting its mode of expression to suit whatever culture it has encountered.

Windhorse Publications aims to continue this tradition as Buddhism comes to the West. Today's Westerners are heirs to the entire Buddhist tradition, free to draw instruction and inspiration from all the many schools and branches. Windhorse publishes works by authors who not only understand the Buddhist tradition but are also familiar with Western culture and the Western mind. Manuscripts welcome.

For orders and catalogues contact

WINDHORSE PUBLICATIONS	WINDHORSE PUBLICATIONS	WEATHERHILL INC
11 PARK ROAD	P O BOX 574	41 MONROE TURNPIKE
BIRMINGHAM	NEWTOWN	TRUMBULL
B13 8AB	NSW 2042	CT 06611
UK	AUSTRALIA	USA

Windhorse Publications is an arm of the Friends of the Western Buddhist Order, which has more than sixty centres on five continents. Through these centres, members of the Western Buddhist Order offer regular programmes of events for the general public and for more experienced students. These include meditation classes, public talks, study on Buddhist themes and texts, and 'bodywork' classes such as t'ai chi, yoga, and massage. The FWBO also runs several retreat centres and the Karuna Trust, a fund-raising charity that supports social welfare projects in the slums and villages of India.

Many FWBO centres have residential spiritual communities and ethical businesses associated with them. Arts activities are encouraged too, as is the development of strong bonds of friendship between people who share the same ideals. In this way the FWBO is developing a unique approach to Buddhism, not simply as a set of techniques, less still as an exotic cultural interest, but as a creatively directed way of life for people living in the modern world.

If you would like more information about the FWBO please write to

LONDON BUDDHIST CENTRE	ARYALOKA
51 ROMAN ROAD	HEARTWOOD CIRCLE
LONDON	NEWMARKET
E2 0HU	NH 03857
UK	USA

ALSO FROM WINDHORSE

KAMALASHILA

MEDITATION: THE BUDDHIST WAY OF TRANQUILLITY AND INSIGHT

A comprehensive guide to the methods and theory of Buddhist meditation, written in an informal, accessible style. It provides a complete introduction to the basic techniques, as well as detailed advice for more experienced meditators seeking to deepen their practice.

The author is a long-standing member of the Western Buddhist Order, and has been teaching meditation since 1975. In 1979 he helped to establish a semi-monastic community in North Wales, which has now grown into a public retreat centre. For more than a decade he and his colleagues developed approaches to meditation that are firmly grounded in Buddhist tradition but readily accessible to people with a modern Western background. Their experience – as meditators, as students of the traditional texts, and as teachers – is distilled in this book.

304 pages, with charts and illustrations
ISBN 1 899579 05 2
£13.99/$27.95

SANGHARAKSHITA

A SURVEY OF BUDDHISM:

ITS DOCTRINES AND METHODS THROUGH THE AGES

Now in its ninth edition, *A Survey of Buddhism* continues to provide an indispensable study of the entire field of Buddhist thought and practice. Covering all the major doctrines and traditions, both in relation to Buddhism as a whole and to the spiritual life of the individual Buddhist, Sangharakshita places their development in historical context. This is an objective but sympathetic appraisal of Buddhism's many forms that clearly demonstrates the underlying unity of all its schools.

'I recommend Sangharakshita's book as the best survey of Buddhism.' *Dr Edward Conze*

576 pages
ISBN 0 904766 93 4
£19.99/$39.95

SANGHARAKSHITA

THE THREE JEWELS: THE CENTRAL IDEALS OF BUDDHISM

The Three Jewels are living symbols, supreme objects of commitment and devotion in the life of every Buddhist.

This authoritative book, by an outstanding Western Buddhist teacher, explains the pivotal importance of the Three Jewels. To understand the Three Jewels is to understand the central ideal and principles of Buddhism. To have some insight into them is to touch its very heart.

264 pages
ISBN 1 899579 06 0
£11.99/$23.95

SANGHARAKSHITA

WHAT IS THE DHARMA?

THE ESSENTIAL TEACHINGS OF THE BUDDHA

Guided by a lifetime's experience of Buddhist practice, Sangharakshita tackles the question 'What is the Dharma?' from many different angles. The result is a basic starter kit of teachings and practices, which emphasizes the fundamentally practical nature of Buddhism.

In turn refreshing, unsettling, and inspiring, this book lays before us the essential Dharma, timeless and universal: the Truth that addresses the deepest questions of our hearts and minds and the Path that shows us how we can renew our lives.

272 pages, illustrated
ISBN 1 899579 01 X
£9.99/$19.95

ANDREW SKILTON

A CONCISE HISTORY OF BUDDHISM

How and when did the many schools and sub-sects of Buddhism emerge? How do the ardent devotion of the Pure Land schools, the magical ritual of the Tantra, or the paradoxical negations of the Perfection of Wisdom literature, relate to the direct, down-to-earth teachings of Gautama the 'historical' Buddha? Did Buddhism modify the cultures to which it was introduced, or did they modify Buddhism?

Here is a narrative that describes and correlates the diverse manifestations of Buddhism – in its homeland of India, and in its spread across Asia, from Mongolia to Sri Lanka, from Japan to the Middle East. Drawing on the latest historical and literary research, Andrew Skilton explains the basic concepts of Buddhism from all periods of its development, and places them in a historical framework.

272 pages, with maps and extensive bibliography
ISBN 0 904766 92 6
£10.99/$21.95

SANGHARAKSHITA

DHAMMAPADA: THE WAY OF TRUTH

The *Dhammapada* is one of the most popular and influential of Buddhist scriptures. The universality of its message, the depth of its teaching, and the refined simplicity of its language have earned it an honoured place in world literature.

It can be taken as a straightforward and practical summary of the essential teachings of the Buddha, but – much more than that – the *Dhammapada* is a poetic representation of a sublime spiritual ideal.

164 pages
ISBN 1 899579 35 4
£9.99/$19.95